GW00838628

The London Clearing Banks

The London Clearing Banks

Evidence by the Committee of London Clearing Bankers
to the Committee to Review the Functioning
of Financial Institutions

November 1977

First published 1978 by the Committee of London Clearing Bankers
Designed by Peter Pickard, ARCA MSIA, London, and Banks & Miles, London
Printed in Great Britain by Blades, East & Blades Limited
Distributed by Longman Group Limited, London
© Crown copyright 1978
ISBN 0 582 03029 3
ISBN paperback 0 582 03030 7
Published in the United States of America by Longman Inc., New York

Contents

Tables and diagrams

Owing to rounding of figures, the sum of the separate items in tables will sometimes differ from the totals shown. The word 'billion' signifies 1,000 million in this submission. Unless otherwise stated, statistics give the sterling equivalent of currency items at middle market rates on reporting dates. The abbreviation 'LCB' is sometimes used for London clearing banks.

Preface

The terms of reference of the Committee to Review the Functioning of Financial Institutions, as set out in the Treasury minute of 5 January 1977, are:

> ". . . to enquire into the role and functioning, at home and abroad, of financial institutions in the United Kingdom and their value to the economy; to review in particular the provision of funds for industry and trade; to consider what changes are required in the existing arrangements for the supervision of these institutions, including the possible extension of the public sector, and to make recommendations."

The scope of the Committee's enquiry could therefore hardly be broader; and in producing this submission the clearing banks have taken the view that anything less than a fully comprehensive survey of all their activities and operations would fall short of the requirements of the enquiry. The length of this submission reflects the extent and diversity of these activities and operations, and their importance to the economy. The submission has been prepared in a form which it is hoped will not only meet the immediate needs of the Committee but also serve as an authoritative work of reference, of interest and value to a wider readership.

The clearing banks have already presented two submissions to the Committee in response to the request by its secretary for evidence relevant to the first stage of its enquiry, in which it set out to examine in particular:

a. the parts played by the various institutions in the arrangements for channelling funds into industry and trade through the banking system and the capital markets;

b. how these functions have changed and developed in recent years, eg in response to changing economic conditions;

c. how decisions to invest or lend money are made – for instance what are the criteria used to choose between alternative projects or investment opportunities, and what are the conditions which borrowers have to satisfy in order to raise money;

d. how effective the financial institutions have been in meeting the demands of industry and trade for finance on reasonable terms;

e. whether there are defects or gaps in the system, and if so how they might be remedied – for instance by changing the way the financial institutions work – so as to improve the flow of savings into industry and trade and stimulate investment.

The two submissions* dealt with the first three and last two of these questions respectively. This present submission incorporates all this original evidence, sometimes in more or less the exact form in which it first appeared, sometimes

*Preliminary Submission to the Committee to Review the Functioning of Financial Institutions: Channelling Funds to Industry and Trade, April 1977; Supplementary Paper to the Preliminary Submission, June 1977.

in greater detail or in a different context. The aim has been to produce a self-contained document in which each major aspect of the clearing banks' 'role and functioning' is fully described and discussed. But within this broad framework, the main emphasis is still on the subject of the financing of industry and trade.

Although the subject of this submission is the clearing banks themselves, it has been necessary to include a certain amount of material about other financial institutions and markets in order to place the banks' role in its proper context. Similarly, although the main purpose of the submission is to assemble factual material about the banks, they are aware that the Committee is empowered to make recommendations and they have therefore themselves chosen to make a limited number of suggestions. The most important of these are the ones made in the supplementary paper to the banks' preliminary submission and which are set out in full in the introductory chapter of this submission.

Throughout this submission the term 'the clearing banks' will be used to describe the six banks whose chairmen formally comprise the Committee of London Clearing Bankers (CLCB) – Barclays, Coutts & Co, Lloyds, Midland, National Westminster and Williams & Glyn's; wherever the shorter term can be used unambiguously they will be referred to simply as 'the banks'. Thus in the context of this submission 'the clearing banks' include neither the Scottish clearing banks (which are referred to collectively as 'the Scottish banks') nor the Co-operative Bank and Central Trustee Savings Bank (which, while functional members of the clearing system, are not members of the CLCB). The branch banks operating in Northern Ireland are also excluded.

Much of the clearing banks' business is now transacted by subsidiary companies. General comments about the banks' activities should therefore be taken to refer to the relevant subsidiary companies as well as to the parent banks themselves. Where statistics are used, however, it has been necessary to adopt a more rigorous convention. Most of the figures quoted in this submission refer to the UK-based business either of the parent banks alone (including Coutts) or of the parent banks together with their banking subsidiaries in England, Wales, the Channel Islands and the Isle of Man: these are referred to collectively as 'the London clearing bank groups'. It will be noted that they exclude the clearing banks' Scottish and Irish subsidiaries, all subsidiaries not formally regarded as banks by the Bank of England (such as certain leasing and factoring companies), all subsidiaries incorporated overseas and all overseas branches. It has been made clear where figures refer instead to the entire clearing bank groups, as in the chapter on profits.

This submission attempts to survey the main developments in the clearing banks and their environment in the 20 years since the Radcliffe Committee was set up. Unfortunately, however, very few of the relevant banking statistics are available in a consistent form for anything like as long as that. In most cases, data about the clearing banks' assets and liabilities have not been provided in this submission for years prior to 1962, when a major overhaul of banking statistics occurred in the wake of the Radcliffe Report. Statistics for the London clearing bank groups have been compiled only since 1972; they are aggregate figures which include transactions between companies within the same group. In addition there have been a number of 'breaks' in the official banking statistics as a result of changes of definition and categorisation, notably in 1971 and 1975. Allowance has been made for these changes wherever possible. Full data on the banks' profits and group balance sheets are available only since 1969, when full profits were first disclosed.

Introduction

Summary

This chapter summarises the main changes in the clearing banks' role in recent years and considers the scope for improving the workings of the financial system as a whole, ending with four main suggestions. The main changes have been the banks' development into international institutions, their diversification and the increasingly competitive nature of their operations. In general, the UK financial system is well equipped to meet the economy's needs, though there are problems involved in providing long-term finance and risk capital for the smaller business. The banks also believe that a 'proprietorial gap' may exist in the system. They do not believe, however, that there are major defects and gaps in their operations. Their main suggestions are: an overhaul of the controls and incentives applied to different types of institution; a review of the machinery for financing smaller companies; a review of the arrangements for providing term finance to industry; and improvements in monetary policy techniques.

The clearing banks' changing role

1.1 The last occasion when the clearing banks gave a comprehensive account of their role for the purposes of an official enquiry was when they provided their evidence to the Committee on the Working of the Monetary System (the Radcliffe Committee) in 1957. It is hard to exaggerate the extent of the changes that have occurred in the 20 years since then, both in the banks themselves and in the financial system within which they operate. The number of clearing banks has been reduced from eleven to six through mergers, while the total number of commercial banks (domestic and foreign) operating in the United Kingdom has expanded from under 125 to over 300. The total resources at the clearing banks' disposal have increased from some £7,000 million to some £50,000 million but their market share of all sterling deposits and short-term savings has fallen from nearly 50 per cent to about 30 per cent. Lending has grown from less than a third of the banks' total resources to more than two-thirds. From being entirely reliant on the funds deposited at their branches by their customers, the banks have been able to tap the new 'wholesale' markets to help finance their lending. From lending almost entirely by way of overdraft, they have developed their contractual term lending to a point where it represents some 40 per cent of all non-personal domestic lending. There has been a vast increase in the numbers of payment items handled by the banks and wholly new systems, heavily dependent on computer technology, have been introduced to cope with them. After years of steady expansion in the banks' branch networks, the number of branches has latterly been declining. Patterns of recruitment into the banks have changed, with women now a clear majority of the workforce, and far more emphasis is now placed on staff training and consultation. Radical changes have been made to the banks' organisational structures and considerable decision-making powers have been devolved to the regions.

1.2   Three further developments, however, have probably been more important than any of these. They are the development of the clearing banks from essentially domestic institutions into international ones; their diversification into a wide range of financial activities not previously associated with clearing banking; and—largely as a result of the first two developments—an increase in the degree of competition between the clearing banks and other institutions. The development of the banks' international business—both London-based and undertaken through their overseas operations—has led to radical changes in their corporate structures and balance sheets and has brought them into increasing competition with other large international banks, from the United States and Continental Europe in particular, not least in their operations on the eurocurrency markets, the growth of which has arguably been the most important financial phenomenon of the post-Radcliffe period. On the domestic front, the clearing banks are now heavily involved, directly or through sub-sidiaries and affiliates, in such fields as instalment credit, leasing, factoring, insurance broking and merchant banking, and are thus in direct competition with institutions which would previously have been regarded as playing a purely complementary role to that of the banks. At the same time, the clearing banks have faced increasing competition from other institutions in their own traditional deposit-taking, lending and money transmission activities. The building societies have emerged as particularly powerful competitors in the market for personal deposits. Competition for domestic corporate lending business has been mounted by both indigenous institutions and foreign ones such as London's large community of American banks. The National Giro has been established to compete in the field of money transmission and, together with the Trustee Savings Banks, has now been empowered to extend that competition to other banking services. This growth of competition was given official blessing in the radical revisions to monetary and credit policy enshrined in *Competition and Credit Control* in 1971 (see paragraph 6.10); and although the secondary banking crisis that followed three years later eliminated some of the participants in the market, the financial system remains far more competitive, particularly in the lending field, than it was 10, let alone 20, years ago.

1.3   The result of all these factors is that the clearing banks have developed along lines much closer to those of the continental 'universal' banks than before, aiming to provide a comprehensive range of domestic and international financial services within a single group of companies. But the blurring of traditional demarcation lines between the clearing banks and other institutions does not mean that they either seek or expect to dominate all the diverse financial markets, old and new, in which they now operate. Deposit banking remains the staple of their existence and conditions all their other banking activities. In particular, it means that by far the largest part of their banking business must be conducted with due regard to the essentially short-term nature of their deposit base. So while they have been able to diversify to a very considerable extent, they cannot transform themselves into predominantly long-term lending or investing institutions. Nor are the constraints on their development solely financial ones. As the banks are the largest employers of labour and owners of premises and equipment of any of the financial industries, there are also important human and physical factors influencing the pace and direction of their development.

1.4   The clearing banks are a major part of a financial system which is as diverse and sophisticated as any in the world. Some of the financial institutions and markets which make up that system are often referred to collectively as 'the City': chief among them are the Stock Exchange and its member firms, the merchant and foreign banks, the discount houses, and the various specialist markets, brokers and dealers operating within the geographical area of the City of London. By contrast, certain financial institutions, such as the building societies and savings banks, are not usually thought of as part of the City at all. This is presumably because their dealings are more with the general public than with companies and other institutions and because they operate through national networks of retail outlets rather than within the City. The clearing banks embrace both sets of characteristics. On the one hand, their head offices are physically situated in the City and much of their specialist head office business is closely related to the activities of other City institutions and markets. On the other hand, the basis of the clearing banks' operations is the business generated at their branches throughout the country, with their customers including millions of private individuals and small companies, as well as large companies and institutions. Thus, while in many contexts it is entirely legitimate to regard the clearing banks as part of the City, the retail nature of so much of their business sets them somewhat apart from most other City institutions.

1.5   The relationship of the various financial institutions and markets to one another is partly competitive and partly complementary. This means that the role of any one institution cannot be judged properly except by reference to the roles played by all the others. Insofar as the clearing banks are less actively engaged than banks in certain other countries in areas such as securities trading and the provision of long-term finance, this is largely because there already exist other UK institutions and markets well equipped to perform those functions. The clearing banks therefore neither expect nor should be expected to perform all the functions that commercial banks have undertaken in countries in which these other institutions and markets are less effective. So while the banks do not believe that their role, or that of any financial institution, should be subject to artificial limitations, neither do they believe that the virtues of specialisation should be totally ignored. It is their intention to continue to adapt to changing circumstances and needs and to compete robustly with one another and with other institutions. But in so doing they cannot afford to neglect the basic clearing banking services which remain the foundation of their business.

Gaps and defects

1.6   The clearing banks believe that the financial system of the United Kingdom is essentially sound and well equipped to meet the needs of the economy as a whole and industry and trade in particular. They do not believe there is a case for radically changing the organisation, supervision or ownership of the country's financial institutions and markets. They believe that the financial system has been effective in the particular task of meeting the demands of industry and trade for finance on reasonable terms. Insofar as the UK economy has performed less well than others in recent decades, particularly in the areas of productivity and investment, they believe that the main reasons for this lie outside the financial system. This, however, does not preclude the possible existence of some specific defects and gaps. Many such gaps have, of course, been filled over the years by the financial system itself, and there is no reason why this process should not continue. Thus just as Finance for Industry (FFI) was reconstituted and Equity Capital for Industry launched in response to alleged gaps in the recent past, so one would expect any similar gaps in the financial system to be plugged if they became apparent in future.

1.7   There are, however, two particular types of finance which, for various reasons, the system has found it comparatively difficult to provide on acceptable terms. The first is term finance for periods in the approximate range of between 10 and 20 years, whether at fixed or variable rates of interest; the clearing banks' deposit structure precludes their engaging directly in more than a limited amount of long-term lending, but they are able to make introductions to the FFI group who are active in this market. The second is risk capital for the smaller developing business, although the banks have taken steps to help redress this problem both by developing their equity finance subsidiaries and through the Industrial and Commercial Finance Corporation (ICFC), one of FFI's two main subsidiaries.

1.8   More fundamentally, the banks believe that there may now exist what might be termed a 'proprietorial gap' in the financial system. That is to say, the proprietorial functions traditionally discharged by the individual entrepreneur and the private shareholder in the past have not been perfectly assumed by today's professional manager and institutional shareholder. There are many reasons for this state of affairs, not least the effect of the tax system on the ability and inclination of private individuals to involve themselves actively in the establishment, ownership and management of businesses in general and new, small businesses in particular. There is a certain amount that the banks have been able to do themselves, or through their subsidiaries and affiliates, to help close the 'proprietorial gap' by generally taking a closer interest in the affairs of their customers than was usual in the past. But there are limits to this process, not least those imposed by the customers themselves who understandably value their independence.

1.9   In terms of what the clearing banks can reasonably be expected to do, given their deposit structure and other relevant considerations, they do not believe that there are major defects and gaps in their own activities. Either directly, or through subsidiaries and associates, they now provide one of the widest ranges of financial facilities of any commercial banking system in the world. And the facilities they do not provide, or provide only in small quantities, are generally available in acceptable amounts from non-clearing banks or elsewhere in the financial system. This, however, is the banks' own view: ultimately the only verdict which can carry conviction will be that of their customers.

Suggestions

1.10   There are a large number of measures which could well enhance the effectiveness of the system as a whole, without being addressed to any particular shortcomings in the system. What follows is not a list of prescriptions for specific maladies, or recommendations for immediate action. Rather it is a list of suggestions, some urged with greater force than others, which may assist the Committee in formulating its own recommendations. It will be noted that most of the suggestions are concerned more with the environment within which the financial institutions have to operate, and the controls to which they are subject, than with the nature and behaviour of the institutions themselves. Before turning to the detailed suggestions, one general point should be made. Few of the suggestions will be worth implementing unless the financial system is allowed to function in conditions of greater economic and political stability than have been experienced in recent years. The main conditions for a general improvement in the effectiveness of the financial system are a reduction in inflation, greater monetary stability, continued containment of the government's borrowing requirement, higher corporate profitability and, above all, an end to successive governments' frequent and disruptive U-turns in industrial and financial policy generally. Thus the banks would suggest that careful consideration should be given to any changes that are made so that the chosen policies may continue in operation without frequent alteration.

1.11   The following are the four main suggestions which the clearing banks wish to make.

a.   **An overhaul of the whole range of controls, regulations, incentives and subsidies applied to different types of financial institution**

At present, the national savings movement, the building societies and the life assurance companies in particular can attract deposits and savings on the basis of fiscal and regulatory advantages not available to other types of institution. Such differentiation may have made sense when the roles of the various institutions were more clear-cut than they are today. But now that institutions are increasingly competing with one another in the same market places, the differentiation has become discriminatory and undoubtedly lessens the efficiency of the financial system as a whole. In particular, the banks would strongly urge a policy of fiscal neutrality towards all types of saving, with incentives applied either universally or not at all. In general, the banks believe that if the authorities wish to differentiate in favour of certain types of economic activity and against others, they should do so by concentrating their incentives and restrictions on users of finance, rather than on institutions. For example, if it is felt desirable to provide incentives for home loans, such incentives should attach directly to all loans of a qualifying type and should not be provided indirectly by treating building societies differently from other institutions. (This implies a greater co-ordination of public policy objectives, so that the financial needs of different sectors such as housing and manufacturing are not the subject of conflicting incentives and controls.)

b.   **A review of the institutional machinery for providing equity or long-term funds to the smaller, developing enterprise**

In addition to bank finance and proprietors' funds, there comes a stage in the development of many smaller companies when they need an injection of external permanent or long-term risk capital. A number of institutions exist to help meet this need, including various subsidiaries of the clearing banks themselves and ICFC, a subsidiary of FFI, in which the banks are majority shareholders. It is the clearing banks' experience, however, that there is considerable resistance on the part of shareholders in private companies to releasing any part of the equity in their companies. If it is suggested that the machinery is still not adequate to meet the latent demand, the banks would submit that the finance most suitable for transformation into long-term funds is primarily that held by life assurance companies and pension funds. Scope exists already for channelling such funds to ICFC through the medium of FFI quoted debenture and loan stocks, although such instruments would become more attractive to investing institutions if government securities did not enjoy preferential tax status.

c.   **Improvements in the facilities for channelling term finance to industry**

In recent years the clearing banks have provided to industry and trade an increasing level of term lending facilities to the extent that it is now doubtful if any further great expansion is possible without giving rise to concern on prudential grounds. The Committee may wish to consider, therefore, whether it would be appropriate to make a recommendation to the authorities for the establishment of official refinance arrangements for medium-term lending, to be available to individual banks in case of need. The financing of major contracts, notably in certain fields of civil engineering and process plant construction, can pose additional problems. Even if the finance is available on appropriate terms, there are difficulties of risk assessment and containment which are not always easy for a single bank or syndicate of banks to manage. There may be a case for introducing some system of insurance or guarantee scheme to cover cases of proven difficulty, such as export contracts outside the specific terms of ECGD arrangements. The banks for their part will continue to consider offering new forms of instrument for savers and depositors in order to increase their own capacity to provide industry with term finance. In particular, they will give serious consideration to the possible development of floating-rate notes as a complement to their existing range of term deposit facilities.

d.   **Improvements in the techniques of monetary policy**

The banks' ability to meet industry's needs in the past has undoubtedly been impaired by their own need to observe certain types of monetary and credit control. Had the authorities been able to operate the *Competition and Credit Control* system in the way they had hoped, with few direct controls on the lending activities of individual institutions, the banks would probably have had no such complaints. But the introduction (and subsequent reintroduction) of the supplementary special deposit scheme faced bankers with the difficult problem of reconciling individual requests for finance with the need to observe what amounted to an overall lending ceiling. In general, the banks believe that industry's interests are best served by monetary controls such as reserve asset and special deposit requirements and open-market operations which apply evenly and without discrimination to the financial system as a whole. In particular, they see no justification for their unique obligation to hold $1\frac{1}{2}$ per cent of their eligible liabilities as non-interest-earning balances at the Bank of England. It represents an unjustifiable cost of intermediation and confers an artificial competitive advantage on non-clearing banks.

The future

1.12   In this submission the clearing banks present a detailed review of the changes that have occurred since the Radcliffe Report. It shows that, during that period and especially during the past decade, the banks have responded to the changing environment in which they work; that they have met the changing needs of their customers in general and industry and trade in particular; and that they have assisted the Bank of England in the implementation of monetary policy in all its aspects. All available evidence suggests that, through a period of radical change, the banks have acted positively and helpfully. There can be no doubt that they will continue to do so as the need arises in future; certainly, there is no reason to believe that changes in the ownership and control of the clearing banks would do anything to enhance the major contribution that they already make to the economic life of the country. As long as they are allowed to operate without undue restrictions or competitive disadvantages, the clearing banks are convinced that their now proven resilience and flexibility will ensure that they continue to provide the range of banking services needed by all sectors of the economy.

Chapter 2
Structure and organisation

Summary   This chapter describes the structure of the five clearing bank groups, and their organisation and management. For several of the banks, the biggest structural changes have been those brought about by the mergers in the late 1960s, since when the clearing banks have all greatly expanded and diversified their business. All the banks have extended their representation overseas in order to meet modern requirements: in so doing Midland and Williams & Glyn's have placed the emphasis on methods involving co-operation with overseas banks, while Barclays, Lloyds and National Westminster have concentrated on extending their own direct representation abroad. At home, the clearing banks have developed merchant banking services and medium-term lending. In the late 1950s all the banks made investments in the finance house sector; these interests were rationalised in the early 1970s so that most clearing banks now have a single wholly-owned finance house subsidiary. Specialist subsidiaries have developed leasing and factoring services, and all the banks are involved in credit cards. All the banks have adopted divisional structures which increase the degree of delegation.

The clearing bank mergers

2.1   The Committee of London Clearing Bankers (CLCB) now has six member banks: Barclays, Lloyds, Midland and National Westminster (the so-called 'big four'), Coutts & Co and Williams & Glyn's. The big four banks are all public companies quoted on the Stock Exchange, and their shares are held by a very wide range of investors, both individual and institutional (see table 1). Williams & Glyn's is wholly owned by a publicly-quoted bank holding company, the National and Commercial Banking Group. Coutts is a wholly-owned subsidiary of National Westminster (see diagram 1). In this chapter the structure of each of the five independent clearing bank groups is described, with particular emphasis on the changes that have taken place during the past 20 years through mergers, acquisitions and the development of new services, stressing the different strategies adopted by different banks. In the latter part of the chapter the organisation and management of the five groups are discussed.

The clearing banks' shareholders   Table 1

The big four banks' shareholders: 31 December 1976

		Percentage number of holdings	Percentage value of holdings
Individuals	Women	44.7	18.8
	Men	36.5	13.2
	Joint accounts	9.4	5.6
Corporate bodies	Insurance companies	0.4	12.1
	Pension funds	0.2	5.5
	Other companies	6.5	16.7
	Universities, schools, etc	1.0	5.4
Nominee companies		1.2	22.7
Total		**437,217**	**£1,683m**

Source: Individual banks.

Ownership of the six London clearing banks   Diagram 1

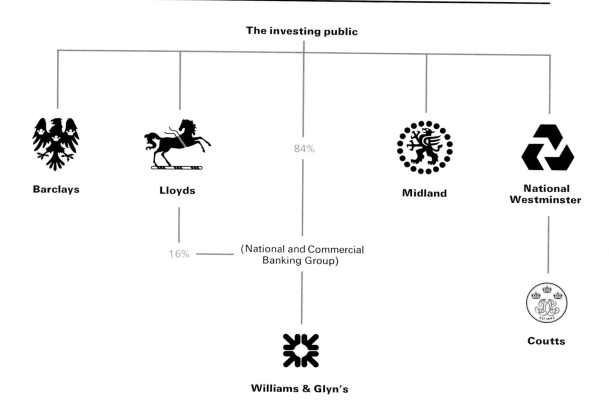

2.2 For several of the banks, the biggest structural changes in the past 20 years have been due to the mergers that took place at the end of the 1960s. Ten years ago there were eleven banks represented on the CLCB. Three of them (Coutts, Lloyds and Midland) were not involved in the mergers, but the other eight have been reduced to three, as follows:

a. In November 1968 Barclays acquired the share capital of Martins Bank; the business of Martins was transferred to Barclays on 15 December 1969 by private Act of Parliament.

b. National Westminster was formed in 1968 and acquired on 8 July 1968 the capital of Westminster Bank and National Provincial Bank; the latter had previously (in 1962) acquired District Bank. The business of all three banks was transferred to National Westminster on 1 January 1970. Coutts, which had been a wholly-owned subsidiary of National Provincial since 1920, became a subsidiary of National Westminster but retained its separate identity.

c. Williams & Glyn's was formed in 1969 and took over on 25 September 1970 the business of Glyn, Mills & Co, Williams Deacon's Bank and the National Bank. The first two had been subsidiaries of the Royal Bank of Scotland. The National Bank had been a public company until 1966, when it was acquired by National Commercial Bank of Scotland, having first sold its Irish business to the Bank of Ireland. The three banks fell under common ownership when their Scottish parents merged in 1968. The enlarged group was reorganised so that the merged Royal Bank of Scotland and Williams & Glyn's each became a subsidiary of a common holding company, National and Commercial Banking Group.

2.3   Table 2 shows how the mergers transformed the pattern of clearing banking in England and Wales. They were the first such mergers of significance since the period immediately following the 1914–18 war, when after a series of amalgamations the pattern of five large banks and a number of smaller ones was established. Official concern at the increased concentration in banking had led to the establishment of the Colwyn Committee on Bank Amalgamations, which reported in 1918. Although the Committee's recommendations were never carried into law, it was accepted that bank mergers were to be subject to approval by the Bank of England in consultation with the Treasury, and that in considering proposals the authorities would adhere closely to the Committee's criteria.

Clearing bank mergers   Table 2

31 December 1968		Balance sheet totals (£m) *	Branches	Staff
Barclays		2,959	2,660	37,000
Martins		580	737	7,900
Barclays		**3,539**	**3,397**	**44,900**
National Provincial		1,362	1,631	20,200
Westminster		1,662	1,441	22,400
District		394	589	5,300
National Westminster		**3,418**	**3,661**	**47,900**
Williams Deacon's	(30 September 1968)	195	280	2,500
Glyn, Mills	(30 September 1968)	93	4	1,100
National Bank	(30 September 1968)	57	35	650
Williams & Glyn's	(30 September 1968)	**345**	**319**	**4,250**
Coutts		**79**	**9**	**1,150**
Lloyds		**2,285**	**2,217**	**29,700**
Midland		**2,459**	**2,712**	**31,700**

*Parent banks only, excluding contra items.
Source: Individual banks.

2.4   The criteria for approving mergers were, essentially, that the merging banks should be complementary rather than overlapping. Such was the case with the acquisition of District by National Provincial in 1962; District was heavily localised in the North West where National Provincial's branch coverage was sparse. Until 1967 it was assumed that mergers among the big five would be frowned upon, and it was thought very doubtful that any of the big five would be allowed to acquire Martins. But in that year the publication of the report of the National Board for Prices and Incomes on bank charges shed further light on official attitudes. It stated that "the Bank of England and the Treasury have made it plain to us that they would not obstruct some further amalgamations if the banks were willing to contemplate such a development".

2.5   The first to move was Martins, which made it clear that it saw its future as part of a larger group and invited bids. However, before the agreed procedure for receiving the bids was complete, Westminster and National Provincial announced in January 1968 that neither was bidding for Martins but that, with official approval, they intended to merge with each other. This caused some surprise because it had not been universally appreciated that the authorities' more liberal attitude extended to mergers among the big five themselves. Very soon afterwards Barclays and Lloyds announced that they too proposed to merge and that in their case the merged bank would bid for Martins. The triple Barclays-Lloyds-Martins merger was referred to the

Monopolies Commission, which opposed it by six votes to four on the view that the weakening of competitive forces which would result would outweigh the benefits to the public. In particular, since the combined bank would have had nearly half the country's clearing bank business, the fear was expressed that such a merger might force the other banks into a defensive merger and thus lead to a duopoly. The Barclays-Martins merger was, however, allowed to go ahead.

2.6   Of the many benefits from the mergers which were envisaged at the time, and which have since been realised, perhaps the most obvious was the opportunity they gave for rationalising branch networks. In many instances the merged banks have been able to combine the business of overlapping outlets, reducing costs without diminishing the standard of service to customers, a subject discussed in more detail in chapter 14. Less obvious, but perhaps more important, were the disadvantages faced by the smaller banks as a result of modern conditions. For example, increasing concentration of business into larger and more powerful units requiring a full range of banking services and an ability to accommodate large lending propositions within the loan portfolio had placed a strain on smaller banks. They were also at a disadvantage in international banking. Large banks are better placed in this field, not only because they are more able to bear the start-up costs of new ventures but also because they enjoy greater prestige abroad. Furthermore, the smaller banks would have found it more difficult to develop ancillary services such as leasing and credit cards. The spur to broadening the range of services to clearing bank customers was partly a need to protect the deposit base against the loss of market share suffered by the clearing banks throughout the 1950s and 1960s, both to other commercial banks and to non-bank intermediaries like the building societies. Some of the smaller clearing banks felt especially vulnerable to these pressures.

2.7   As has already been implied, both the big mergers in 1968 involved geographical overlap, but there was an element of complementarity also. Martins was heavily weighted towards its original home territory, the North West, where Barclays was not strongly represented. Westminster, despite a vigorous programme of diversification during the 1960s, retained a bias towards London and the home counties, an area of comparative weakness for National Provincial. A comprehensive geographical coverage became more valuable as the clearing banks diversified, since the costs of developing new services were thereby spread over a wider customer base. The mergers also generated valuable economies of scale and opportunities for rationalisation in the banks' computerisation programmes. There were, for example, 31 separate computer systems in operation in the companies making up the National Westminster group at the time of the merger. The savings were most marked in the branch accounting systems. Notable economies of scale have also been exploited in management resources, large deposit taking, cash handling, stationery and staff training.

Investments in other deposit banks

2.8   Traditionally it has been the clearing banks' policy not to operate under their own names in Scotland and Ireland, although very recently all the 'big four' banks have begun to open a limited number of Scottish branches. The clearing banks have, however, for a long time had shareholdings in the Scottish clearing banks. A series of mergers analogous to those in England has reduced the number of Scottish banks from six to three over the past 20 years, with consequential changes in the clearing banks' shareholdings (see diagram 2). Of the six Scottish banks in existence 20 years ago, three were independent (Bank of Scotland, Royal Bank of Scotland and Commercial Bank of Scotland) and three were controlled by English banks (British Linen Bank by Barclays, Clydesdale Bank by Midland, and National Bank of Scotland by Lloyds). Clydesdale has not been affected by mergers since then (though it had absorbed another Midland subsidiary in 1950). The National Bank of Scotland merged with Commercial Bank in 1958 to form National Commercial Bank of Scotland, leaving Lloyds with a 37 per cent interest in the enlarged equity; then in 1968, as already mentioned, National Commercial Bank merged with Royal Bank, and Lloyds were left with 16.4 per cent of the new holding company, National and Commercial Banking Group. Finally, in 1969 Barclays sold British Linen Bank to Bank of Scotland in exchange for a 35 per cent shareholding in the latter. Barclays and Lloyds have common directors with Bank of Scotland and National and Commercial Banking Group respectively, but they do not seek to intervene in their day-to-day management. Likewise Clydesdale has its own board, fully responsible for all aspects of its business.

Ownership of the three Scottish clearing banks   Diagram 2

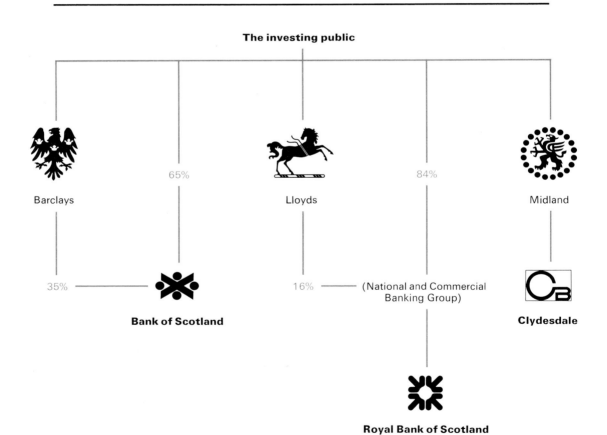

2.9   In Ireland the number of associated banks has fallen from nine to four over the same period. All four banks operate in both parts of Ireland, but two are based in Northern Ireland and both are wholly owned by clearing banks, Northern Bank by Midland and Ulster Bank by National Westminster. Northern Bank was acquired by Midland in 1965; it absorbed the Belfast Banking Company (a long-standing Midland subsidiary) in 1970. The clearing banks also have interests in certain other smaller domestic deposit banks in the United Kingdom. The Yorkshire Bank, with 183 branches in Northern England and the North Midlands and one in London, is owned jointly by four clearing banks. The Isle of Man Bank, the main bank on the island, is owned by National Westminster. Lewis's Bank, with 11 offices mostly in branches of the Sears department store group, is owned by Lloyds, which acquired it from Martins in 1967.

International banking

2.10 Scarcely less radical in its impact than the mergers of 1968–70 has been the great expansion and diversification of the banks' business since that time. This has been achieved partly by developing new services 'in house', partly by acquisitions, partly by the establishment of new outlets, and partly by undertaking joint ventures with other banks. The area where the development has been most marked is international banking. A full account of the changes in the international banking environment over the past 20 years is given in chapter 10, and the clearing banks' response to these changes is described in chapters 11 and 12; in particular, chapter 12 sets out in detail the expansion in the banks' overseas representation. In the present chapter the development of the banks' international business is described in outline, together with the changes in group structure that it has entailed. Subsequent sections of this chapter do the same for the development of new services at home, notably in the fields of merchant banking and instalment credit.

2.11 Twenty years ago the clearing banks' international business consisted mainly of providing the services necessary to their UK customers in connection with their foreign trade and foreign travel: foreign exchange, documentary credits, bill negotiations and collections and travellers' cheques. The provision of banking services in the United Kingdom for overseas correspondent banks and their customers was also important. The banks' own representation overseas was generally limited to Western Europe (chiefly France), but two of the clearing banks (Barclays and Lloyds) also had important investments in specialist British overseas banks. In Barclays' case the investment was a controlling interest, but nevertheless Barclays DCO ('Dominion, Colonial & Overseas') was an independent public company run separately from the parent bank. Lloyds had a 26 per cent holding in Bank of London and South America (BOLSA); it also had a network of branches in India and Pakistan, but these were sold in 1961. At that time the banks relied in the main on being represented overseas by correspondent banks rather than on a local presence.

2.12 Since then the growing internationalisation of business generally, the growth of foreign trade, the rise of the eurocurrency markets and the decline of sterling have necessitated profound changes in the banks' approach to international business. In particular, it became clear in the late 1960s that existing correspondent relationships were no longer adequate to meet the growing needs of customers for an internationally-oriented banking service. Two main approaches were possible towards the problem of how best to develop overseas links, and individual banks differed in where they placed the emphasis. One approach, on which Midland and Williams & Glyn's have chiefly relied, was to act in association with other European banks. The other possibility was for a bank to establish its own direct representation overseas. An extension of the correspondent relationships has been the formation of 'clubs' of European banks which formalise co-operation between member banks and, to a varying extent, provide a basis for joint ventures in other parts of the world. Partly because its 'club' is the most highly developed, Midland has felt little need to establish extensive direct representation abroad. By contrast, Barclays, Lloyds and National Westminster have concentrated on building up their own overseas presence, and have made only limited use of co-operative ventures.

2.13 Apart from the use of consortia and 'clubs' to develop representation overseas, several clearing banks have also taken shareholdings in London-based consortium banks, some of them specialising in particular geographical regions of the world, or in particular types of business. Some banks also participate in large 'multi-purpose' consortium banks: Midland & International Banks (Midland), Orion Bank (National Westminster) and United International Bank (Williams & Glyn's). A similar participation by Westminster in International Commercial Bank was sold after the merger, and a joint venture between National Provincial and Rothschilds was also discontinued. A list of the clearing banks' investments in consortium banks, including those relating to the 'clubs', is given in table 48 on page 269.

2.14 As their international business developed, Barclays and Lloyds regarded it as essential to obtain full ownership of the British overseas banks with which they were chiefly associated, in order to avoid conflicts of interest between different bodies of shareholders. Accordingly, Barclays bought out the minority shareholders in Barclays DCO in 1971 and changed its name to Barclays Bank International (BBI). Lloyds accomplished the corresponding process in two stages. First, in 1971 a new bank was formed by merging Lloyds' own wholly-owned subsidiary Lloyds Bank Europe with BOLSA. Shortly before, BOLSA had itself obtained full ownership of its associate, the Bank of London and Montreal. With the help of additional share purchases Lloyds secured a controlling interest in the newly-merged bank, but a minority interest (held mainly by the public but partly by an American bank) remained. Then in 1973 Lloyds bought out the minority interest and in 1974 renamed the bank Lloyds Bank International. These acquisitions gave both banks extensive networks of branches in developing countries. Both also had branches in New York and Europe, and Lloyds had in addition a separate subsidiary in New Zealand, the National Bank of New Zealand (acquired in 1966). National Westminster lacked the developing country involvement, but it did have the European business of Westminster Foreign Bank (now called International Westminster Bank). All three banks in the early 1970s set about increasing their direct representation in Europe and North America and establishing a presence in Asia. As described in chapter 12, this was done by opening branches or representative offices or by acquiring local banks, so that today they are represented in all the world's important financial centres, as is illustrated in tables 49, 50 and 51 on page 270.

2.15 While this expansion was taking place, the old-established business of Barclays in Africa and the Caribbean and of Lloyds in Latin America declined in relative importance. In many cases the branches in the various territories were incorporated into local banks, often with government or other local shareholders, with a resultant loss of flexibility. As well as their own operations in developing countries, the clearing banks also have shareholdings in the two remaining independent British overseas banks, Grindlays Bank and Standard Chartered Bank. Lloyds first gained an interest in Grindlays through the sale of its branches in India and Pakistan in 1961, and after capital reorganisations in 1969 and 1975 its effective interest is now 21 per cent. Citibank have 49 per cent and the public 30 per cent; the interests of Lloyds and of the public are held through a quoted holding company, Grindlays Holdings. Midland increased its shareholding in Standard Chartered from 4 per cent to 16 per cent in 1975; in the same year National Westminster disposed of its 8 per cent interest. Until late 1977 Barclays owned 8 per cent of Australia and New Zealand Banking Group, which is now domiciled in Australia.

2.16   As well as the expansion in their overseas representation, the London-based business of the clearing banks has greatly increased, especially with the growth of the eurocurrency market, and the older functions based on trade finance and international payments have diminished in relative importance. In the Barclays group, the business of Barclays' own foreign department was transferred to BBI in 1972, and BBI became the vehicle for all the group's international and overseas business. In the other banks the parent banks retain their traditional foreign business; eurocurrency business may be conducted either chiefly by the parent (Midland, Williams & Glyn's), chiefly by the international subsidiary (Lloyds) or by both (National Westminster). In National Westminster the overseas representation is also split between the parent and International Westminster Bank. For management purposes, however, all that group's international business is organised into a single division, as it is in Barclays, Midland (except in the case of Samuel Montagu) and Williams & Glyn's.

Merchant banking and term lending

2.17   The evolution of merchant banking activities within the clearing bank groups can be traced back to the development of the London money markets in the late 1960s, especially the sterling inter-bank and certificate of deposit markets, the local authority loans market and the eurocurrency markets. Mainly because of official liquidity controls, the clearing banks were prevented from operating in those markets in their own names, and from competing effectively for the deposits of large customers. Accordingly they began to bid competitively for deposits through subsidiaries, often 'bidding subsidiaries' established specially for the purpose. These subsidiaries obtained deposits either from the market or directly from customers and deployed them in the market at a small profit. With their access to term deposits they also provided suitable vehicles for the early development of medium-term lending to customers. After the introduction of *Competition and Credit Control* in 1971 the clearing bank parents were free to bid for deposits and the original rationale for the bidding subsidiaries disappeared. The function of bidding for deposits from branch customers was in most cases transferred to the parent bank, and eurocurrency business for the most part either to the parent or to an international subsidiary. But given the specialist expertise that had been built up in sterling medium-term lending and sterling 'wholesale' money-market dealing, the banks found it convenient to keep the bidding subsidiaries in being for one or both of these purposes.

2.18   In the early 1970s the clearing banks began greatly to increase their medium-term lending and at the same time to broaden the range of merchant banking services they offered. The former bidding subsidiaries were natural vehicles for doing both, though in most banks the parent bank's own term lending function is also now very important. The merchant banking services developed include corporate financial advice, capital issue facilities, investment management, loan syndication and acceptance credits: in fact the banks now offer all the services usually associated with the accepting houses and the other leading merchant banks. The subsidiaries concerned are Barclays Merchant Bank, Lloyds Associated Banking Company, County Bank (National Westminster) and Williams, Glyn & Co. The division of functions within the various groups differs, however. Barclays Merchant Bank is more specialised since it does not undertake investment management (which is the province of Barclays Bank Trust Company). Williams, Glyn & Co is mainly confined to corporate advice, loan syndication and eurobond underwriting: almost all the lending is done by the parent bank. Lloyds Associated Banking Company is rather different; it does some term lending, but its main function is the old one of taking wholesale deposits from customers and lending on to the market, which Lloyds still finds it convenient to keep separate. In the Lloyds group corporate finance and investment management are both handled within the parent bank.

2.19 Midland has chosen a different route towards developing merchant banking services. Instead of relying entirely on building them up on an in-house basis over a period of time, Midland took advantage in 1973 of a relaxation of the previous Bank of England guidelines on bank takeovers to acquire Montagu Trust, the holding company for Samuel Montagu & Co, an established accepting house, in which a 33 per cent holding had been acquired in 1967. The following year it acquired Drayton Corporation, a smaller merchant banking concern, and the business of both companies and of Midland's own former bidding subsidiary was amalgamated under the Samuel Montagu name.

2.20 As well as the term lending done within their own banks, whether in the merchant banking subsidiaries or elsewhere, the banks have two jointly-owned ventures specialising in medium and long-term finance. Finance for Industry (FFI) is 15 per cent owned by the Bank of England and 85 per cent by the London and Scottish clearing banks. The shareholding banks subscribed additional equity capital of £14.5 million in 1973, a further £25 million in 1974, and in 1976 £4 million to enable FFI to subscribe for shares in Equity Capital for Industry. Some of the individual banks have subsidiaries and associates which provide risk capital to industrial and trading companies. The clearing banks are also co-shareholders with the Bank of England in the Agricultural Mortgage Corporation (AMC). The roles of FFI and AMC are described in chapters 8 and 9.

Instalment credit and related services

2.21 Most of the clearing banks took shareholdings in finance houses in the late 1950s as a convenient means of participating in the growing market for instalment credit, especially consumer credit, which for a variety of reasons they were not well placed to enter directly. Two banks took full control of their finance house affiliates from the outset, Midland with Forward Trust and National Provincial with North Central Finance, but the others were content with smaller participations. Immediately after the bank mergers the position was as follows. Barclays had 28 per cent of United Dominions Trust (UDT) and 18 per cent of Mercantile Credit (the latter inherited from Martins). Lloyds had half of Lloyds and Scottish, a joint venture with Royal Bank of Scotland, and 25 per cent of Bowmaker. Midland, as already remarked, owned Forward Trust, and National Westminster not only owned North Central but also had 18 per cent of Mercantile Credit (from Westminster Bank) and 38 per cent of Astley Industrial Trust (from District Bank). As well as its indirect interest in Lloyds and Scottish, Williams & Glyn's inherited a one-third stake in St Margaret's

Trust (from the National Bank), which was increased to 100 per cent just before the merger.

2.22   It was evident that this tangle of shareholdings needed to be tidied up, and most banks have taken the view that, because of the development of their own lending and the consequent growing overlap between their own services and those of their finance house affiliates, it is necessary to have full control of one finance house. Accordingly most of the minority shareholdings have been eliminated. Barclays sold its UDT holding in 1972 and took full control of Mercantile Credit in 1975. Lloyds sold its interest in Bowmaker in 1969; Lloyds and Royal Bank of Scotland remain the principal shareholders in Lloyds and Scottish, but because of the introduction of a public shareholding (against the general trend) their shareholdings have each been diluted to about 40 per cent. National Westminster strengthened its involvement in the sector by acquiring Lombard Banking in 1970 and amalgamating it with North Central the following year. Its holding in Mercantile Credit was sold in 1972; Astley had been absorbed by Mercantile in 1969. The result of these moves is that the greater part of the industry is controlled by one bank or another. Three of the largest houses (Mercantile, Lombard North Central and Forward Trust) are integral parts of clearing bank groups. A fourth (North West Securities) is owned by Bank of Scotland, and another (Hodge Group) by Standard Chartered Bank. Lloyds and Scottish has two dominant bank shareholders. Only UDT, Bowmaker and First National Finance Corporation have no bank affiliations.

2.23   As well as developing traditional instalment credit business both for personal and for industrial customers, the banks have built up their leasing business, a particularly fast-growing activity in recent years. This has been done either through the finance house subsidiaries or through specialist subsidiaries like Lloyds Leasing, Midland Montagu Leasing and Williams & Glyn's Leasing. The banks have also joined leasing partnerships, most notably Airlease International (set up in 1969), which leases ships as well as aircraft. Another, more specialised, leasing partnership is Omnium Leasing, created for the purpose of leasing a complete oil refinery. Lloyds and Scottish and Midland Montagu Leasing are shareholders in Computer Leasings, along with International Computers (ICL) and other partners. Midland has in addition a separate joint venture with ICL for leasing computers, while Lloyds has a joint venture with British Aircraft Corporation (Lloyds Associated Air Leasing). Another fast-growing activity in recent years has been factoring. Barclays, Midland and National Westminster each have specialist factoring subsidiaries, while Lloyds and Williams & Glyn's are involved through Lloyds and Scottish.

Other services

2.24   One entirely new service evolved by the clearing banks in the past few years, which supports both their money transmission and their lending activities, is credit cards. The first British credit card was Barclaycard, set up in 1966 and operated as a department of Barclays Bank. The other bank-owned credit card, Access, was launched in 1972. It is a joint venture between Lloyds, Midland, National Westminster and Williams & Glyn's. Administration is handled by a separate jointly-owned company, but when cardholders take advantage of the extended credit arrangements (described in chapter 8) each bank is responsible for lending to its own cardholders. National Westminster also has a 49.7 per cent interest in the UK-based operations of The Diners Club.

2.25   Outside the main stream of their banking operations the clearing banks now offer a number of ancillary services, either through the parent banks themselves or through specialist subsidiaries. These form the subject of chapter 13. Some are of long standing, such as the executor and trustee services, but others have been introduced recently. For the most part the new services have been developed on an in-house basis; for example, all the banks have broadened the range of their investment, insurance and tax advisory services, and all have introduced a number of computer-based services, some closely related to the money transmission functions, others not. Only in relatively few cases have acquisitions been made. Two examples were the Unicorn unit trust group (Martins 1967) and the Centre-File computer bureau (Westminster 1968); in each case other clearing banks have developed corresponding services themselves. Midland, however, has made three important acquisitions which to a greater or lesser extent are outside the usual range of services offered by the clearing banks.

2.26   The first of these was Thomas Cook, in which Midland obtained a controlling interest in 1972 as the leading partner in a consortium which bought the company from the government. The minority shareholders were bought out early in 1977. Thomas Cook is a tour operator, a retail travel agent, a retail and wholesale foreign exchange dealer and a major issuer of travellers' cheques; it is represented in many countries round the world. The second was Bland Payne, one of the largest insurance broking groups in the world, which was acquired as part of Montagu Trust in 1973. As well as offering the UK-based services of a Lloyd's broker, both to domestic and overseas customers, Bland Payne has a number of overseas establishments, notably in Australia and the United States. It is also involved in shipbroking and in insurance underwriting, the latter through the management of Lloyd's underwriting syndicates and the ownership of two small insurance companies. The third Midland diversification was London American Finance Corporation (LAFCO), in which it obtained a controlling interest in 1975; FFI is the minority shareholder. LAFCO specialises in export finance and export marketing, both in this country and elsewhere.

Group organisation

2.27   The development and diversification of the clearing banks' business described in the foregoing sections has meant that their corporate structures have become much more elaborate. The principal companies in each group are listed in table 52 on page 271; for companies engaged in banking or similar activities the balance sheet totals as at the latest reporting date are shown in millions of pounds. Table 53 on page 272 lists the more important UK associated companies and trade investments. The increased ramifications of the business have created a need for changes in management structures. At the apex of the pyramid stands the group board. The custom of including among its membership non-executive directors representative of industry and commerce at large continues, and provides a depth of experience and commercial judgement as well as a valuable means whereby the banks keep in touch with their customers' needs. A need has been felt, however, to increase the number of executive directors. The chairman of a clearing bank has always been a full-time appointment, but it is now often the practice for there to be a number of full-time deputy chairmen and vice-chairmen, and to include on the board some of the general managers who may have responsibilities either for the group as a whole (such as the group chief executive) or for particular parts of it. The chairmen of the larger operating subsidiaries are also frequently main board directors.

2.28 Below board level, all the banks have now established a divisional structure, which entails a greater degree of delegation than was customary in earlier days. The two banks most affected by mergers, National Westminster and Williams & Glyn's, both opted for particularly radical changes in their organisation. Each has a number of functional divisions reporting to the main board, embracing both profit centres (such as domestic banking and international banking) and cost centres (such as management services and business development). In both banks the heads of the more important divisions sit on the main board; they report in the first instance to the chief executive or his deputy. In Williams & Glyn's the divisional organisation encompasses the whole group; in National Westminster the domestic banking subsidiaries (Coutts, Ulster Bank and Isle of Man Bank) are, however, run independently.

2.29 Barclays is divided into two main divisions, UK division and international division, and two specialised divisions, Barclays Merchant Bank and Barclays Bank Trust Company. Each is controlled by its own board of directors, has its own chief executive, and is responsible for all its own supporting services. Each therefore enjoys a considerable degree of independence both from the others and from above. The UK division is controlled by the board of a separate management company which directly manages the domestic clearing bank business (although the business itself remains vested in Barclays Bank) and which oversees Mercantile Credit and certain other UK subsidiaries. The group board is therefore confined to general oversight of the business, group strategy and the allocation of group resources between divisions; its membership does, however, overlap with that of the divisional boards, and indeed the group chairman and deputy chairman are the chairmen of the international and UK divisions respectively. Both the main divisional boards include non-executive directors.

2.30 In the Midland group the parent bank has two main profit centres, for domestic and international business respectively, each reporting to one of the two chief general managers, who are main board directors. The support service functions are cost centres under their joint control. The various operating subsidiaries are each controlled by their own boards which are fully responsible for their day-to-day business, with their chief executives reporting to the parent company through the appropriate chief general manager. Likewise in Lloyds the more important subsidiaries are independently run. The parent bank has six main divisions, branch banking, overseas department, trust division and three support divisions; branch banking is headed by five joint general managers, the others by specialist general managers. All these general managers report to the chief general management (chief general manager, deputy chief general manager and two assistant chief general managers). Cohesion between the parent bank and the subsidiaries is maintained through the group chief executive and his deputy, and, of course, through cross directorships.

Organisation of domestic banking

2.31 All the banks organise their domestic clearing bank business on a regional basis; this is important for the delegation of lending decisions, as well as for general administration. The exact pattern differs from one to another, and some have stronger traditions of decentralisation than others. In Barclays the present pattern can be traced back to the private banks that existed before the amalgamations of the early years of the century. Barclays now has a two-tier system of seven regional offices and 35 local head offices. Each regional head office is headed by a regional general manager. Each local head office is headed by a team of executive local directors; the larger ones have local boards including non-executive local directors. Although Barclays remains the most decentralised of the banks, its cohesion has been increased in recent years by the more frequent movement of local directors, both between one district and another and between districts and head office. The banks making up the National Westminster group were small enough not to feel any pressing need for a decentralised structure. Westminster Bank had, however, begun to decentralise in 1967, and hired McKinsey & Co in 1968 to assist in reforming its organisation. After the merger, McKinsey were retained, and as well as recommending the divisional structure mentioned in paragraph 2.28 they advised a system of eight regions for the domestic division, each headed by a regional executive director who sits on a regional board with non-executive regional directors. Under the regions are 72 area offices headed by area managers, who enjoy wide delegated powers.

2.32   Midland was another bank with a traditionally centralised organisation, but where a less centralised structure has been developed to meet the needs of customers and an expansion of business. Today there are 24 regional head offices headed by regional directors, each of whom reports to one of five general managers in head office. A separate corporate finance division within the domestic banking sector is responsible for relations with very large corporate customers throughout the United Kingdom, as well as providing support and liaison for all term lending facilities. Similarly in Lloyds' branch banking division each of the five joint general managers is responsible for a specific geographical area; these areas are divided into 17 regions controlled by regional general managers and each with its own regional board. Williams & Glyn's domestic business is spread over three of the bank's divisions, one for Northern England, one for Southern England and one for the City of London. Within the first two divisions responsibility for the branches is further split between regional groupings and, below that, area offices each controlling about a dozen branches.

Management techniques

2.33   The past two decades have seen throughout the business community a growing sophistication in company management. The clearing banks have kept fully abreast of these developments, and have sought to apply them both in their own businesses and in assisting their customers (especially the smaller ones) through their advisory services (see chapter 9). To meet the needs of their increased and more diversified business the banks have established formalised strategic planning systems, embracing the direction of future business and the allocation of capital and personnel resources; at the same time, the introduction by most of the banks of 'management by objectives' has given branches and departments the opportunity to assess their performance against targets set in the light of the banks' overall corporate objectives.

2.34   At a more technical level, new marketing techniques have been applied to support the banks' efforts to diversify their business and broaden the service to customers. Computerisation, although aimed in the first instance at the banks' branch accounting systems, has led to much more sophisticated management information systems. Extensive use is made of systems analysis, operational research and computer modelling as management tools. Organisation and methods teams have examined the way work is arranged and duties divided, assessed administrative and clerical procedures, studied office mechanisation, office layouts and working conditions, and have thereby made an important contribution to improving productivity. Particular attention has been paid through clerical work improvement plans to measuring and enhancing the efficiency of clerical work, and to planning future staffing requirements more accurately. Staff reporting systems have been upgraded to provide for improved performance appraisal for individual staff members. Succession planning has been introduced for the more senior management positions, and extensive use is made of both internal and external management courses.

2.35   By all these means the banks have ensured that the expansion of their business to meet the need of customers for a wider range of services has been accompanied by an increase in efficiency, which enables the banks' new services to be offered on competitive terms while keeping down the cost of their traditional services.

Chapter 3
Money transmission

Summary   This chapter describes the role of the clearing banks in providing the money transmission services on which the nation depends for making payments. Virtually the entire cash distribution system depends on the clearing banks, which also handle most non-cash payments. A distribution network exists to move banknotes from the Bank of England to and from bank branches. Cheques are the most important means of payment after cash: on average six million a day are cleared through the general and town clearing systems. Costs have been kept down by automating the sorting process. The banks have also established a credit clearing for standing orders, counter credits, wages and other payments by businesses. Many of these payments are now handled electronically by Bankers' Automated Clearing Services. Other bank methods of making payments include credit cards, bankers' drafts, telephonic transfers, travellers' cheques and various forms of international payment. Given the dominance of cash and cheques, talk of a 'cashless' and 'chequeless' society is premature and the banks expect to devote as much attention to improving existing services as to developing new ones.

Introduction

3.1   The clearing banks' prime role is that of financial intermediation: that is, they channel funds from those who have them to those who need them. What distinguishes the clearing banks from most other banks is the extent to which this role has been based upon the provision of current account facilities and money transmission services. Most non-clearing banks also provide current account facilities but these are almost always a relatively minor part of their business. Moreover, for the actual transmission of funds these banks are dependent on the services of the clearing banks, with the exception of the Co-operative Bank and the Central Trustee Savings Bank, which are now functional members of the clearing house in their own right. By developing these services the clearing banks have not only provided much of the infrastructure on which the nation depends for the conduct of its financial transactions but also ensured their ability to provide the deposit-taking and lending services described in the chapters that follow.

3.2   Practically every payment which is made in England and Wales depends, directly or indirectly, on services provided by the clearing banks. (In Scotland the Scottish clearing banks play a similar role.) It is estimated that well over 50,000 million payments are made in Britain every year, which is equivalent to about 4 payments each day for everyone over the age of 16. Of these, all but about 2,500 million payments (less than 5 per cent of the total) are made in cash (notes and coins). Virtually the entire cash distribution system depends on the clearing banks, which undertake the task of issuing notes and coins to their customers and of receiving cash deposits. In addition to the banks' own personal and business customers, other banks and financial institutions and the Post Office are major users of the clearing banks' cash services.

Money transmission activity

Table 3

Market shares in non-cash payments (Great Britain, 1976)

Institutional market shares:		Numbers of payments Millions	Percentages
	London clearing banks	1,970	81
	Scottish clearing banks	155	6
	Post Office and National Giro	200	8
	Trustee Savings Banks	35	1
	Co-operative Bank	25	1
	Other	45	2
	Total	**2,430**	**100**
Types of non-cash payment:		Numbers of payments Millions	Percentages
	Cheque	1,580	65
	Credit transfer	330	14
	Standing order	180	7
	Direct debit	110	5
	Postal order	160	7
	Credit card	70	3
	Total	**2,430**	**100**

Figures exclude payments made to withdraw cash, and exclude government payments in cash from Post Offices using order book foils.

Source: Inter-Bank Research Organisation.

3.3 The clearing banks also handle most of the non-cash payments made in Britain. Table 3 provides some indication of the central position that the banks hold in non-cash payments mechanisms. It also contains the best available estimates of non-cash payments made during 1976, classified according to the institution providing the service. It can be seen that over 80 per cent of all non-cash payments made in Britain (and nearly 90 per cent if only England and Wales are considered) are handled by the London clearing banks. The most important types of non-cash payment, with estimated volumes for 1976, are also shown in table 3. For each of these different methods of making payments (except postal orders) the clearing banks handle over 80 per cent of payments made. The number of non-cash payments has been increasing recently at over 7 per cent per annum, reflecting the spread of the banking habit and greater use of banking services by existing customers. The main flows of payments using bank money transmission services are shown in table 4. It can be seen that the most important single flow is from individuals to businesses. Individuals make almost half of all payments and businesses receive well over half of all payments.

Payment flows

Table 4

Analysis of payments by bank money transmission methods

Percentages	Paid to:	Individuals	Businesses	Government and public utilities	Total for 1975
Paid by:	Individuals	1	38	8	47
	Businesses	16	22	4	42
	Government and public utilities	9	1	1	11
Total for 1975		**26**	**61**	**13**	**100**

Source: Inter-Bank Research Organisation.

3.4 The resources employed by the clearing banks in providing money transmission services are very considerable. About 60 per cent of the banks' UK staff are involved, representing a total of some 120,000 employees. The value of capital resources employed approaches £1,000 million and the total operating cost is about £800 million per annum. Taken together, the London clearing banks' money transmission business represents a substantial industry in its own right. In no other major country do commercial banks shoulder such a large share of the payments system. Elsewhere they generally receive greater assistance from the central bank in cash distribution (a topic developed in chapter 17) and in clearing non-cash payments.

Cash distribution services

3.5　The most fundamental service in banking is that which enables the customer to deposit cash and draw it out again. Customers for cash services at the clearing banks' 12,000 branches include private individuals drawing cash, employers requiring cash for wages, retailers depositing their takings, transport undertakings, the Post Office and many others. To meet this demand requires a major cash distribution network. Banknotes are printed by the Bank of England and are made available at its head office and branches. Notes are issued only to clearing banks and to a small group of other banks. The notes are collected from the Bank of England by bullion vans owned by the banks, or by security carrier companies employed by the banks, and are transported to the banks' cash centres, of which there are about 100. From these, the notes are taken by bullion van to the bank branches. The system for coin distribution is somewhat different: the Royal Mint will send coins to bank cash centres or directly to bank branches, but only if it is satisfied that there is not already a surplus of that denomination in circulation. Notes and coin which are surplus to a branch's requirements, and notes which are too soiled to be reissued, are returned to the bank's cash centre by bullion van. Notes are thence returned to the Bank of England. The Royal Mint, on the other hand, does not normally accept coin back from the banks, which must therefore find storage space for substantial quantities of surplus coin.

3.6　In order to be able to supply any reasonable demand for any denomination of notes or coin, the branches must hold substantial stocks of cash. Throughout 1976, the clearing banks held an average of about £700 million in cash at branches and cash centres. No interest can be earned on these holdings by the banks: however, the banks' loss is the government's gain since the banks pay the Bank of England when notes are drawn and the interest thus earned by the Bank of England is paid to the Treasury. In a rather different way, funds received by the Royal Mint for coin sold to the banks are also credited to the Treasury. Quite apart from the loss of interest, the banks incur heavy costs in physically handling cash, especially coin. They are constantly improving the methods by which they handle, transport, sort, pack, count and issue it; in particular, they have a responsibility to their staff and customers to pioneer developments in security arrangements.

3.7　In addition to the standard services of withdrawing and depositing cash at a customer's own branch, the clearing banks have introduced two additional services. The first of these, the reciprocal cash withdrawal system, enables bank customers to draw cash from branches of other banks using a bank cheque card (described in paragraph 3.13) or by special arrangement. Thus a customer is able to take advantage of the extensive network of branches of all the clearing and other deposit banks participating in the scheme if his own bank does not have a conveniently located branch. The second major innovation to affect customers is the introduction of automatic cash dispensers, which allow customers to withdraw money without having to go to a bank counter. The first cash dispensers in the world were installed by a clearing bank in 1967. Since then cash dispensers have been widely installed and there are now over 2,000 in use, most of them available at all hours. One clearing bank has the largest network of on-line cash dispensers in the world. These are linked directly to the bank's computers and enable the customer to withdraw up to a prescribed daily limit provided his account is in funds or within an authorised overdraft limit. Cash dispensers have been developed by the banks individually rather than jointly, and each bank has adopted its own philosophy for the installation and marketing of cash dispenser services. This has resulted in a rapid pace of development and continual pressure both on the banks and on the manufacturers supplying them to improve equipment and services. The number of cash dispensers in operation has more than doubled in the past four years, as shown in table 5. It can be seen that most of the growth in recent years has come from the installation of on-line dispensers.

Cash dispensers Table 5
Numbers in use

December		1972	1973	1974	1975	1976
	Off-line	883	975	1,135	1,212	1,220
	On-line	12	203	468	601	737
	Total	**895**	**1,178**	**1,603**	**1,813**	**1,957**

Source: CLCB Statistical Unit.

3.8 The clearing banks' role in cash distribution is not confined to Bank of England notes and Royal Mint coins. Within the United Kingdom, the Scottish and Northern Irish banks issue their own notes and these find their way into England and Wales in significant quantities. Although they are not legal tender in England and Wales, the clearing banks accept these notes as deposits to customers' accounts and make special arrangements to return them to Scotland or Northern Ireland for payment. The clearing banks are also the main domestic source of foreign currency for those travelling abroad and they keep stocks of currency in their tills for this purpose.

Cheques and credit transfers

3.9 The origin of payments by cheque can be traced back to the days of the goldsmith bankers: rather than withdraw gold deposited with a goldsmith to settle a transaction, customers realised that the goldsmith could be asked to transfer gold from the payer's account to that of the payee. The document authorising this transfer developed into the modern cheque, which after cash is still by far the most common method of making payments in Britain. At the same time, it was necessary to create a system for transferring deposits between different banks and for settling the resulting indebtedness between the banks. The origins of the clearance of cheques are to be found in the coffee houses of Lombard Street, where clerks from the private banks would meet to exchange their small bundles of cheques for cash settlement. The amalgamation of numerous private banks and the formation of the joint stock banks at the end of the last century were the beginning of the branch network of today. The system for the clearance and settlement of cheques has evolved over many years under the auspices of the Bankers' Clearing House. As a result of rationalisation during the second world war, there are now two main cheque clearings: the town clearing and the general clearing.

3.10 The town clearing comprises cheques for £5,000 or more drawn on and paid in at about 100 branches of the clearing banks, the Bank of England, the Co-operative Bank and the Central Trustee Savings Bank in the City of London; these cheques are exchanged and settled on the day they are paid in.

The town clearing is largely concerned with stock market, money market and foreign exchange market transactions. This facility for the same-day transfer of funds between bank accounts is believed to be unique and enables the transmission of large-volume funds to be achieved quickly and smoothly. This is particularly valuable where international transactions are concerned and contributes to the City's strength as an international financial centre. Although the town clearing is small in volume (only 5 million items were handled in 1976 compared with 1,468 million in the general clearing), it handles 90 per cent of the total value of all items cleared. Details of clearing volumes are given in table 6.

Voucher clearings   Table 6
Volumes handled by London clearing banks

Figures in red are percentages			Annual number millions		Daily number millions	Average annual growth rate
			1972	1976	1976	1972–76
Debit clearings	Town	Inter-bank	3.6	4.4		
		Inter-branch	0.8	0.9		
		Total	**4.4**	**5.3**	**0.02**	4.6
	General	Inter-bank	784	1,044		
		Inter-branch	343	424		
		Total	**1,127**	**1,468**	**5.8**	6.8
Credit clearing		Inter-bank	117	159		
		Inter-branch	133	171		
		Total	**250**	**330**	**1.3**	7.2
Total voucher clearings			**1,381**	**1,803**	**7.1**	6.9

Source: CLCB Statistical Unit.

3.11   The general clearing statistics in table 6 cover all other cheques drawn on clearing banks and paid into branches throughout the country, including cheques drawn on and paid in at separate branches of the same bank; these inter-branch items, however, do not pass through the clearing house but are handled by the clearing departments of the individual banks. In normal circumstances cheques passing through the general clearing are exchanged in London on the working day following their payment into a bank, with debit to the drawers' accounts and settlement between the banks taking place the next working day; thus cheques are normally cleared within two working days, although the branch into which the cheque was paid will not know whether it has been honoured until the following day. Inter-bank settlement for both the town and general clearings is achieved by transfers between the accounts that the banks hold at the Bank of England. By appointing a clearing bank to act as its agent, a non-clearing bank can also have its cheques cleared through the clearing house, as can the government with payments initiated by the Paymaster General's office.

3.12   By the late 1950s, the banks had given much thought to the possibility of automatically sorting and listing cheques on computer-controlled equipment. All cheques, wherever paid in, must eventually reach the branch on which they are drawn for signature verification and examination of other details. This 'homing' of the cheque is achieved relatively simply by requiring each branch to sort and list cheques paid in into batches for each bank. These batches are delivered each morning to the clearing departments of the banks on which they are drawn where they are sorted into branch order. With cheque volumes increasing year by year at a rate of some 5 to 7 per cent, the need to automate this process became more pressing. The clearing banks eventually introduced a system for the automatic handling of cheques and this system has now existed for the past 15 years. This development is an example of inter-bank co-operation producing an efficient and cost-effective system which has undoubtedly contributed to the containment of operational costs.

3.13 The increase in the banking habit, with the resultant rise in the number of cheques used to pay for goods and services, required some form of identifying document to support the validity of cheques made out to traders: this need was met by the introduction of the bank cheque card (or cheque guarantee card). The bank cheque card in its current form has two principal purposes: to enable the holder to encash a cheque for up to £50 at the majority of branch banks in Great Britain and Ireland, and two cheques for up to £30 each (shortly to be increased to £50) at many banks in Europe; and to guarantee the payment of a cheque issued by the holder of the card in respect of goods or services up to a value of £50. The original bank cheque cards were of widely differing designs and manufactured to different standards, and it was considered that it would be a great advantage to traders and bank customers alike if the multiplicity of cards were standardised; in 1969, a number of English, Scottish and Irish banks agreed to adopt a standard format. At the same time some European banks, including the major British banks, set up a scheme recognising each other's cheque cards and since 1974 all cards have been marked with the Eurocheque symbol. The number of cheque cards in issue (including Barclaycards held by Barclays customers, for whom they serve also as cheque cards) is shown in table 7. They are still issued free to customers in spite of the considerable costs involved, including those of fraud. It was the sharp increase in losses sustained by banks as a result of fraud that made them reluctant, despite inflation, to increase the value of the guarantee. Nonetheless, in response to public demand, the value was increased for domestic purposes from £30 to £50 from 1 August 1977.

Cheque cards   Table 7
Numbers in issue

December	1972	1973	1974	1975	1976
	4,534,000	5,400,000	6,614,000	8,369,000	9,466,000

Source: CLCB Statistical Unit.

3.14 Another innovation in the 1960s was the credit clearing, though its origins can be traced back to the 1930s. Since that time a system had existed whereby standing order payments were made by the creation of a 'credit advice' showing the name of the payee, the branch holding the account and other relevant information. These 'advices' were sorted into batches at the head offices of the remitting banks and delivered to the head offices of the addressee banks accompanied by banker's payments for the total of the batch. An arrangement had also existed whereby trade, salary and pension payments could be prepared by companies for handling by the banks in the same way as standing order payments. Moreover, the banks had been prepared to accept over their counters credits for accounts at branches of other banks; each credit was forwarded directly to the relevant branch, accompanied by a form of banker's payment which could be cleared through the cheque clearing. In 1960, a formalised credit clearing was inaugurated as the medium for handling all these types of payment, as well as dividends and interest payments. The credit clearing, which handles more than 1 million items daily (see table 6), is similar to the cheque clearing in procedures, transmission time and settlement time, but for a number of reasons it has not been possible to introduce automated handling in quite the same way as for cheques. Instead, certain elements of the credit clearing are now handled separately by electronic methods. These include the majority of standing order payments and some payments of trade debts, wages, salaries and pensions. As with the cheque clearing, the banks which are not members of the clearing house enjoy access to the credit clearing through agency arrangements.

Electronic methods of payment

3.15   One of the earliest applications of computers in the clearing banks was in the handling of credit transfer payment vouchers for standing orders. As soon as substantial progress had been made by the banks in converting current account procedures to computer systems, as described in chapter 14, the opportunity existed to eliminate vouchers and exchange inter-bank payments between computer systems by means of magnetic tapes. The electronic transfer of payments between banks duly started in April 1968 with the creation by the clearing banks of the Inter-Bank Computer Bureau. Now organised as a separate company called Bankers' Automated Clearing Services Limited (BACS) with its own purpose-built computer centre, the organisation has grown into the world's largest automated clearing house, with a total staff of about 200 handling 262 million items in 1976. Non-clearing banks and other financial institutions have agency arrangements with BACS, while customers of the clearing banks and other banks are able to initiate payments by presenting magnetic tapes directly to BACS. The number of non-bank users of BACS has increased rapidly from 520 in 1971 to 2,249 by the end of 1976.

3.16   The ability to produce a magnetic tape containing payments data eliminates the clerical effort necessary for voucher production, avoids the use of stationery and economises on the use of the computer equipment itself, because magnetic tape production is many times faster than voucher production. The number of payments handled by BACS has grown very rapidly and, as diagram 3 shows, the growth rate of automated payments has until recently been twice as fast as that of the voucher clearings. Standing order payments accounted for 43 per cent of the volume of items handled by BACS in 1976, direct debits for 38 per cent and automated credit transfers for 19 per cent. (The detailed breakdown is shown in table 8.)

Automated clearings   Table 8

	Millions of items		Average annual
	1972	1976	growth rate (per cent)
Direct debits	55	100	16.2
Standing orders	98	114	3.8
Other credit transfers	13	48	38.6
Total processed by BACS	**167**	**262**	12.1
Standing orders processed by banks	8	34	41.2
Total automated clearings	**175**	**296**	**14.1**

Source: CLCB Statistical Unit.

3.17   Almost all standing order payments (which are also known as payments by banker's order) are now processed entirely electronically. Each bank prepares a daily magnetic tape of payments to be made on behalf of its customers to customers of other banks and delivers it to BACS, which then sorts the information received and produces for each bank a magnetic tape of credits to be made to customers of that bank. This tape, in turn, is used to credit the recipients' accounts. Standing order payments between customers of the same

Clearing activity

Diagram 3

Number of items handled by the London clearing banks
in the inter-bank and inter-branch clearings

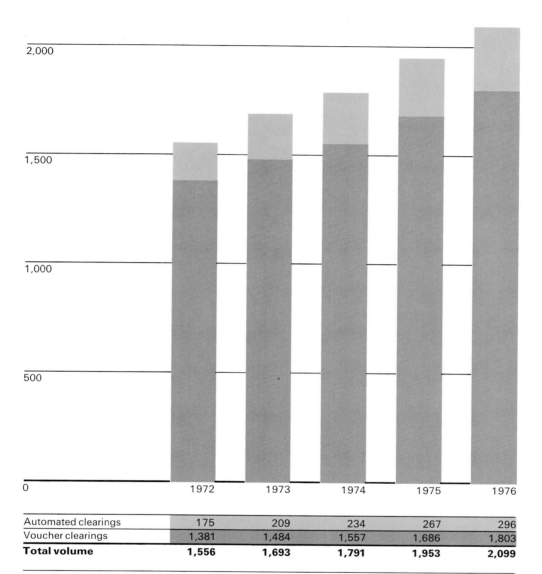

Millions

	1972	1973	1974	1975	1976
Automated clearings	175	209	234	267	296
Voucher clearings	1,381	1,484	1,557	1,686	1,803
Total volume	**1,556**	**1,693**	**1,791**	**1,953**	**2,099**

Source: CLCB Statistical Unit

bank are now all processed electronically within the bank, whereas formerly
some were passed through BACS.

3.18 Regular standing order payments to institutions (for example, life assurance
premiums, hire purchase instalments and payments to building societies) need
to be reconciled in the offices of the recipients, with the result that considerable
time can elapse between the due date of payment and the knowledge that the
payment has been received or, more importantly, not received. To overcome
this problem, the banks devised the direct debit scheme: instead of the bank
originating the payment in the form of a credit transfer, the payee is permitted
to originate the payment by way of a debit transfer. Thus, the onus for
obtaining the payment is on the payee, who now learns of non-payment
through the return of the unpaid direct debit within a few days. As with
standing order payments, it is necessary for the bank to have authority from
the payer that regular payments should be made by this method, and consent

of the payer is also required when a direct debit is to be substituted for a standing order. Originally, direct debits were handled by introducing paper vouchers into the cheque clearing, but with the formation of BACS, payees were encouraged to provide data about their debits on magnetic tape for processing by BACS. Participating institutions are required to give the banks an indemnity, unlimited in amount, so that an invalid debit may be instantly reimbursed by the debiting institution without question and without limitation in time, thus protecting the customer. Because the banks underwrite the indemnity, they have, of necessity, restricted the participants in the scheme to institutions of undoubted integrity.

3.19   When a company produces a substantial volume of credit transfer payments, it will generally find it advantageous to use BACS. Often credit transfers are produced by computer systems in any case and the payer can deliver a magnetic tape directly to BACS. The automated credit transfer is particularly used by companies and organisations with large numbers of wage and salary credits to be distributed directly to employees' accounts. It is estimated that more than 70 per cent of all salary payments credited to bank accounts are now made through BACS.

Other bank methods of making payments

3.20   A relatively new, but rapidly growing, method of making payments is by using one or other of the credit cards issued by the clearing banks. Some 6 million individuals hold bank credit cards but, since some people hold both, there are about 7 million cards in issue. About half this number are regularly used for making purchases. The total number of payments made in 1976 by using credit cards is estimated to have been about 70 million, excluding transactions to draw cash from bank branches. (The extended credit facilities available to cardholders are discussed in chapter 8.)

3.21   The clearing banks provide two services for customers who require to make payments without the payee having to wait for a cheque to be cleared to be sure of receiving the money. One method is the issue of banker's drafts, which are cheques drawn by a bank on its own head office; they are generally used for settling large value transactions such as house purchase. The banker's draft is given by the payer to the payee and can then be paid in to the payee's account and cleared exactly like a cheque. For urgent transactions the telephonic transfer system can be used; coded telephone messages are sent by the payer's bank to that of the payee, which ensure that the funds are transferred the same day.

3.22   The banks provide their customers with various methods of making international payments. A customer may instruct his bank to make a transfer abroad, either directly to the recipient or to his bank account. This is achieved by the UK bank sending a message to a correspondent bank abroad to credit or pay the required amount to the payee. Until recently, the bank would have used the mail, cable or telex to instruct a correspondent bank abroad to make the required payment but, from May 1977, it has been possible for British banks to use the SWIFT system to send payment instructions to certain countries. SWIFT (Society for Worldwide Interbank Financial Telecommunication) is a private data communication system between more than 500 banks in 15 countries which allows international payment instructions to be sent instantaneously, using the latest methods of computer-controlled message switching. The clearing banks were founder members and played a leading part at every stage from its inception to its successful implementation in 1977. Alternative methods for international payments include foreign currency drafts, where the UK bank draws a draft on a foreign affiliate or correspondent bank and the recipient pays it into his account as if it were a domestic cheque.

3.23 Travellers' cheques provide a convenient and safe method of making payments and obtaining local currency in foreign countries; the tremendous expansion in business travel, as well as tourism, over the past 20 years, has resulted in a large increase in activity. As well as issuing their own sterling travellers' cheques, the clearing banks can supply customers with foreign currency travellers' cheques issued by themselves or their subsidiaries or by correspondent banks. Sterling travellers' cheques are often supplied to overseas visitors to the United Kingdom through agency arrangements with correspondent banks, although encashment facilities for foreign banks' travellers' cheques are provided at all clearing bank branches.

Charges for money transmission services

3.24 Except for services provided for certain government departments and nationalised industries (as explained in chapter 16), the clearing banks do not operate common tariffs or systems of charging. There are, therefore, differences in the way in which charges are applied and in the rates charged for particular services, although certain general features are common to the charging policies of each bank. Each bank, for instance, has a published tariff for private accounts, incorporating a provision for the account to be conducted free of charge if a specified minimum balance or minimum average balance is maintained, and for a specified charge for each debit entry if the account is overdrawn or if the minimum balance is not maintained. Any charge is abated by a specified percentage of the average cleared credit balance, calculated so as to take into account the value to the bank of such balances.

3.25 Smaller business accounts are also conducted on the basis of a simple scale of charges which takes into account the number of entries, both debit and credit, which pass through the account. The rates vary from bank to bank and do not generally form part of a published tariff. Here too provision is made for the charge to be abated by the value of any cleared credit balances maintained. The charges for larger business accounts are generally negotiated between the bank and the customer, and are usually expressed either as a rate per entry, or as a percentage of turnover passing through the account. The rates take into account the customer's anticipated usage of all the more common money transmission services; more specialised services are usually charged for separately. The value of credit balances maintained will be taken into account when establishing the charges. In some cases the customer undertakes to maintain a given minimum balance on current account to defray the cost of the service, and no explicit charges are levied.

Future developments in the banks' money transmission services

3.26 Comments on future methods of making payments sometimes show an unrealistic optimism about the pace of change. Much has been made of the imminent arrival of the 'cashless' and 'chequeless' society. In fact, as shown at the outset of this chapter, at least 95 per cent of all payments are still made in cash and 65 per cent of the remainder are made by cheque. Cash is uniquely well fitted for making small value payments, since the total cost of an average cash transaction is very much less than the cost of alternative methods. Cheques also have unique properties which make them far more flexible than most rival methods of payment. Cash and cheques have existed for centuries and there is no reason to suppose that they will be rapidly replaced.

3.27   Therefore, the clearing banks expect to devote as much attention to improving existing services as to developing entirely new ones. The development of automatic cash dispensing has recently entered a new phase with the introduction of the first 'autotellers' which are connected directly to the banks' computers and can be used for establishing the customer's current balance, requesting a bank statement or new cheque book, making deposits and simple transfers, as well as for obtaining any amount of cash up to a predetermined limit. Some of these machines have already been installed in shops, factories and other public places and this development will continue.

3.28   The clearing banks are constantly studying ways of improving the cheque clearing system in order to contain the inevitable increase in costs. Much has been achieved behind the scenes by heavy capital expenditure in up-to-date processing machinery. Moreover, in 1977 the clearing banks authorised the development of a major system for replacing much of the town clearing by an electronic switching system called Clearing House Automated Payments System (CHAPS). This system will enable clearing and non-clearing banks to initiate large value payments electronically, thus speeding the payment process and eliminating the need for paper vouchers and manual handling. Settlement will take place on the day of transmission, as in the town clearing. The development potential of CHAPS is considerable, since it could ultimately be used not only to replace many of the payments now passing through the town clearing but also to extend the benefits of town clearing to smaller payments or to those made outside the City.

3.29   The banks will continue to promote the facilities of BACS as a way of reducing or controlling the number of paper vouchers which require processing. As an example, they have held extensive discussions with the Department of Health and Social Security to investigate how benefits might be paid to bank account holders by automated credit transfer. A more fundamental change in payments methods may well be the introduction of electronic funds transfer at the point of sale. The technology of electronic cash registers and of magnetic cards is sufficiently advanced for it to be feasible to make instantaneous transfers from a shopper's account to a retailer's account at the time that goods are purchased. However, it is unlikely that such methods will be in common use before the 1980s.

3.30   The banks' ability to develop and market their money transmission services must be constrained by the amount that the market is prepared to pay. High interest rates in 1973 and 1974 enabled charges on personal accounts to be reduced substantially. However, price controls and the reluctance of the users of these services to bear their full cost have made it impossible to take account of subsequent increases in labour and other costs. As a result, charges now cover only about 20 per cent of the cost of providing the services, and there is a considerable degree of cross-subsidisation between the users of money transmission services and other bank customers. The banks must therefore concentrate on holding down the costs of existing services at least as much as on developing new ones. (The individual clearing banks are currently providing detailed information on these matters to the Price Commission which is undertaking a sectoral investigation into money transmission charges.)

Deposit taking

Summary

This chapter describes the main types of sterling deposit held with the clearing banks, their maturity structure and sources, and the banks' market share in deposit-taking as a whole. Individual institutions' market shares depend on a variety of factors including the level of loan demand, the competitive advantages enjoyed by some institutions and the interest rates offered. Current accounts are non-interest-bearing accounts used for making payments; despite the growth in account holders the level of balances has grown more slowly than other deposits and the accounts have also become ever more expensive for the banks to operate. The other main type of retail deposit is called the 7-day deposit (though withdrawals are usually allowed without notice). Since 1971 the banks have made greater use of large-scale deposits raised on the 'wholesale' markets. These include large deposits taken in the branches, inter-bank and other deposits raised on the money markets, and certificates of deposit. The banks' deposit structure is predominantly short-term, but the stability of that structure is greater than the notional maturities might suggest. The banks engage in 'maturity transformation' since they cannot match all their term loans with deposits of equal maturity. The personal sector is the main provider of the banks' sterling deposits. The banks are in competition with a wide range of institutions for deposits and over recent years have lost market share, in particular to the building societies.

Introduction

4.1   It is largely the money transmission services described in the previous chapter that have provided the basis for the clearing banks' central role in the UK financial system. By providing these services the banks have generated the current account credit balances which represent the bedrock of their resources, even though they now amount to a smaller proportion of total resources than they used to. The banks' current accounts have in their turn been one of the chief influences on the development of the banks' role as providers of finance.

4.2   There are two main ways in which the types of bank deposit can be analysed. The first involves a three-way distinction between current accounts, deposit accounts (together referred to as retail deposits) and wholesale deposits. The second involves a two-way distinction between sight deposits (mainly current accounts but also wholesale overnight and call deposits) and time deposits. These two approaches have been adopted in the analyses of the bank deposits contained in tables 54 and 55 respectively on page 273, with a further distinction being drawn in each case between sterling and foreign currency deposits. The latter have grown considerably in importance from a low base a decade ago, and accounted for about a third of the deposits of the clearing bank groups at the end of 1976. This chapter, however, is concerned chiefly with the banks' sterling deposits; foreign currency deposits are discussed in chapter 11. Before examining the component parts of the banks' sterling deposit structure in greater detail, it is necessary to make some general points about the major influences on the level of bank deposits as a whole.

4.3   The chief of these influences are the general state of the economic environment in which the banks have to operate—not least the level of national income and wealth—and the extent of the competition for deposits, both between one bank and another and between the banks as a whole and other financial institutions. The government and Bank of England act to control the total supply of money, of which bank deposits are the major component, by the methods described in chapter 6. These actions, together with the preferences of individual depositors, determine the total level of bank deposits. Individual institutions, of course, may seek to increase their deposits by a greater proportionate amount than the expansion of the money supply as a whole; but clearly they cannot all do so. The market shares of total deposits held by different banks and deposit-taking institutions are themselves dependent on a variety of factors. They include the composition of an institution's customer base, the location of its branches, the quality of its service and its general efficiency. Three further factors, however, are worth considering in a little more detail.

4.4   The first of these is loan demand. Traditionally most deposit-taking institutions, the clearing banks included, could have been described as 'deposit-driven'; that is to say, their main concern was to deploy the deposits received in the normal course of business as best they could. This is still essentially the position of a number of institutions, notably the savings banks. However, in recent years it has become increasingly less true of commercial banks. The development of the wholesale money markets in particular has enabled bankers to modify the traditional approach, since they can now enter into lending commitments in the knowledge that any shortfall in branch deposits can be made good in the markets. Indeed, many non-clearing banks without retail deposits are now effectively 'advances-driven'.

4.5   The second factor is the artificial competitive advantages enjoyed by some institutions in their deposit-taking activities. The chief of these advantages are total or partial freedom from monetary and credit controls, and the fiscal advantages extended to the depositors of certain institutions, notably the savings banks and building societies. The case for terminating such discriminatory advantages is argued in chapter 18. The third factor arises largely from the first and second, and is the actual amount of interest that institutions are prepared to pay to attract depositors—or, in the case of current accounts, the quality and cost of the services provided. The banks are constrained in their interest rate policies by a number of factors, which include not only their ability to deploy their deposits at a profit but also various artificial constraints, notably the official pressure on the banks from time to time to keep their rates down.

Current accounts

4.6   Current accounts are the accounts customers maintain with banks to enable them to withdraw cash on demand, issue cheques and make use of the banks' other money transmission services. Such accounts operate either in credit or (by prior arrangement) in debit; when considering the current accounts as a form of bank deposit the term refers only to the credit balances held in these accounts. Credit balances on current accounts of the clearing banks are non-interest-bearing, though most customers receive an abatement of their charges for transmission activity on the basis of a notional interest rate allowance.

Current accounts are maintained by both personal and business customers, and each sector provides roughly half the total credit balances. Virtually every business enterprise in the country has at least one such account, although many of them are in debit. In addition, non-clearing banks maintain settlement balances with the clearing banks, though in the statistics these are classified as wholesale deposits rather than current accounts. Because current accounts can be used so effectively to make payments, they are a relatively close substitute for cash; indeed, credit balances on current account are included in even the narrower definition of the money supply (M1).

4.7   The clearing banks are not by any means the only providers of current account services but, largely because of their widespread branch networks, they hold the overwhelming majority of all current accounts, both by number of accounts and by value of credit balances. However, the clearing banks now face competition in their current account business from the National Giro and Trustee Savings Banks, although the market shares of these institutions are still small. The total number of current accounts maintained by the clearing banks has been growing at an annual rate of about 4 per cent in recent years and rose from 15.9 million at the end of 1971 to 19.4 million at the end of 1976. So far as personal business is concerned, it is estimated that in 1976 some 38 per cent of all adults in the United Kingdom held current accounts with one or more of the London clearing banks (the figure for England and Wales would be about 42 per cent). The banks have had considerable success in extending the banking habit throughout the community; and during the 1970s the socio-economic profile of the banks' current account customers moved closer to that of society as a whole (see table 9). However, despite the growth in account numbers, current account balances have grown more slowly over the past 15 years than interest-bearing deposits and indeed have failed to keep pace with inflation; this is at least in part because high interest rates have increased the cost to the depositor of holding excess balances in his current account.

Savings by socio-economic group Table 9
Analysis of savings in 1975/76

Percentages		AB	C1	C2	DE
	Total sample	12.7	23.5	32.5	31.2
	LCB current accounts	22.9	33.5	27.8	15.8
	LCB savings/deposit accounts	19.3	28.0	30.6	22.1
	Other banks	15.6	27.2	33.0	24.3
	Building societies	19.9	30.7	29.1	20.3
	National Savings Bank	14.6	25.1	32.0	28.4
	Trustee Savings Banks	7.1	20.9	37.6	34.5
	Life assurance	12.6	24.5	36.0	26.8
	Unit trusts	24.7	27.0	26.5	21.8
	Stocks and shares	39.2	28.6	17.5	14.6

Source: Target Group Index.

4.8   Current accounts have not only tended to decline as a percentage of total deposits; they have also become progressively more costly to generate. The clearing banks estimate that in 1976 the cost of operating their current account services was equivalent to the payment of an interest rate of around 7 per cent on outstanding current account balances even after allowing for costs recovered by bank charges. So although no explicit interest is paid on current accounts, they are far from being a free resource to the bank.

Other retail deposits

4.9   In addition to operating current accounts, the banks have long used their branch networks to attract interest-bearing deposits as well. The chief of these are the banks' 7-day deposits. Deposits of any amount are accepted though for the most part they comprise relatively small savings from the personal sector. They are technically subject to seven days' notice, although it is normal practice for the banks to waive this requirement, adjusting interest payments in lieu of notice. So, although deposit accounts cannot be used for making payments, they are among the most liquid forms of savings after current accounts, and are in competition with other relatively liquid forms of personal savings such as building society and savings bank accounts. In addition, some of the clearing banks operate savings accounts which also earn interest and provide limited cash withdrawal facilities at any of the bank's branches, rather than just the account-holding branch as with 7-day deposits. However, savings accounts represent an extremely small proportion of total deposits. Savings deposits and 7-day deposits are amalgamated for statistical purposes, and together with current accounts are frequently referred to as retail deposits, indicating that they are almost entirely generated through the branches.

4.10   Between 1962 and 1974 7-day deposits grew at a faster rate than current account balances, although from table 10 it will be seen that the annual pattern varied considerably. They rose from 39 per cent of total retail deposits in 1962 to 46 per cent in 1976, having been over 50 per cent in 1974. There was particularly strong growth in the period 1972–74 when a rapid increase in the money supply was accompanied by historically high interest rates paid on 7-day deposits. Since 1974, however, 7-day deposits have been very sluggish, latterly as a result of falling interest rates, and for much of 1977 have been declining. The number of 7-day deposit and savings accounts rose from 9.3 million in 1971 to 11.4 million in 1976; by then about 18 per cent of all adults in the United Kingdom were believed to be 7-day deposit account holders.

Branch retail deposits   Table 10

Sterling deposits of parent banks only

November £ million	1962	1963	1964	1965	1966	1967	1968	1969	1970	1971	1972	1973	1974	1975	1976
Current accounts	4,294	4,714	4,971	4,922	4,892	5,315	5,438	5,265	5,594	6,312	6,932	7,179	7,498	8,806	9,499
Deposit accounts	2,772	2,828	3,044	3,434	3,620	3,880	4,283	4,372	4,614	4,612	4,874	6,060	8,038	8,337	8,238
Total	**7,066**	**7,542**	**8,015**	**8,356**	**8,512**	**9,195**	**9,721**	**9,637**	**10,208**	**10,924**	**11,806**	**13,239**	**15,536**	**17,143**	**17,737**

Source: CLCB Statistical Unit.

4.11   Before the introduction of *Competition and Credit Control* (CCC) in 1971, the interest rate paid on 7-day deposits was agreed between the clearing banks and had for some time been 2 per cent below Bank rate. Since that time each bank has fixed and published its own rate. However, it was recognised at the time of CCC that the greater freedom afforded to the banks might lead them to compete for individuals' savings invested in savings banks or building societies. Consequently, the authorities reserved the right to protect those institutions by imposing limits on the terms offered by the banks for savings deposits; and from September 1973 to February 1975 they restricted the interest payable on bank deposits of less than £10,000 to a maximum of 9½ per cent. Although there have been divergences from time to time between the rates offered by individual clearing banks for 7-day deposits, competitive pressures since 1972 have tended to result in uniformity. The difference between deposit rate and lending base rate has varied between 1½ and 4½ per cent, with a tendency to widen evident since January 1975. However, more relevant than the link with base rate is the cost of the banks' other deposits, and it should be noted that the difference between deposit rate and money market rates has narrowed during 1977. The undoubted safety of the clearing banks in the eyes of the general public, and the convenience that 7-day deposits offer, lead customers to maintain balances on these accounts despite the higher interest rates that can be obtained elsewhere from time to time.

Sterling wholesale deposits

4.12   Until the 1960s, virtually all clearing bank deposits were current account or 7-day deposits. However, in the 1960s a market developed for deposits of large sums lodged mainly by financial institutions and large corporations for varying periods and receiving higher rates of interest than the clearing banks' 7-day deposit rate; these are referred to as wholesale deposits. Until CCC the clearing banks generally did not bid for such deposits directly, as the requirement to maintain the official 28 per cent liquidity ratio would have made the business unprofitable, and at that time their interest rate agreements were operative; however, their subsidiary companies, some specially formed for the purpose, did take deposits from the wholesale market. The constraints on the parent banks were removed with the introduction of CCC, and since then both parent banks and subsidiaries have operated in the market. The proportion of wholesale deposits increased rapidly until by 1973 it was over 45 per cent of the clearing bank groups' total sterling deposits, although since then the proportion has been somewhat lower as demand for lending has been depressed (see table 54 on page 273).

4.13   As a source of funds for the clearing banks, the wholesale deposit market has three distinct component parts: deposits of £10,000 and over received through the branch network; inter-bank and other large deposits placed either directly by the institution concerned or through money brokers; and the issue of negotiable certificates of deposit. The rates paid on the second and third of these are determined on the open market. Interest rates for the wholesale deposits received through the branch system are communicated to the branches daily, but for larger sums of over £50,000 or so rates for individual deposits are negotiated separately on the basis of the prevailing open-market rates.

4.14   The volume of wholesale deposits that the clearing banks require at any one time represents the balance of funds they need, over and above their more stable current and deposit accounts, to finance their lending and liquidity needs. When the demand for borrowing is strong, therefore, the volume of market deposits sought by the banks will tend to rise, and vice versa. The volume and cost of wholesale deposits fluctuate on a daily basis with the ebbs and flows of commercial loan demand, the movements of funds between the public and private sectors, and the operations of the Bank of England on the various financial markets. As profitable opportunities arise, and to maintain a continuing market presence, the clearing banks operate both as borrowers and as lenders in the markets; balances with other banks and certificates of deposit are, however, held largely for liquidity reasons.

4.15   Sterling certificates of deposit (CDs) were first issued in October 1968 following the successful development of a market in dollar certificates of deposit, which were introduced in the United States early in 1961 and in the United Kingdom in May 1966. A CD is a document issued by a bank certifying that a deposit has been made with that bank which is repayable to the bearer upon surrender of the certificate at maturity. To the 140 or so banks which have been given permission to issue them, sterling CDs allow large sums to be raised at fixed rates of interest and for fixed periods from a wide range of sources. The main attraction to the holder is that CDs earn about the same rate of interest as a fixed-term deposit but they can, if necessary, be realised before maturity. They can be sold at any time at the prevailing market price on the secondary market which is operated chiefly by the discount houses. Largely because of their ready marketability, CDs can be issued with longer maturities than most other wholesale deposits – an important consideration in view of the growth in the banks' term lending. From the start, banks themselves have held an appreciable portion – currently about 60 per cent – of all sterling CDs in issue, and the market in CDs has developed largely as an extension of the inter-bank deposit market. The value of sterling CDs outstanding expanded rapidly after the implementation of CCC and quickly outpaced that of London issues of dollar CDs. However, after 1973 the issues of sterling CDs declined and by the end of 1976 had fallen from the November 1973 peak of £6,111 million to £3,340 million. The total amount of CDs issued by the clearing banks and their subsidiaries has moved in line with this general trend: from 1971 to 1973, issues of sterling CDs were, in fact, one of the main means by which clearing banks expanded their resources. The total outstanding issued by the clearing bank groups rose from £1,478 million in April 1972 to a peak of £3,540 million in November 1973, in parallel with a more modest rise in sterling deposits from the inter-bank market. The subsequent fall in demand for bank credit led to less reliance on CDs and inter-bank funds, and by the end of 1976 clearing bank group issues of CDs had fallen to £1,685 million.

Maturity structure

4.16   The short-term nature of the clearing banks' sterling deposits is illustrated in diagram 4 which shows that three-quarters of the total is made up of deposits repayable in less than eight days, mainly current accounts and 7-day retail deposits. Only about 6 per cent of deposits are of maturities of six months and over, which shows that the banks' wholesale deposits are also predominantly of short-term maturity. Because of depositors' preference for liquidity, short-term interest rates will (other than in exceptional circumstances) be lower than long-term rates. The clearing banks have traditionally made use of short-term deposits to keep the cost of their lending lower than it would otherwise be. However, the combined effects of increasing operating costs and reducing volumes of retail deposits in real terms have eroded the competitive edge which the clearing banks once had in setting their lending rates.

4.17   In assessing the maturity structure of the banks' deposits, an important distinction must be made between notional and actual maturity, and between the stability of individual deposits and that of deposits as a whole. The fact that current account balances are withdrawable on demand and other retail deposits at seven days' notice is no guide to the actual length of time for which the balances will be held on the banks' books; while in any case the fluctuations in the balances on individual accounts largely cancel one another out. As the Radcliffe Report concluded, "individual balances go up and down, depositors come and depositors go, but the total on current account goes on for ever". So although the banks must cater for a degree of day-to-day volatility, long experience enables them to assume that their deposit base as a whole will remain reasonably stable. Given this stability, and the banks' ability to augment their branch deposits on the wholesale markets, they can lend a significant portion

Personal holdings of financial assets

Diagram 7

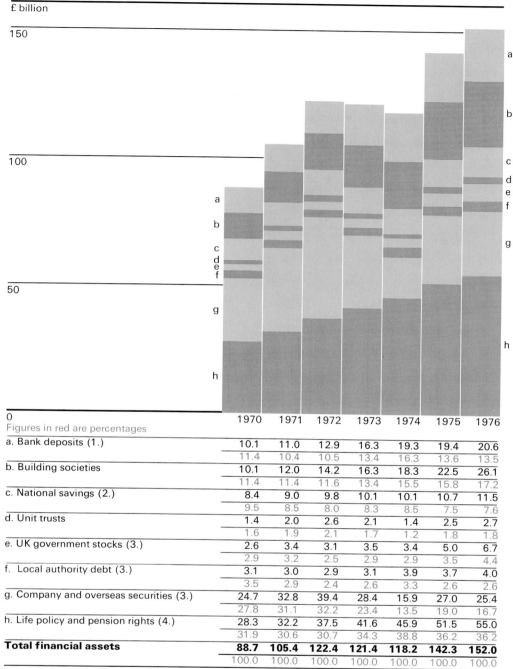

£ billion

	1970	1971	1972	1973	1974	1975	1976
a. Bank deposits (1.)	10.1	11.0	12.9	16.3	19.3	19.4	20.6
	11.4	10.4	10.5	13.4	16.3	13.6	13.5
b. Building societies	10.1	12.0	14.2	16.3	18.3	22.5	26.1
	11.4	11.4	11.6	13.4	15.5	15.8	17.2
c. National savings (2.)	8.4	9.0	9.8	10.1	10.1	10.7	11.5
	9.5	8.5	8.0	8.3	8.5	7.5	7.6
d. Unit trusts	1.4	2.0	2.6	2.1	1.4	2.5	2.7
	1.6	1.9	2.1	1.7	1.2	1.8	1.8
e. UK government stocks (3.)	2.6	3.4	3.1	3.5	3.4	5.0	6.7
	2.9	3.2	2.5	2.9	2.9	3.5	4.4
f. Local authority debt (3.)	3.1	3.0	2.9	3.1	3.9	3.7	4.0
	3.5	2.9	2.4	2.6	3.3	2.6	2.6
g. Company and overseas securities (3.)	24.7	32.8	39.4	28.4	15.9	27.0	25.4
	27.8	31.1	32.2	23.4	13.5	19.0	16.7
h. Life policy and pension rights (4.)	28.3	32.2	37.5	41.6	45.9	51.5	55.0
	31.9	30.6	30.7	34.3	38.8	36.2	36.2
Total financial assets	**88.7**	**105.4**	**122.4**	**121.4**	**118.2**	**142.3**	**152.0**
	100.0	100.0	100.0	100.0	100.0	100.0	100.0

Figures in red are percentages

1. Includes deposit banks, National Giro, accepting houses, overseas and other banks and discount market, less 2½ per cent to allow for non-profit-making institutions.

2. Includes National Savings Bank, Trustee Savings Banks, National Savings Certificates, Save-as-you-Earn, Premium Savings Bonds, etc.

3. Estimated market values.

4. Includes Government Actuary Department's estimates of occupational pension rights.

Source: Anatomy of UK Finance 1970–75 by Christopher Johnson
(based on Diamond Commission Reports on the Distribution of Income and Wealth).

4.22   The growth in the deposits of UK residents with all the identified repositories has been almost exactly the same over the past 14 years as that of gross domestic product at current prices – about 325 per cent in each case. However, within this figure different repositories expanded at dramatically different rates. Diagram 8, derived from the figures in table 57, highlights the changes, in both absolute and relative terms, in the main forms of deposit and saving between 1962 and 1976. At one extreme there was a virtual twentyfold increase

Comparative growth of deposit holdings

Sterling deposits of UK residents

Diagram 8

1962
Grand total:
£16,523m

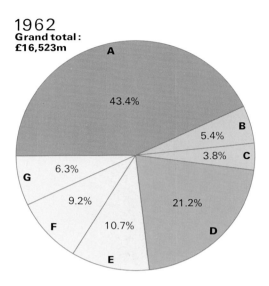

A 43.4%
B 5.4%
C 3.8%
D 21.2%
E 10.7%
F 9.2%
G 6.3%

1976
Grand total:
£69,759m

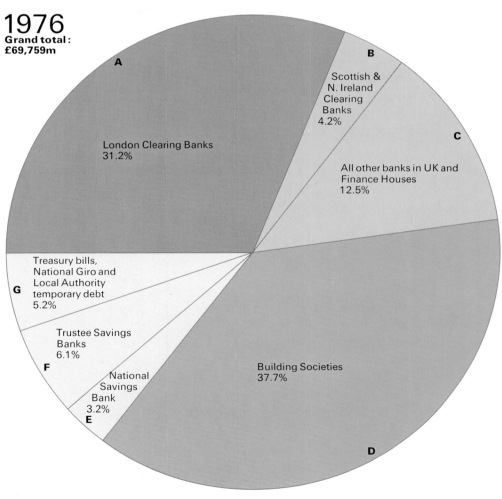

A London Clearing Banks 31.2%
B Scottish & N. Ireland Clearing Banks 4.2%
C All other banks in UK and Finance Houses 12.5%
D Building Societies 37.7%
E National Savings Bank 3.2%
F Trustee Savings Banks 6.1%
G Treasury bills, National Giro and Local Authority temporary debt 5.2%

Source: Financial Statistics.

in deposits with non-clearing banks (including foreign banks in London and the clearing banks' own banking subsidiaries); at the other extreme there was a mere 25 per cent increase in deposits with the National Savings Bank. Between these extremes, the clearing banks showed below-average growth of just over 200 per cent while the other large savings medium, the building societies, grew by nearly 650 per cent. Admittedly these two figures exaggerate the differences in the total deposit growth of the clearing banks and building societies, because of the exclusion of the banks' subsidiaries. On the other hand, they underestimate the difference in the growth of the retail deposits of the banks and the building societies because the clearing bank figures include some wholesale deposits after 1971. The building societies overtook the clearing banks in aggregate deposits for the first time in 1971 and after losing some ground in 1974 recovered their lead in 1975 and substantially increased it in 1976. Some of the competitive advantages which helped them to do so are discussed in chapter 18.

4.23 The growth in the market share of the building societies is the main reason why banks as a whole have suffered a decline in their share of total deposits over the 14-year period, despite the rapid growth of non-clearing banks. The market share of the clearing banks alone has fallen from 43 to 31 per cent while that of the building societies has risen from 21 to 38 per cent. The comparative growth rates of clearing bank retail deposits and building society share and deposit account balances are plotted against the rise in the retail price index in diagram 9. Only in two of the 14 years covered by the diagram— 1973 and 1974—did the clearing banks' deposits grow at a faster rate than those of the building societies, probably as a result of the comparatively high level of interest then paid on 7-day deposits. The faster growth shown by the

Comparative deposit growth rates   Diagram 9

Branch retail deposits and building society deposits (1962 = 100)

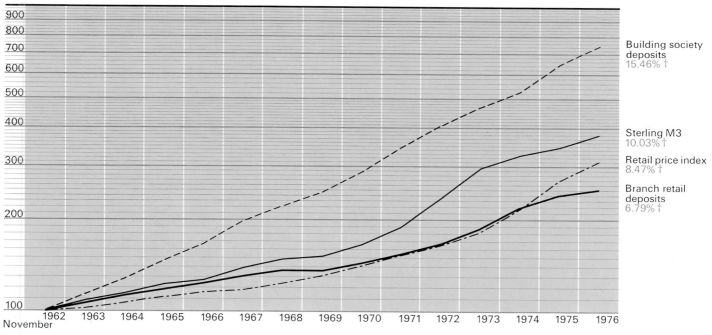

† Compound annual rates of increase 1962 − 1976 (figures in red)
Sources : CLCB Statistical Unit and Financial Statistics

building societies in other recent years similarly reflects the high rates of interest they have been able to offer, partly by virtue of the composite-rate tax arrangements from which their tax-paying depositors benefit. The shift in market share from banks to building societies probably represents the most important change in the deposit-taking picture over the past decade or so.

4.24   Despite the growth in the market shares of non-clearing banks, mentioned in paragraph 4.22, the clearing banks remain the predominant banking repositories for the funds of the general public in the United Kingdom. From table 55 on page 273 it can be computed that at December 1976 the clearing bank groups still held nearly 69 per cent of the total bank deposits (sterling and foreign currency) of UK non-bank residents, and 63 per cent of total sterling deposits (including those held by other banks). Table 12 traces the changes in the clearing banks' market share of UK non-bank residents' sterling bank deposits since 1971. It fell to its lowest level in 1973 but recovered significantly in the following year, partly as a result of the difficulties experienced by some of the non-clearing banks.

Market shares of sterling deposits   Table 12

Deposits of UK non-bank residents

December Percentages	1971	1972	1973	1974	1975	1976
LCB parents	71.6	65.8	62.7	68.2	67.3	65.7
LCB subsidiaries	28.4	6.3	7.0	7.4	7.9	7.9
Other banks		27.9	30.3	24.3	24.8	26.5
All banks in UK	**100.0**	**100.0**	**100.0**	**100.0**	**100.0**	**100.0**

Source: CLCB Statistical Unit.

Chapter 5

Liquidity and capital adequacy

Summary   This chapter describes the prudential constraints the clearing banks observe in order to ensure their ability to meet their obligations to depositors at all times. The most important of these constraints are self-imposed and would apply even in the absence of control from without. Because of the need to repay depositors, clearing banks must maintain a substantial margin of liquid assets. The extent of that margin depends mainly on the maturity structure of the banks' assets and liabilities. To meet immediate cash withdrawals they maintain stocks of notes and coin at their branches. To meet clearing settlements they maintain current accounts at the Bank of England, which can be replenished by adjustments to their holdings of money-market liquid assets. Behind these assets stands the banks' 'strategic reserve' of gilt-edged securities. In addition to maintaining adequate liquidity the banks must demonstrate their solvency by showing an appropriate margin of assets over liabilities, even after providing fully for bad and doubtful debts. Less attention is now paid to crude capital/deposit ratios, and more to measures that reflect the varying degrees of risk attached to different assets. It has become common practice to compute the ratio of 'free capital' to deposits. Although the clearing banks operate internal control and audit systems, they welcome the fact that the Bank of England's responsibilities for the health of the banking system are being extended and formalised; however, they are concerned about the implications of the proposed deposit protection scheme. The clearing banks participated in the 'lifeboat operation' so as to contain the crisis of confidence in 1973/74 and to protect depositors.

Introduction

5.1   Chapter 4 described the sources of the clearing banks' deposits. Before describing their lending activities it is necessary to examine the main constraints to which the banks are subject in deploying these deposits. Essentially two types of constraint are involved. On the one hand, the banks' actions must pay due regard to the monetary and credit controls which are imposed on the banks to ensure their compliance with official economic policy objectives. These controls are the subject of chapter 6. On the other hand, the banks must ensure that they are always able to repay their depositors; this obligation requires the banks' adherence to appropriate standards of liquidity and capital adequacy. Although these two concepts are closely related they will be discussed separately in this chapter. They apply to both sterling and currency business; this chapter concentrates on sterling business, while paragraphs 11.14 and 11.19 cover the particular considerations that affect currency business.

5.2   The most important prudential constraints on their liquidity and capital adequacy are those which the banks impose on themselves. These constraints are rooted in the well-tried practice of prudent banking and have served to retain the confidence of the banks' depositors, without which their businesses would collapse. Self-imposed prudential constraints existed long before the banks were subject to official supervision or regulation and they would still apply in the total absence of control from without.

Liquidity

5.3   The first obligation of any deposit-taking institution is to ensure its ability at all times to meet any withdrawal by its depositors under any circumstances which may reasonably be envisaged. If any bank were ever to fail to meet this obligation, it would lose the confidence of its depositors and the ability to continue in business. There is also a closely related obligation to meet any demand by its borrowing customers to take up any previously agreed loan facilities. For the clearing banks in particular, these two obligations condition all their activities, since their deposits are practically all short-term and they have provided large overdraft facilities on which their customers can draw on demand. Deposit withdrawals and drawings on loan facilities may be financed by new deposits, obtained if necessary by active bidding by the bank on the wholesale money markets. However, no bank can assume that it will be able to meet all calls solely by attracting new deposits: it might well have to pay unacceptably high rates of interest to attract the funds it needed, or deposits to the required amount might not be available. It is to guard against both eventualities that all banks hold a substantial margin of liquid assets.

5.4   Gauging the volume and type of liquid assets that a bank needs to hold cannot be reduced to a precise formula. A number of separate considerations must be borne in mind, of which the most important is the maturity structure of the bank's assets and liabilities. If all advances were financed by deposits of equal maturity, very little liquidity would be needed. In fact, however, all banks engage in 'maturity transformation' or 'mismatching' by using their deposits to finance loans of longer maturities. Indeed, a degree of mismatching is essential if the banks are to satisfy the requirements of their borrowers for continuity of finance while at the same time meeting the liquidity needs of their depositors; what is essential is that each bank should properly control the extent of such mismatching. As a general rule, the greater the mismatching of maturities between a bank's deposits and loans, the greater its need for liquidity. It should be noted that the mismatching of maturities can expose the banks to risks of financial loss as well as to liquidity problems whenever the interest rates on the loans and investments are fixed for longer periods than those of the deposits. Banks can largely insulate themselves against these risks by lending at variable rather than fixed rates of interest, so that regardless of any differences in the maturities of their assets and liabilities there are no differences in the timing of changes in the respective interest rates. All overdraft lending is variable-rate, and so is most term lending. A further type of mismatching can arise when assets denominated in one currency are financed by liabilities denominated in another. Because of the risks of financial loss that would result from adverse movements in exchange rates, the banks generally avoid such mismatching even when exchange control regulations permit it.

5.5   Comparing the maturities of a bank's assets and liabilities in order to assess the extent of any mismatch is complicated by the fact that the effective maturity of a deposit or loan may be considerably longer than the notional maturity. This is particularly true of a bank's retail deposits and its overdraft lending. Although a high proportion of the clearing banks' lending is technically repayable on demand, they would hope never to have to seek immediate repayment of a loan for liquidity reasons. A clearing bank can from long experience assume that its deposit base as a whole will remain reasonably stable providing it retains the confidence of its depositors. But to retain that confidence its liquidity must comfortably exceed what is needed for normal day-to-day transactions, even though it could never be enough to cover every possible eventuality.

5.6 It might be thought that the clearing banks' liquidity needs would have been diminished as the proportion of current account balances in their deposit mix has fallen. In fact, however, this is not the case. Wholesale deposits, which have grown correspondingly in importance, require even more liquidity cover. Although these deposits cover the whole spectrum of maturities, they are heavily concentrated at the shorter terms, with a significant proportion lodged overnight or at call. Individual banks cannot rely on maturing deposits being renewed, and in practice wholesale deposits are more volatile than retail deposits. It is for this reason that the need to assess the extent of any mismatch between a bank's assets and liabilities and its resulting requirement for liquidity is particularly acute in the case of its wholesale market operations.

5.7 The clearing banks maintain substantial balances of notes and coin at their branches to meet immediate demands such as personal drawings and the wages requirements of industry and trade. At the end of 1976, approximately £750 million was held as cash in tills, or $2\frac{1}{2}$ per cent of sterling deposits. The proportion is very much smaller for the non-clearing banks. These funds do not count as reserve assets for the purposes of monetary controls; nor do they produce revenue. Indeed, because of security and transport costs, cash handling is a very expensive function to fulfil.

5.8 Most of the daily fluctuations in the clearing banks' deposits and advances arise not from cash withdrawals but from clearing settlements including those associated with the banks' operations on the wholesale markets. To meet these movements the clearing banks maintain non-interest-bearing current account balances with the Bank of England. At present these have to average $1\frac{1}{2}$ per cent of eligible liabilities, considerably more than the banks consider to be necessary, as is argued in chapter 17. In order to maintain this Bank of England balance, daily adjustments are made to holdings of liquid assets such as money at call, Treasury bills, commercial bills, certificates of deposit and short-term inter-bank lending. In practice, the main adjustments are made to the last two of these items, as described in chapter 18.

5.9 Beyond their holdings of liquid assets, the clearing banks have a 'strategic reserve' in the form of their holdings of gilt-edged securities. At the end of 1976 these amounted to some £1,800 million, equivalent to about 6 per cent of sterling deposits. In earlier years the banks' investment portfolios were much larger, and were seen not just as a strategic reserve but as an alternative to advances as a remunerative outlet for the banks' resources. Indeed, during and after the war the banks' investment portfolios were larger than their loan portfolios. In the post-war period the growing demand for bank finance has partly been accommodated by running down investments; this process was already under way at the time of the Radcliffe Report in 1959 (when gilt-edged investments were 28 per cent of deposits) but gathered pace during the 1960s. In the early 1970s gilt-edged holdings (in some banks at least) probably reached an irreducible minimum. The banks still sometimes add to their portfolios at times when deposits are growing but loan demand is weak; there were, for example, net additions in 1975. But gilt-edged securities are held primarily for liquidity purposes nowadays. Consequently the average maturity is very short. About a quarter of the portfolio is in stocks maturing in less than one year (which qualify as reserve assets). A further substantial fraction matures within two years. Very little (currently less than 5 per cent) is in stocks with lives of over five years. Stocks at the longer end of the banks' portfolio gain in terms of liquidity with the passage of time and become reserve assets eventually. Thus one important motive for buying them is the facility for pre-arranging a flow of liquid assets to meet future needs.

5.10   The various liquid assets held by the banks are set out in detail in table 58 on page 275. If gilt-edged securities and inter-bank lending are included, the various sterling liquid assets amount to over a third of the clearing banks' sterling deposits. This may appear cautious given the evident stability of the banks' deposit base. However, these liquid assets include the reserve assets of various kinds which the banks are obliged to maintain at not less than $12\frac{1}{2}$ per cent of their eligible liabilities for monetary policy purposes, as described in chapter 6. This obligation applies to every day's closing balances. So even though the banks' liquid assets might be adequate to meet an abnormally large withdrawal of deposits, they might still be inadequate to prevent their reserve assets falling below the permissible minimum. In a dire emergency the authorities might be prepared to accept this for a short period, but the banks cannot presume so. Consequently the banks must maintain liquidity well in excess of their reserve assets in order to provide for abnormal withdrawals, as well as to meet day-to-day requirements, thereby demonstrating unequivocally to depositors the banks' ability to meet their obligation to repay.

Capital adequacy

5.11   To maintain the confidence of their depositors banks must demonstrate not only their liquidity but also their solvency. It is essential that the value of their assets should exceed their liabilities by a margin appropriate to the extent and nature of their business. This margin of capital is needed to absorb losses that could arise, for example, from an unforeseen fall in the value of assets, whether through the effects of a sharp rise in interest rates on the value of their investments or through a severe spate of bad debts. It should be empha- sised that the banks always make full provision for all known bad and doubtful debts. As well as making specific provisions against individual loans which the banks know, or suspect, will not be fully repaid, the banks maintain a general provision for doubtful debts which is intended to provide for the inherent risk in lending. The general provision is intended to cover bad debts not yet identified that might reasonably be expected to arise on the current portfolio of advances in the normal course of business; like the specific provisions, it is subtracted from the value of advances in the banks' published accounts and does not therefore appear as part of their published capital resources. These capital resources – share capital, reserves and certain other items – are required to ensure the solvency of the bank even under abnormal conditions.

5.12   To supplement their share capital and reserves the banks have raised further funds in the form of loan capital, denominated both in sterling and foreign currencies and subordinated to the claims of depositors. In the event of the failure of the business, repayment of these loans would not begin until deposi- tors' claims had been met in full. Accordingly they serve as a further protection to depositors, although the claims of subordinated lenders would be met in priority to those of shareholders. One of the principal attractions of loan capital to a bank is that it is available in foreign currencies and can be used to support deposits in the same currency, thereby protecting capital/deposit ratios from fluctuations in exchange rates. However, there are limits to the amount of capital that a bank can raise in the form of subordinated loans. Neither the bank's shareholders nor its subordinated lenders would be prepared to see its overall debt/equity ratio overextended. In the last resort the equity of the bank is needed to ensure that losses can be absorbed without forcing the bank at best into a capital reconstruction and at worst into liquidation.

5.13   There has been much debate both about the appropriate measure of capital adequacy and about the appropriate levels for the various ratios that can be calculated. A crude approach is simply to relate total capital resources to total deposits. The banks are aware that such a ratio is in practice monitored by many of their depositors (especially overseas banks) and it is important for that reason. The clearing banks' capital ratios on this basis are currently between 6 and 8 per cent, which they believe are comparable with or higher than those of major banks in other countries. The limitation of such an approach is that it pays no regard to the nature of the different types of asset that a bank holds. The approach which is now being adopted increasingly is one which seeks to identify the amount of capital required to cover these different types of asset. The amount required will depend on the extent of the risk that the assets may not realise their full value.

5.14   At one extreme certain types of money market assets, such as Treasury bills, require little or no capital cover; since the risks of a fall in value or of default by the debtor are negligible, it is not unreasonable for them to be financed almost entirely by deposits. The market value of gilt-edged investments, however, can fluctuate and a degree of capital cover is therefore appropriate. Advances to customers do not fluctuate in value in the same way but there is the rather different risk that they may not all be repaid in full. In the case of certain investments both types of risk apply, while the assets making up the infrastructure of the banks (essentially their premises, equipment and trade investments) require the highest degree of capital cover of all. This reflects not only the fact that they may fall in value but also their limited marketability. Property values fluctuate at the best of times, and in the event of a crisis a large property portfolio might be extremely difficult to sell at reasonable prices. In the case of the banks' purpose-built equipment and some of their trade investments, it would not be safe to assume that their book value could be realised on the open market. It is for these reasons that it is now commonly accepted that infrastructure assets should not normally be financed by deposits (just as the fixed assets of an industrial or commercial undertaking should not normally be financed by short-term funds). For the same reasons, the banks have only a limited role to play in the provision of equity finance to industry and trade. The public at large is not privy to sufficiently detailed information about the degree of risk of the banks' assets to compute sophisticated capital/asset ratios. But as a compromise between these ratios and the old-fashioned capital/deposit ratio, it is now common practice to compute the ratio of a bank's 'free capital' (total capital less infrastructure assets) to its deposits.

5.15   During the past few years the clearing banks' ratios of free capital to deposit liabilities have at times fallen to uncomfortable levels, and the banks have duly raised additional capital, both equity and subordinated debt. Even so, their free capital ratios appear less generous when compared with the position in some other countries than their total capital ratios. It is a source of continuing concern that post-tax profits have recently been insufficient to preserve the banks' free capital ratios, after meeting the capital investment needs of the business and after paying modest dividends to shareholders. This matter is discussed fully in chapter 15.

Supervision

5.16   It has already been stated in this chapter that the most important prudential constraints on the banks are self-imposed. All the banks have developed their own internal control and audit systems designed to ensure that every aspect of the banks' activities complies with standards laid down by their head offices and thus that the banks' depositors are adequately protected against loss. The development of these systems has been greatly aided by modern computer technology which permits the production of itemised balance sheet data and facilitates the day-to-day monitoring of the activities of all divisions and branches. A different kind of check is exercised by advance controllers, who assess loans and the risks attached to them on an individual basis. In addition, the banks' inspection staff conduct their own independent investigations; they visit all branches periodically and are called in whenever there is any suggestion of fraud, either internal or external. These various control systems operate independently of one another and are supplemented by the external investigations undertaken by the banks' auditors.

5.17   Apart from these self-imposed controls, it has long been part of the responsibility of the Bank of England to ensure that all the banks under its aegis operate to high prudential standards: the clearing banks for their part have always appreciated this involvement by the Bank of England, not least as a further source of reassurance to depositors. Until recently the Bank's supervisory role was exercised in a fairly informal manner, and was limited in the main to those institutions which it formally recognised as banks. Although the number of banks thus controlled had increased significantly in the 1960s and early 1970s, there remained many institutions engaged in deposit taking and lending with which the Bank had few dealings.

5.18   Since the secondary banking crisis of 1973/74, the supervisory arrangements have become more formal, and are expected to become more formal still with the passage of legislation based on the government's White Paper of August 1976, *The Licensing and Supervision of Deposit-Taking Institutions*. By extending the Bank's supervisory role to all deposit-taking institutions, the legislation should help to prevent the sort of reckless behaviour on the part of many such enterprises which precipitated the 1973/74 crisis. For that reason the clearing banks welcome the main licensing and supervision proposals of the White Paper. They await with interest the detailed proposals for the criteria to be applied in granting licences and in assessing the liquidity and capital adequacy of the licensed institutions.

5.19   For their own part, the clearing banks expect the legislation to formalise the present arrangements for supervising the 'primary' banking sector, worked out as a result of consultation between the banks and the Bank of England in the wake of the 1973/74 crisis. The main features of these arrangements were described in an article, jointly agreed by the Bank and the London and Scottish clearing banks, in the *Bank of England Quarterly Bulletin* of September 1975. The article emphasised the importance of maintaining adequate levels of free capital, while accepting that in the case of the clearing banks it was not necessary to deduct the full value of premises from total capital in arriving at a figure for free capital. This reflected the fact that many of the clearing banks' premises were relatively small and readily marketable. The article also

cent between September 1973 and February 1975. This was done to help protect building societies from the effects of high interest rates, and therefore directly distorted competition between the two types of institution. A particularly distasteful feature of this measure was that it required the banks to discriminate against their smaller customers.

Selective credit controls

6.21   Although official lending guidance in quantitative terms was dropped in 1971, the Bank of England continues to issue qualitative guidance on the direction of bank lending. The use of guidance rather than the more formal techniques found in some other countries confers a degree of flexibility in implementation which is welcome. The clearing banks stress, however, that they always do everything they can to adhere both to the letter and the spirit of the official requests. The present guidance, issued in August 1977, in essence requires banks to give preference to manufacturing industry and to exports and import-saving; and to maintain particular restraint on lending to persons, to property companies and for purely financial transactions. Additionally, in their lending to persons banks are asked to observe the same restraints as apply under the terms control orders to hire purchase contracts.

6.22   The guidance on property lending merely ratifies what the clearing banks would be doing in any case. Given the severe problems in the property market the banks would certainly have wished to limit their commitments to the sector and were already doing so when the present guidance was first issued; they would not, of course, have done so in such a way as to add unnecessarily to their customers' difficulties, and the terms of the guidance did not require them to do so. As for the rest of the guidance, the banks have always done everything they can to support manufacturing industry and exports. Recently the weakness of loan demand has been such as to enable the banks to achieve this objective without detriment to other customers. They would be less happy if the guidance prevented them from adequately meeting the needs of sound, efficient enterprises in non-manufacturing sectors. The banks also have some reservations about the restriction of their personal lending. Their personal customers provide them with a high proportion of their deposits, and they often wish that they could be more helpful when such customers need to borrow.

6.23   The banks have a more general comment to make on selective credit controls, which applies in particular to the present constraints on consumer credit. Whereas the need to maintain control over the monetary aggregates is accepted by almost everybody because of the need to maintain the purchasing power of the currency, there is no such automatic presumption that controls over the allocation of credit between one sector and another are necessary or desirable. Each such control needs to be justified on its own merits, as do controls over any other forms of economic activity. This is not always done. Indeed at times controls have been imposed on lending for particular purposes when it might have been more sensible to control the activity itself rather than the extension of credit towards it. If, for example, the authorities wish to restrict the consumption of durable goods, there are strong grounds for saying that the rate of tax on these goods should be increased rather than that there should be restrictions on the related credit. First, fiscal measures would be more effective, given that the very nature of credit makes it difficult in practice to relate financial flows to purchases of particular goods. Secondly, they would be more equitable; to prevent people in financial deficit from acquiring the goods in question while those who have credit balances on their accounts are perfectly free to do so seems to be unreasonable. Thirdly, if fiscal measures were used, the full economic costs and benefits involved could be more clearly perceived and evaluated.

6.24   The economic effects of bank lending extend far beyond the immediate borrower, since the company or individual who borrows from a bank uses the money for some further economic purpose, which will have effects of its own. Therefore well-intentioned regulation of too specific a nature can have quite unexpected and undesired overall results; for instance, a company in a 'preferred' credit sector could well suffer a loss of business if its customers were being deprived of credit. Any attempt to apply more detailed controls over the allocation of credit to particular industries would encounter overwhelming difficulties in view of the conglomerate nature of many of the larger corporations; inevitably the directions would bear most heavily on smaller companies whose business was of a homogeneous nature.

6.25   Terms control on consumer credit has in practice usually been applied as a convenient and swift means of effecting a short-term reduction in consumer demand. It was with this in mind that it was reimposed in 1973; yet it has remained in force ever since, throughout the deepest recession since the war. It is doubtful whether it is justified even as a short-term measure, given the damage it does to the vigour and competitiveness of the consumer durable industries. The banks note the conclusion of the Crowther Committee on consumer credit: "Terms control should find no place among the weapons of economic policy. Its value is far outweighed by the inequities it creates and by the difficult practical problems to which it gives rise." As far as the banks are aware, this view has not been convincingly refuted.

Lending:
the banks' role and record

Summary   This chapter considers the main factors which influence bank lending and attempts a general assessment of the clearing banks' record in lending to industry and of the effectiveness of the financial system as a whole. The banks' lending role developed from their deposit-taking activities and is still conditioned by them. The banks are constrained by the need to honour agreed lending facilities, and also by competitive forces which have eroded their market share of lending. At times when the banks are not fully lent, the reason is usually sluggish demand. Bank finance is used by industry to finance fixed investment as well as working capital. Gearing has shown a long-term tendency to increase, as has the importance of bank finance within total corporate indebtedness. There is no evidence that investment has been held back for lack of bank finance, and the banks feel that neither the total amount they lend nor its allocation between sectors of the economy is open to attack. An analysis of advances by category of borrower confirms the importance of manufacturers as bank borrowers, even though they have made less use of agreed borrowing facilities than other categories. Only half the banks' sterling lending to the financial category is extended to the property sector. The banks doubt whether the performance of the financial system as a whole has been a reason for the country's poor economic record.

Introduction

7.1   The clearing banks' lending role evolved from their deposit-taking and money transmission business, the overdraft developing from the convenience of the current account and the use of the cheque to form the foundation of the clearing banks' present-day lending activities. Loans and advances are the banks' most important assets, although in the exceptional circumstances of the war and post-war years a higher proportion of depositors' funds was invested in gilt-edged securities and it was not until 1960 that the pre-war ratio of advances to deposits was regained. Since that time the ratio has risen significantly, and the political and economic importance attached to the clearing banks' lending activities has increased. While this importance is fully appreciated by the banks themselves, it is necessary to bear in mind throughout the discussion which follows that their obligations to their depositors still condition all their lending activities.

7.2   The various domestic lending facilities which the banks provide, and the terms and conditions on which they are made available, will be surveyed in chapter 8; chapter 9 will examine the banks' lending relations with smaller businesses, while international lending will be chiefly covered in chapter 11. The purpose of the present chapter is to set the scene for this detailed survey of the banks' lending activities by looking at their role as providers of finance in the context of industry's financial needs, by considering the allocation of their lending between the main sectors of the economy and by attempting an overall judgement of the effectiveness with which their role is discharged. In view of the importance of industrial and commercial companies as recipients of bank finance, and the topicality of the subject of industrial finance, many of the points in this chapter are of particular relevance to this subject.

7.3   The amounts lent by the banks to their customers, the terms on which they are lent and their allocation between different customers are determined by a variety of factors, some of which bear on the total supply of loanable funds and some of which affect the demand for those funds. Most of the principal supply factors have already been identified in the previous three chapters, but are worth recapitulating at this stage before proceeding to the demand factors. They include the level of deposits in the economy as a whole; the clearing banks' share of those deposits, which depends partly on competitive forces and partly on official activities and controls; the banks' need for adequate liquidity and capital, which precludes them from lending all their deposits or from lending improvidently; and the operation of credit controls, which influence the directions in which the banks may lend. So whatever lending policies the banks themselves may adopt, and whatever demand they may face from their customers, there are important external constraints on what they are able to accomplish in practice.

7.4   The relative importance of these various constraints has altered as the clearing banks' advances have increased as a proportion of their total resources. Since the Radcliffe Committee reported in 1959, the sterling advances of the clearing banks have increased from less than 40 per cent of their net sterling deposits to over 70 per cent, as illustrated in diagram 10. Between 1945 and 1959 lending had been subject to continuous restraint, principally through the control of the Capital Issues Committee, and the change since then has confirmed the expression by the banks' representatives to the Radcliffe Committee of "their strong desire to meet all their customers' reasonable requirements for temporary finance". The increase in lending was achieved up to about 1974 in part by switching out of gilt-edged securities and other liquid assets; but since then, because of the need to maintain adequate liquidity, additional lending has had to be covered by increases in the volume of deposits. The clearing banks' competitive position in the deposit market, which was discussed in chapter 4, therefore has a direct bearing on their lending activities.

7.5   In addition to the external constraints on the supply of loanable funds, and the demand factors discussed in the following section, there are two other factors which have a considerable effect on the actual amounts lent by the clearing banks. They are the banks' need to honour agreed borrowing facilities and the effects of competition from other banks and lending institutions.

7.6   The clearing banks respond to customers' requests for finance by agreeing borrowing facilities; once a bank has arranged a facility it is under a firm commitment to make the money available. However, 'drawdown' (or the actual use made of the facility) is dependent entirely on the customer. Loan arrangements tend to be available for drawing within a specified period, which can be extended if there has been any delay in a project; overdraft facilities by their very nature fluctuate according to the customer's day-to-day needs. Thus of the £36,381 million of facilities available in May 1977, only 60 per cent were actually taken up (see diagram 18 on page 89). In the short term, cyclical variations in the demand for bank finance can lead to a sluggishness in bank lending; and for brief periods before a recovery in loan demand occurs there may seem to be considerable unused lending capacity. Indeed much of the recent growth in medium-term lending took place when industry's demand

Distribution of sterling assets

London clearing bank parents' principal sterling assets as a
percentage of total sterling deposits: November annually

Diagram 10

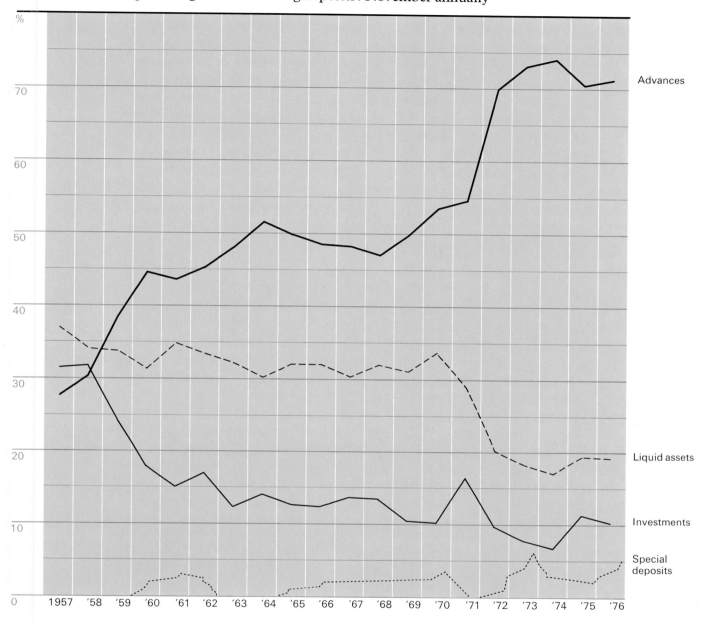

1. Total sterling deposits comprise current, deposit and other accounts including net wholesale deposits.
2. Liquid assets include cash, balances at the Bank of England and call money; with effect from
   November 1971 they comprise reserve assets plus cash and certain market loans.

Source: Bank of England Statistical Abstract.

for conventional overdraft finance was at a low ebb. But the banks can never
afford to forget the more or less automatic recovery in overdraft lending which
takes place during the upsurge of an economic cycle. Largely because the
banks have a virtually contractual obligation to honour the overdraft facilities
agreed with their customers, some apparently surplus lending capacity may
sometimes be inevitable.

7.7   Over the past ten years the clearing banks, while remaining the market leaders,
have suffered some erosion of their share of the total sterling bank lending
market. This is illustrated in diagram 11. In the early part of the period this

Market shares of advances   Diagram 11

London clearing banks' proportion of all U K bank lending
to U K residents

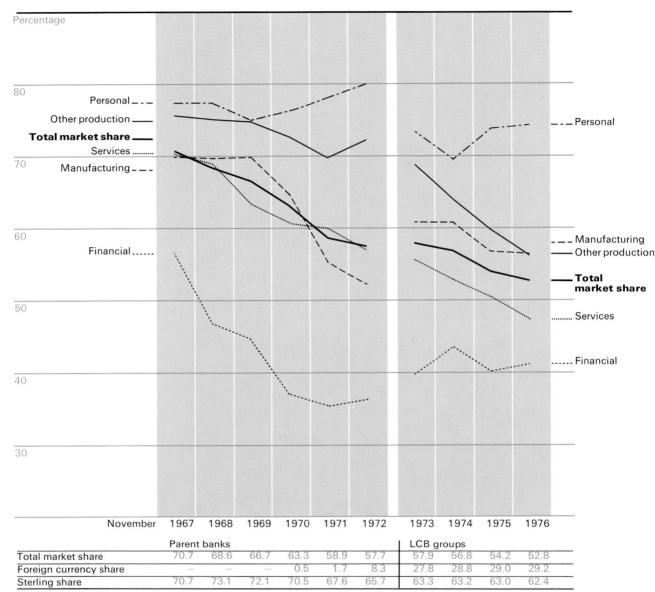

		Parent banks					LCB groups			
November	1967	1968	1969	1970	1971	1972	1973	1974	1975	1976
Total market share	70.7	68.6	66.7	63.3	58.9	57.7	57.9	56.8	54.2	52.8
Foreign currency share	–	–	–	0.5	1.7	8.3	27.8	28.8	29.0	29.2
Sterling share	70.7	73.1	72.1	70.5	67.6	65.7	63.3	63.2	63.0	62.4

Source: CLCB Statistical Unit.

was largely the result of official controls being applied chiefly, if not exclusively, to the clearing banks, whilst the activities of other banks (including the clearing banks' own subsidiaries) were allowed freer rein. The further loss of market share during the period immediately following the implementation of *Competition and Credit Control* in 1971 largely reflects the increasing involvement in the sterling lending markets of the American banks. The clearing banks' share of total sterling lending by all banks has stabilised since 1973, although in the context of sterling lending as a whole it is relevant to note that the building societies have continued to expand at a faster rate than the banks.

7.8   Within the various constraints on the supply of loanable funds, the banks would not suggest that they are always fully lent, in the sense of lacking any scope to expand their lending further at a particular time, although they would contend that throughout most of the post-war period the headroom has been extremely limited. But at times when the banks have appeared to have scope for higher lending, the situation has arisen primarily as a result of lack of demand for bank finance by their industrial and commercial customers. For this reason the banks are vitally concerned with the factors which influence this demand.

Industry's demand for bank finance

7.9 Industrial and commercial companies represent the clearing banks' main lending market; and the banks accordingly have a strong incentive to identify and meet their demand for finance. This demand is determined by two factors. The first is the extent to which businesses' need for finance exceeds their ability to generate it from their own operating results. The second is their decision to seek that finance from banks as opposed to other financial institutions or markets. Both of these factors reflect some influences which are long-term in nature, some which are cyclical and must therefore be taken into account in comparing one year with another, and some which are due to special circumstances.

7.10 Bank finance can be used for a wide variety of business purposes; but the chief of these, as is illustrated by table 13, is to finance investment in fixed capital, stocks and work in progress. There is no clear consensus as to the relative importance of the factors which influence this. However, as far as industrial and commercial companies are concerned, there is some evidence

Companies' sources and uses of funds
Industrial and commercial companies

Table 13

£ million Figures in red are percentages		1971		1972		1973		1974		1975		1976	
Sources	Undistributed income (saving) and capital transfers	4,977	68.4	5,664	54.7	7,815	52.0	8,193	54.7	8,506	68.5	11,848	66.7
	Bank and other borrowing	969	13.3	3,146	30.4	5,297	35.2	4,472	29.8	913	7.4	3,033	17.1
	UK capital issues	375	5.2	616	6.0	158	1.1	−13	−0.1	1,037	8.4	791	4.5
	Overseas*	952	13.1	921	8.9	1,765	11.7	2,336	15.6	1,962	15.8	2,095	11.8
	Total sources	**7,273**	100.0	**10,347**	100.0	**15,035**	100.0	**14,988**	100.0	**12,418**	100.0	**17,767**	100.0
Uses	Gross domestic fixed capital formation	3,468	47.7	3,900	37.7	4,825	32.1	6,078	40.6	6,983	56.2	7,745	43.6
	Rise in value of stocks and work in progress	758	10.4	940	9.1	3,764	25.0	6,147	41.0	2,278	18.3	5,163	29.1
	Cash expenditure on trade investments and on acquiring subsidiaries	556	7.6	971	9.4	1,474	9.8	755	5.0	567	4.6	803	4.5
	Liquid assets including government stocks	1,227	16.9	2,364	22.8	2,607	17.3	0	—	1,854	14.9	1,874	10.5
	Overseas*	222	3.1	665	6.4	1,988	13.2	1,788	11.9	1,767	14.2	3,092	17.4
	Other and unidentified	1,042	14.3	1,507	14.6	377	2.5	220	1.5	−1,031	−8.3	−910	−5.1
	Total uses	**7,273**	100.0	**10,347**	100.0	**15,035**	100.0	**14,988**	100.0	**12,418**	100.0	**17,767**	100.0
	Self-financing ratio †		117.8		117.0		91.0		67.0		91.8		91.8

*Overseas trade credit, capital issues overseas, overseas direct investment in securities, and intra-company investment.

†Undistributed income and capital transfers as a percentage of gross domestic fixed capital formation and rise in value of stocks and work in progress.

Source: Financial Statistics.

from recent studies by the Bank of England* that their rate of capital accumulation (fixed capital formation as a percentage of the stock of fixed capital assets at current replacement cost) is influenced by the relation between the rate of return earned on capital invested and the cost of the finance required to install it. During the past 15 years the rate of return on capital has been falling, as shown

*Bank of England Quarterly Bulletin March and June 1976 and June 1977.

Companies' real cost of capital and rates of return   Diagram 12
Industrial and commercial companies; post-tax figures

†Provisional estimates

Source: The Bank of England Quarterly Bulletin June 1977.

in diagram 12, and after 1972 it fell below the cost of capital. Movements in the ratio of return to cost correspond quite closely to the decline in the rate of capital accumulation. This suggests that an important factor limiting industrial and commercial companies' demand for finance has been the deteriorating view they have taken of the prospective net returns on investment as a result of observing the returns actually being earned. Moreover, these actual returns have affected the companies' current and prospective ability to raise finance internally from retained profits, as well as from external sources.

7.11   The contribution made by external sources of finance to the financing requirements of industrial and commercial companies is illustrated in table 14. Borrowing by these companies, in the form of debentures, loan stocks, preference shares, and bank advances net of liquid assets, increased as a proportion of the replacement cost of fixed assets and stocks, from 14.7 per cent in 1960 to 26.6 per cent in 1974. There was a fall in the ratio in 1975 and 1976 because borrowing slackened while accelerating inflation increased the replacement cost of stocks and work in progress and, to a lesser extent, of fixed assets as well. Apart from this brief interlude, gearing has shown a long-term tendency to increase on the basis of nominal valuations. When debentures, loan stocks and preference shares are taken at their market value, gearing can be seen to have risen to a peak in 1966, eased slightly and then remained fairly stable until falling in the two latest years.

Companies' debt ratios
Industrial and commercial companies

Table 14

Percentages	Ratio of borrowing to capital employed *		Ratio of bank advances to total borrowing †
End-year	Nominal	Market	
1960	14.7	10.3	31.6
1961	14.9	10.7	34.7
1962	18.7	15.3	33.6
1963	19.7	16.6	35.4
1964	21.0	17.4	39.2
1965	21.6	17.7	40.5
1966	24.6	21.2	37.5
1967	24.9	21.0	36.7
1968	25.4	19.3	37.0
1969	23.7	18.5	41.9
1970	24.6	18.8	43.0
1971	20.4	18.9	46.6
1972	20.3	17.9	54.8
1973	23.5	17.9	60.7
1974	26.6	18.4	64.6
1975	20.7	15.9	68.8
1976‡	20.1	16.0	72.6

* Ratio of outstanding debentures, loan stocks, preference shares, and bank borrowing net of liquid assets, to the (backward-looking) tax-adjusted capital stock at replacement cost. Debentures, loan stocks and preference shares are at nominal or market values as indicated.

† Ratio of bank advances to total nominal indebtedness.

‡ Provisional estimates.

Source: Bank of England Quarterly Bulletin June 1977.

7.12 The ratio of bank advances to the nominal value of borrowing by industrial and commercial companies is also illustrated in table 14. It shows a rising trend which has accelerated markedly since 1970. The continued rise in the ratio in 1975 – when bank advances rose much less than in the preceding few years – and again in 1976 was partly because the sterling value of existing currency advances, which were equivalent to over £4,000 million, increased owing to the depreciation of the sterling exchange rate. Uncertainty about future rates of inflation could be a reason why companies choose to borrow from banks on a short-term basis, rather than commit themselves to the higher nominal interest rates involved in borrowing on the capital markets over a longer term.

7.13 The changes over the past decade in industrial and commercial companies' relative dependence on additional bank borrowing are further illustrated in diagrams 13 and 14. These diagrams concentrate on each year's flow of additional bank lending (including commercial bills as well as advances) in relation to the year's financial requirements. The annual increase in bank lending of all kinds as a percentage of the companies' gross fixed investment plus the increase in the book value of stocks (including stock appreciation), fluctuated between 6 per cent and 24 per cent in the 1964–71 period. Its minimum was in the recession year of 1966, its maximum in 1970 just after the peak of the recovery. This fluctuation may reflect the fact that companies tend to treat bank borrowing as a residual source of funds in the short term, to be turned to when other (mainly internal) sources of finance are inadequate. Thus total requirements fall in recession when investment tends to be cut back more sharply than the fall in retained profits, and rise when investment expands rapidly during recovery. A similar pattern is apparent when additional bank borrowing is related to the total external sources of funds of industrial and commercial companies. Bank borrowing represented 54 per cent of external funds in 1964, fell to 20 per cent in 1966, and recovered to 64 per cent in 1970.

Companies' sources of external funds
Industrial and commercial companies

Diagram 13

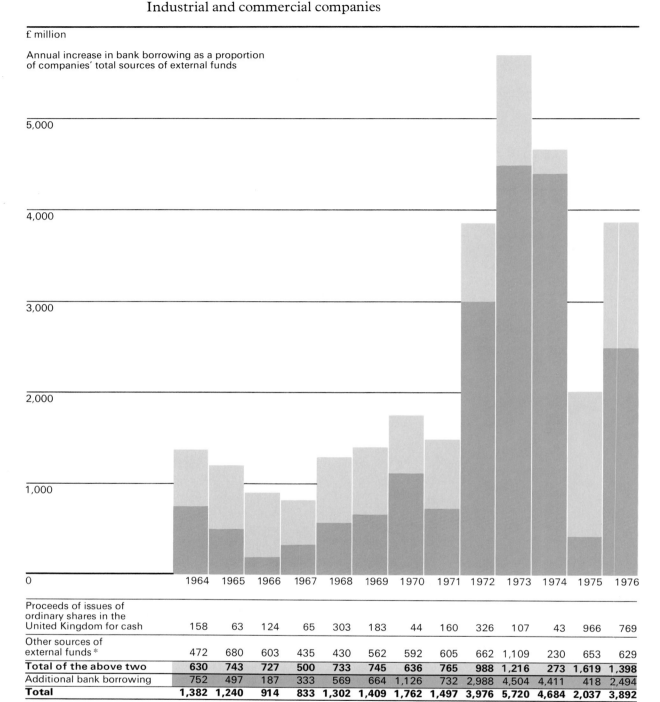

£ million

Annual increase in bank borrowing as a proportion
of companies' total sources of external funds

	1964	1965	1966	1967	1968	1969	1970	1971	1972	1973	1974	1975	1976
Proceeds of issues of ordinary shares in the United Kingdom for cash	158	63	124	65	303	183	44	160	326	107	43	966	769
Other sources of external funds *	472	680	603	435	430	562	592	605	662	1,109	230	653	629
Total of the above two	**630**	**743**	**727**	**500**	**733**	**745**	**636**	**765**	**988**	**1,216**	**273**	**1,619**	**1,398**
Additional bank borrowing	752	497	187	333	569	664	1,126	732	2,988	4,504	4,411	418	2,494
Total	**1,382**	**1,240**	**914**	**833**	**1,302**	**1,409**	**1,762**	**1,497**	**3,976**	**5,720**	**4,684**	**2,037**	**3,892**

*Issues of debentures and preference shares for cash, other loans and mortgages, capital issues overseas, and overseas direct investment in securities.

Sources: National Income and Expenditure; Financial Statistics.

7.14   After 1971 the normal cyclical movements were swamped by a substantial shift to greater dependence on bank borrowing. As a proportion of the total external funds of industrial and commercial companies, it rose to 75 per cent in 1972, 79 per cent in 1973, and 94 per cent in 1974, dropped back to 21 per cent in 1975 but rose again to 64 per cent in 1976. As a proportion of gross investment plus stockbuilding, bank borrowing rose to 62 per cent in 1972, declined to 52 per cent in 1973, and thence to 36 per cent in 1974 as the delayed cyclical upswing in investment developed, fell away to 4 per cent in 1975 but recovered to 19 per cent in 1976.

Companies' investment and bank borrowing
Industrial and commercial companies

Diagram 14

Annual increase in bank borrowing as a
percentage of gross fixed investment plus
increase in the book value of stocks and
work in progress

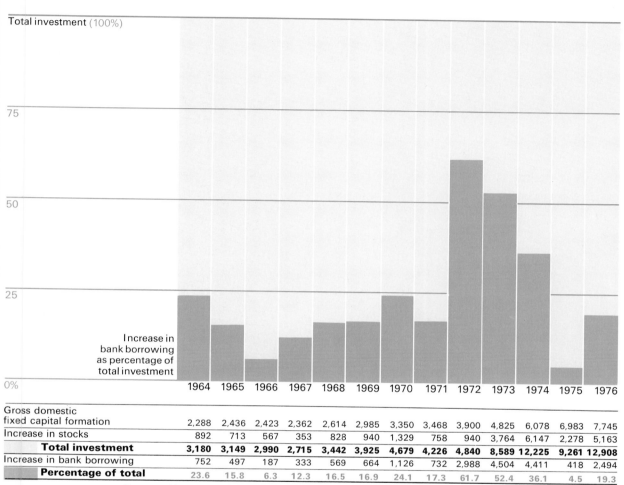

	1964	1965	1966	1967	1968	1969	1970	1971	1972	1973	1974	1975	1976
Gross domestic fixed capital formation	2,288	2,436	2,423	2,362	2,614	2,985	3,350	3,468	3,900	4,825	6,078	6,983	7,745
Increase in stocks	892	713	567	353	828	940	1,329	758	940	3,764	6,147	2,278	5,163
Total investment	**3,180**	**3,149**	**2,990**	**2,715**	**3,442**	**3,925**	**4,679**	**4,226**	**4,840**	**8,589**	**12,225**	**9,261**	**12,908**
Increase in bank borrowing	752	497	187	333	569	664	1,126	732	2,988	4,504	4,411	418	2,494
Percentage of total	23.6	15.8	6.3	12.3	16.5	16.9	24.1	17.3	61.7	52.4	36.1	4.5	19.3

Sources: National Income and Expenditure; Financial Statistics.

7.15 In 1972, and to some extent in 1973, these high percentages exaggerated the extent to which industrial and commercial companies were increasing their net indebtedness to the banks, because in those years companies were also (in the aggregate) accumulating bank deposits and other liquid assets on an unusual scale. In other words, there was a greater resort to the overall services of banks as financial intermediaries, partly as a result of the greater degree of competition between them, as well as greater dependence upon borrowing from banks by industrial and commercial companies in the aggregate. This greater dependence developed strongly in 1974 when the growth of company savings was inhibited by price controls and the developing recession and, combined with the effects of stock appreciation, failed to match the continuing growth of investment expenditure to its cyclical peak. At the same time, the general collapse of confidence closed the main alternative source of external finance, the new issue market, whose activity was drastically reduced in 1974.

7.16 While the banks responded to industrial and commercial companies' financial needs as they arose, there is little doubt that companies themselves subsequently became anxious to bring their dependence upon bank finance back within more normal bounds, as opportunities occurred. During 1975 and 1976 these were provided by reductions in investment spending, a substantial revival of the new issue market, mainly in the form of rights issues, and latterly a recovery of profits. The result was the decline mentioned above for 1975 in the ratios of additional bank borrowing both to investment (including stock-building) and to all sources of funds. During 1976 the ratios rose again; this was partly the result of special and temporary influences on bank borrowing in the disturbed state of the foreign exchange and financial markets in the latter half of 1976. The ratios declined again in 1977, though towards the end of the year demand for bank finance appeared to be returning, mainly to finance stockbuilding, but also to support the expected revival of fixed investment which was by then showing some signs of materialising. The experience of 1974/75 illustrates the complementary roles which can be performed by banks and the stock market in supplying companies with the additional funds they require. In 1974 the shock to confidence which virtually closed the market for new capital was absorbed by the expansion of bank finance; in 1975 and to some extent also in 1976, the revival of the stock market enabled companies to make the requisite readjustments to their balance sheets.

7.17 Some data which bear upon the demand for external finance are plotted in diagram 15. This shows the extent to which industrial and commercial companies' gross investment in fixed capital and stocks has exceeded (or fallen short of) their flow of retained profits and capital transfers since the beginning of 1964. This component of their need to borrow clearly fluctuates with the business cycle, although as the diagram shows it does not have the same peaks and troughs. The diagram also plots additional lending to industrial and commercial companies by the whole UK banking sector. The relationship between the two lines suggests that the volume of bank lending does move in the way required to accommodate the need of industrial and commercial companies to borrow to finance any shortfall of internally-generated funds when investing in fixed capital and stocks. Although the amount and timing of bank borrowings are determined by the companies themselves rather than by the banks, the diagram suggests that the banks are prompt to meet corporate demand for finance once it has been expressed. Thus in 1968 and 1972, both years of recovery, bank lending increased rather sooner than the upturn in investment less internal funds. In 1972 this largely reflected the increased freedom conferred on bank lending by *Competition and Credit Control*. The same trend was apparent in 1976.

7.18 The evident responsiveness of the banks to demand for finance as it changes during the business cycle does not exclude the possibility that they are not responsive enough in the long term. It might be said, for example, that the continuous line in the diagram (industrial and commercial companies' investment less their savings) has been held down by the hatched line (bank lending to them) at all points. It is noticeable, however, that when bank loans became more freely available from the end of 1971, as reflected in the upward movement of the hatched line, it was some time – well into 1973 – before industrial and commercial companies increased their investment relative to their saving. The diagram suggests that whatever stopped them doing so was not the failure of banks to expand their lending in response to increased demand.

Analysis of lending

7.19 The pattern of clearing bank lending between the different sectors of the economy is determined largely by the demands of the banks' customers,

Companies' demand for finance
Industrial and commercial companies

Diagram 15

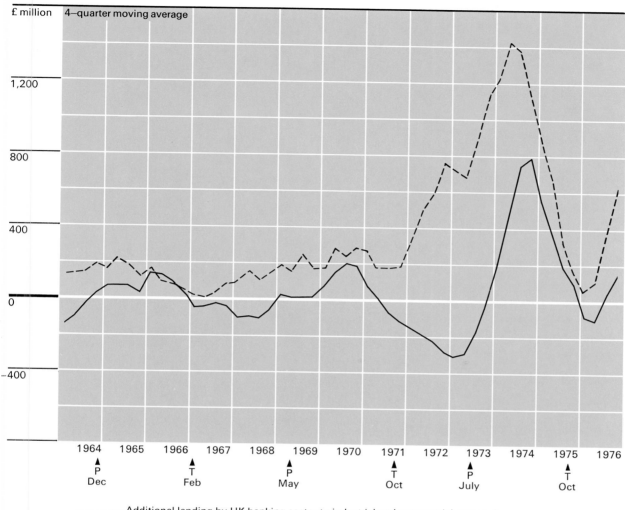

- - - - - Additional lending by UK banking sector to industrial and commercial companies

————— Industrial and commercial companies' gross investment in fixed capital and stocks less retained profits and capital transfers.

P and T relate to the peaks and troughs of the business cycle as estimated by the Central Statistical Office.

Sources: Economic Trends and Financial Statistics.

reflected in the first instance in requests for facilities and then in the use actually made of the facilities agreed. These demands themselves reflect the pattern of financial deficits and surpluses in the economy, the state of the business cycle, the level of interest rates and other basic economic circumstances. Other factors are the monetary and credit controls operated by the Bank of England, especially if these have a selective dimension and lead to a distortion in the allocation of lending from what would otherwise have been the case. The clearing banks themselves do not set out to strike a particular balance between different sectors of the economy in their lending activities, though their overall allocation of funds between the private and public sectors is to some extent conditioned by their need to hold gilt-edged securities and other public sector investments for liquidity purposes.

7.20   The pattern of financial assets and liabilities of all banks in the United Kingdom is illustrated in table 15, which compares the sources of bank finance by major economic sector with the distribution of that finance between the same sectors.

Sources and distribution of banking funds
Table 15

UK banking sector – sterling and foreign currency

31 December 1976	Sources of funds (deposits)		Distribution of funds (lending)	
	£ billion	Percentage of domestic deposits	£ billion	Percentage of domestic lending
Public sector	1.0	2.6	15.3	30.2
Industrial and commercial companies	11.2	29.1	23.3	45.9
Personal sector*	20.7	54.0	7.7	15.2
Financial institutions other than banks	5.5	14.3	4.5	8.7
Total domestic sectors	**38.4**	100.0	**50.8**	100.0
Non-residents	90.8		85.5	
Non-deposit liabilities (net)	7.1			
Total	**136.3**		**136.3**	

*Comprises individuals, unincorporated businesses and private non-profit-making bodies.

Source: Financial Statistics.

Among the main conclusions to be drawn from it are that the banking sector attracts more deposits from non-residents than it lends to them, while on the domestic front it predominantly channels deposits from the personal sector to the public sector and to industrial and commercial companies. Financial institutions other than banks are of minor importance as a source of funds for the banks and of even less importance as recipients of bank finance.

7.21 Another way of analysing the allocation of bank advances (though not investments) is by industrial classification rather than by broad sector as in table 15. For the banking sector as a whole, an analysis by industrial category is contained in diagram 16; for the clearing banks the same analysis is shown in diagram 17, and the full analysis is given in table 60 on page 276. These figures confirm the importance of industry and trade as recipients of bank finance; though for different reasons all these diagrams and tables slightly understate the banks' total involvement in the provision of industrial and commercial finance (the diagrams and table 60 because bill finance is not covered by advances, and table 15 because 'industrial and commercial companies' do not include nationalised industries, the trading activities of local authorities and unincorporated businesses). It should also be borne in mind that clearing bank lending which is channelled through some of their specialist subsidiaries is not classified according to the ultimate borrower when the subsidiaries are not themselves classed as banks: the ultimate borrowers are, in fact, predominantly in the manufacturing and other production categories. Lending by the clearing banks to their leasing companies is included in the services category, while lending to the factoring subsidiaries and some instalment credit subsidiaries is recorded in the financial category.

7.22 Before examining the clearing banks' lending activities sector by sector, it is necessary to recall a point made in paragraph 7.6. Although lending facilities are agreed between the banks and their customers, the actual use made of those facilities is a matter for the customers themselves. It will be seen from diagram 18 that there are considerable variations between the main categories of borrower in the extent to which they actually utilise the facilities available to them. This is particularly true of overdrafts which by their very nature fluctuate according to the customers' day-to-day needs.

7.23 Lending to the manufacturing category by the clearing bank parents reached a peak of 40.8 per cent of advances to UK residents in 1970. There was a sharp drop to 30.9 per cent in 1971 when advances to the category fell by £400 million. It will be noted from diagram 16 that the manufacturing

Advances by all banks in United Kingdom
Analysis of advances in sterling and foreign currencies

Diagram 16

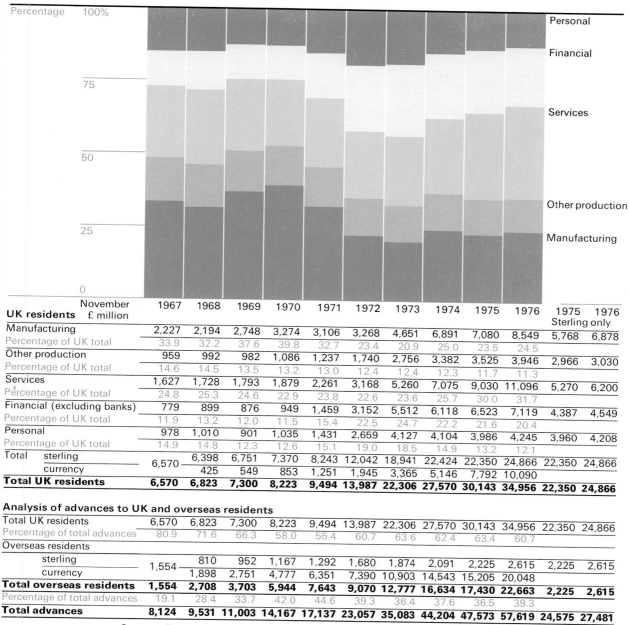

UK residents £ million	November 1967	1968	1969	1970	1971	1972	1973	1974	1975	1976	1975 Sterling only	1976 Sterling only
Manufacturing	2,227	2,194	2,748	3,274	3,106	3,268	4,651	6,891	7,080	8,549	5,768	6,878
Percentage of UK total	33.9	32.2	37.6	39.8	32.7	23.4	20.9	25.0	23.5	24.5		
Other production	959	992	982	1,086	1,237	1,740	2,756	3,382	3,525	3,946	2,966	3,030
Percentage of UK total	14.6	14.5	13.5	13.2	13.0	12.4	12.4	12.3	11.7	11.3		
Services	1,627	1,728	1,793	1,879	2,261	3,168	5,260	7,075	9,030	11,096	5,270	6,200
Percentage of UK total	24.8	25.3	24.6	22.9	23.8	22.6	23.6	25.7	30.0	31.7		
Financial (excluding banks)	779	899	876	949	1,459	3,152	5,512	6,118	6,523	7,119	4,387	4,549
Percentage of UK total	11.9	13.2	12.0	11.5	15.4	22.5	24.7	22.2	21.6	20.4		
Personal	978	1,010	901	1,035	1,431	2,659	4,127	4,104	3,986	4,245	3,960	4,208
Percentage of UK total	14.9	14.8	12.3	12.6	15.1	19.0	18.5	14.9	13.2	12.1		
Total sterling	6,570	6,398	6,751	7,370	8,243	12,042	18,941	22,424	22,350	24,866	22,350	24,866
currency		425	549	853	1,251	1,945	3,365	5,146	7,792	10,090		
Total UK residents	**6,570**	**6,823**	**7,300**	**8,223**	**9,494**	**13,987**	**22,306**	**27,570**	**30,143**	**34,956**	**22,350**	**24,866**

Analysis of advances to UK and overseas residents

	November 1967	1968	1969	1970	1971	1972	1973	1974	1975	1976	1975	1976
Total UK residents	6,570	6,823	7,300	8,223	9,494	13,987	22,306	27,570	30,143	34,956	22,350	24,866
Percentage of total advances	80.9	71.6	66.3	58.0	55.4	60.7	63.6	62.4	63.4	60.7		
Overseas residents												
sterling	1,554	810	952	1,167	1,292	1,680	1,874	2,091	2,225	2,615	2,225	2,615
currency		1,898	2,751	4,777	6,351	7,390	10,903	14,543	15,205	20,048		
Total overseas residents	**1,554**	**2,708**	**3,703**	**5,944**	**7,643**	**9,070**	**12,777**	**16,634**	**17,430**	**22,663**	**2,225**	**2,615**
Percentage of total advances	19.1	28.4	33.7	42.0	44.6	39.3	36.4	37.6	36.5	39.3		
Total advances	**8,124**	**9,531**	**11,003**	**14,167**	**17,137**	**23,057**	**35,083**	**44,204**	**47,573**	**57,619**	**24,575**	**27,481**

Sources: Bank of England Quarterly Bulletin and CLCB Statistical Unit.

category's borrowing from banks in the United Kingdom as a whole also fell at that time. The figures for recent years indicate some loss of market share in lending to the manufacturing category by the clearing bank groups (see diagram 11 on page 78). This partly reflects the fact that this category includes a high proportion of the very large UK companies on which American and other non-clearing banks have concentrated their attention. However, in the four years since 1973 for which group figures have been available, the clearing banks' advances to the manufacturing category have always accounted for a higher proportion of their total advances to UK residents than has been the case for other banks: in November 1976 the percentages were 26.2 and 22.5 respectively. From diagram 18 it is noticeable that borrowers in the manufacturing category have tended in recent years to show a relatively high margin of undrawn facilities. Between May 1975 and May 1977, facilities made available to manufacturing industry by the clearing banks were increased

Advances by London clearing banks
Analysis of advances in sterling and foreign currencies

Diagram 17

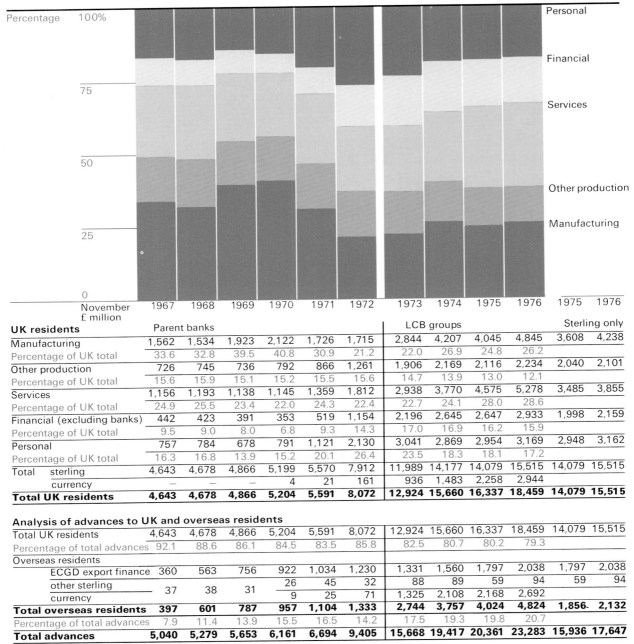

November £ million	1967	1968	1969	1970	1971	1972	1973	1974	1975	1976	1975	1976
UK residents	Parent banks						LCB groups				Sterling only	
Manufacturing	1,562	1,534	1,923	2,122	1,726	1,715	2,844	4,207	4,045	4,845	3,608	4,238
Percentage of UK total	33.6	32.8	39.5	40.8	30.9	21.2	22.0	26.9	24.8	26.2		
Other production	726	745	736	792	866	1,261	1,906	2,169	2,116	2,234	2,040	2,101
Percentage of UK total	15.6	15.9	15.1	15.2	15.5	15.6	14.7	13.9	13.0	12.1		
Services	1,156	1,193	1,138	1,145	1,359	1,812	2,938	3,770	4,575	5,278	3,485	3,855
Percentage of UK total	24.9	25.5	23.4	22.0	24.3	22.4	22.7	24.1	28.0	28.6		
Financial (excluding banks)	442	423	391	353	519	1,154	2,196	2,645	2,647	2,933	1,998	2,159
Percentage of UK total	9.5	9.0	8.0	6.8	9.3	14.3	17.0	16.9	16.2	15.9		
Personal	757	784	678	791	1,121	2,130	3,041	2,869	2,954	3,169	2,948	3,162
Percentage of UK total	16.3	16.8	13.9	15.2	20.1	26.4	23.5	18.3	18.1	17.2		
Total sterling	4,643	4,678	4,866	5,199	5,570	7,912	11,989	14,177	14,079	15,515	14,079	15,515
currency	–	–	–	4	21	161	936	1,483	2,258	2,944		
Total UK residents	**4,643**	**4,678**	**4,866**	**5,204**	**5,591**	**8,072**	**12,924**	**15,660**	**16,337**	**18,459**	**14,079**	**15,515**

Analysis of advances to UK and overseas residents

	1967	1968	1969	1970	1971	1972	1973	1974	1975	1976	1975	1976
Total UK residents	4,643	4,678	4,866	5,204	5,591	8,072	12,924	15,660	16,337	18,459	14,079	15,515
Percentage of total advances	92.1	88.6	86.1	84.5	83.5	85.8	82.5	80.7	80.2	79.3		
Overseas residents												
ECGD export finance	360	563	756	922	1,034	1,230	1,331	1,560	1,797	2,038	1,797	2,038
other sterling	37	38	31	26	45	32	88	89	59	94	59	94
currency				9	25	71	1,325	2,108	2,168	2,692		
Total overseas residents	**397**	**601**	**787**	**957**	**1,104**	**1,333**	**2,744**	**3,757**	**4,024**	**4,824**	**1,856**	**2,132**
Percentage of total advances	7.9	11.4	13.9	15.5	16.5	14.2	17.5	19.3	19.8	20.7		
Total advances	**5,040**	**5,279**	**5,653**	**6,161**	**6,694**	**9,405**	**15,668**	**19,417**	**20,361**	**23,283**	**15,936**	**17,647**

Source: CLCB Statistical Unit.

by £2,202 million (or 26 per cent); but actual borrowing by manufacturing increased by only £446 million (or 10 per cent). Thus while the clearing banks have demonstrated their support for manufacturing industry over the past few years, manufacturers have been reluctant borrowers.

7.24   In table 16 some data are provided which relate the increase in clearing bank advances to manufacturing industry to its investment expenditure, a substantial proportion of which is normally financed from undistributed profits. The figures are five-year aggregates intended to smooth the large year-to-year fluctuations in manufacturing investment in the course of the business cycle. Although the clearing banks have lost some of their share of total bank lending to the manufacturing sector, nevertheless, over the past 15 years as a whole, the increase in their lending has contributed a rising proportion of the sums required to finance

Lending commitments and utilisation
London clearing bank groups' total sterling and currency facilities

Diagram 18

£ million

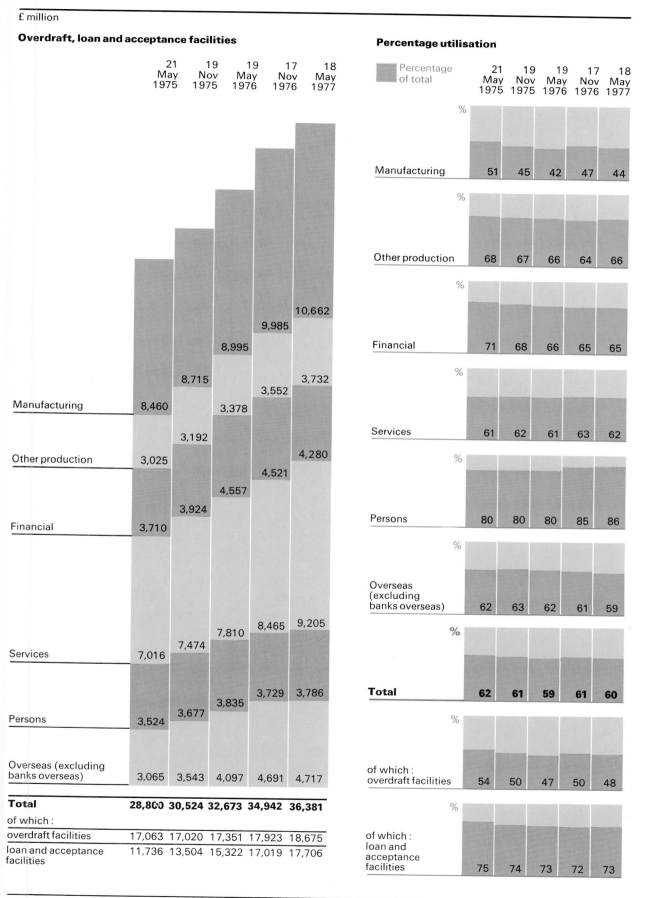

Overdraft, loan and acceptance facilities

	21 May 1975	19 Nov 1975	19 May 1976	17 Nov 1976	18 May 1977
Manufacturing	8,460	8,715	8,995	9,985	10,662
Other production	3,025	3,192	3,378	3,552	3,732
Financial	3,710	3,924	4,557	4,521	4,280
Services	7,016	7,474	7,810	8,465	9,205
Persons	3,524	3,677	3,835	3,729	3,786
Overseas (excluding banks overseas)	3,065	3,543	4,097	4,691	4,717
Total	**28,800**	**30,524**	**32,673**	**34,942**	**36,381**
of which: overdraft facilities	17,063	17,020	17,351	17,923	18,675
loan and acceptance facilities	11,736	13,504	15,322	17,019	17,706

Percentage utilisation

	21 May 1975	19 Nov 1975	19 May 1976	17 Nov 1976	18 May 1977
Manufacturing	51	45	42	47	44
Other production	68	67	66	64	66
Financial	71	68	66	65	65
Services	61	62	61	63	62
Persons	80	80	80	85	86
Overseas (excluding banks overseas)	62	63	62	61	59
Total	**62**	**61**	**59**	**61**	**60**
of which: overdraft facilities	54	50	47	50	48
of which: loan and acceptance facilities	75	74	73	72	73

Source: CLCB Statistical Unit

Manufacturing industry: Table 16
advances and investment expenditure
Increase in advances in relation to investment expenditure

£ million	1962–66	1963–67	1964–68	1965–69	1966–70	1967–71	1968–72	1969–73	1970–74	1971–75	1972–76
UK manufacturing industry gross domestic fixed capital formation plus increase in the book value of stocks	8,368	8,827	9,732	10,463	11,637	12,297	13,294	15,978	21,627	24,488	30,574
London clearing bank parents increase in advances to manufacturing sector, November to November	550	486	414	638	683	155	153	947	1,670	1,261	2,228
Second line as a percentage of first line	6.6	5.5	4.3	6.1	5.9	1.3	1.2	5.9	7.7	5.1	7.3

Sources: National Income and Expenditure; CLCB Statistical Unit.

manufacturing industry's investment in fixed assets and stocks. (See paragraphs 7.9–7.18 for a fuller discussion of the relationship between bank finance and industrial investment.)

7.25 Compared to other banks in the United Kingdom, a relatively high proportion of the clearing banks' advances has also gone to the 'other production' category in each of the ten years 1967–76. This is largely because the category embraces two sectors in which the banks recognise special responsibilities – agriculture and construction, discussed more fully in paragraphs 9.16–9.19. Over one third of advances to the 'other production' category (£912 million out of £2,415 million in May 1977) is accounted for by agriculture, which on some measures is the largest single industry in the United Kingdom and one which still has a major contribution to make to the economy. The industry is almost all in small units and the clearing banks, with their national network of branches, are the main lenders to it.

7.26 Although the manufacturing and 'other production' categories' direct share of clearing bank advances has fallen over the past ten years, these two categories account for 90 per cent of the take-up of the special export finance facilities which are classified as lending to overseas residents. In view of the lower interest rates available under these schemes, companies with the option of using special export finance rather than conventional bank finance have switched to the former, thus artificially decreasing the banks' lending in these categories. If export finance lending is added to the figures shown in diagram 17 for the manufacturing and other production categories, the result is an increase in such lending from 38 to 44 per cent of the enlarged total in November 1976. The clearing banks are not aware that any request for assistance for productive purposes by creditworthy customers has been refused except as a result of official constraints on aggregate bank lending. Lending to these categories has never been inhibited by the remaining lending activities of the clearing banks and any reasonable demand for finance by these customers would undoubtedly be met.

7.27 Much of the banks' lending to the service industries is directed towards smaller enterprises, notably retailers, and accordingly receives separate treatment in chapter 9. Here it should be pointed out that the services category also includes the banks' lending in the form of advances to the public sector. Lending to public utilities and local and national government includes the eurocurrency loans described in chapter 11 as well as sterling lending to help meet the working capital needs of public corporations. As the public sector is responsible for maintaining the country's infrastructure as well as for providing a wide range of essential services such as gas and electricity, the banks consider these advances to be indirectly in support of UK industry and trade.

Advances to the financial category
London clearing bank groups' lending

Diagram 19

£ million

Analysis of advances as at 16 February 1977 : **Total £23,905m**

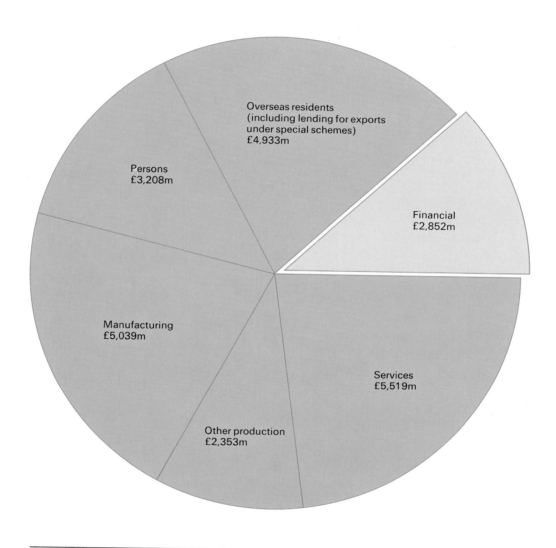

Overseas residents
(including lending for exports
under special schemes)
£4,933m

Persons
£3,208m

Financial
£2,852m

Manufacturing
£5,039m

Services
£5,519m

Other production
£2,353m

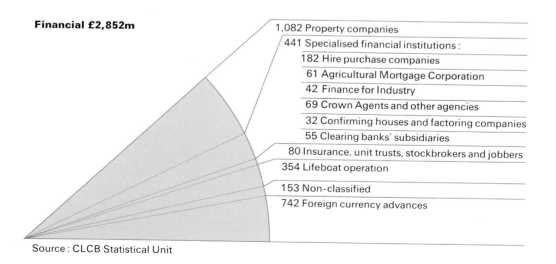

Financial £2,852m

1,082 Property companies

441 Specialised financial institutions :

182 Hire purchase companies

61 Agricultural Mortgage Corporation

42 Finance for Industry

69 Crown Agents and other agencies

32 Confirming houses and factoring companies

55 Clearing banks' subsidiaries

80 Insurance, unit trusts, stockbrokers and jobbers

354 Lifeboat operation

153 Non-classified

742 Foreign currency advances

Source : CLCB Statistical Unit

7.28   Lending to the financial category is sometimes wrongly assumed to be solely concerned with property investment and speculation. In fact, as diagram 19 shows, the property category accounted in February 1977 for only half the sterling lending to the financial category; included in the property category are housing estate developers (though not builders, who are included in the 'other production' classification), housing associations and estate agents. In view of the criticism that property lending has attracted in recent years, and the importance of the collapse of property values in precipitating the secondary banking crisis of 1973/74, it has been felt appropriate to provide some detailed factual information about the property market and the way it is financed in appendix D.

7.29   Advances to the property category represent a relatively small proportion of the clearing banks' total lending to UK residents. From table 61 on page 277 it will be seen that for the parent banks alone the figure reached a peak of 8 per cent in 1972 and has subsequently declined to about 6 per cent. Figures on a group basis first became available in 1973 and show that even in that year lending to the property sector accounted for only 9 per cent. It should be added that a substantial part of these advances comprised bridging loans pending funding from longer-term sources. The clearing banks always adhere closely to the official directives on bank lending. However, their ability to effect a reduction in their property lending in response to requests for restraint in 1972 and subsequent years was limited by their obligation to honour agreed commitments and, later, by a reluctance to withdraw facilities or realise security which would result in forced sales of property on an already seriously depressed market. Nevertheless, property lending has now been reduced in absolute as well as relative terms, and it is not unreasonable to assume that the difficulties of the market would have led to such a reduction in any case, even without official directives. Also included in the financial category is that part of the advances made by the clearing banks under the lifeboat operation to institutions which are not statistically classified as banks; support group lending to statistical banks is classified as inter-bank lending. (The lifeboat operation is described in chapter 5.)

7.30   In the basic analysis of advances contained in diagram 17, the other two borrowing categories shown are persons and overseas residents. The personal category has always accounted for a very much smaller percentage of bank lending than of bank deposits, mainly because the personal sector is almost invariably in financial surplus but also because it has been the subject of frequent official lending restrictions. The banks have developed a wide range of lending facilities for their personal customers, described in chapter 8, and personal lending rose substantially in the liberal lending climate of 1971–73, since when it has remained more or less static in response to official directives. The banks wish that economic conditions permitted them to make more use of these facilities in order to meet their personal customers' occasional borrowing needs, not least in view of their long-term importance to the banks as depositors. The banks' lending to overseas residents (described in chapter 11) has, by contrast, grown steadily as a proportion of the total. It will be seen from diagram 17 that the sterling lending under this heading is predominantly in connection with ECGD-backed lending to finance British exports. The banks' heavy involvement in the provision of finance for North Sea oil, which involves both their domestic and their international lending operations, is also discussed in chapter 11, with a comprehensive review contained in appendix C.

The clearing banks' lending record

7.31 The main arguments of this chapter are that the amounts available for lending by the clearing banks are heavily influenced by the factors mentioned in paragraph 7.3 and that the actual use made of these amounts is determined mainly by the banks' own customers. However, this does not mean that the banks' role in the lending process is a purely passive one. On the contrary, the actual lending facilities they offer and the terms and conditions on which they are made available are matters over which they enjoy a considerable measure of control. It is these aspects of the banks' lending record which are described in detail in chapter 8 and on which the banks are fully prepared to be judged. The remainder of this chapter sets the scene for the more detailed evidence which follows by making some general comments about the clearing banks' overall lending record, and in particular about their effectiveness in meeting the demands of industry and trade for finance on reasonable terms.

7.32 There are no clear-cut standards of 'effectiveness' by which to judge the banks' lending record; the term is a vague one and any overall assessment is bound to be largely subjective. Nevertheless, in considering the effectiveness with which the banks respond to the demand for finance it may be helpful to consider five distinct questions: Do the banks lend enough in aggregate? Do they allocate their credit appropriately between different sectors of the economy? Do they lend enough to particular borrowers? Are the terms on which they lend reasonable? And do they support their customers enough in other ways?

7.33 The clearing banks believe that after allowing for the supply and demand factors already described in this chapter there is little they can do on their own to increase the level of their aggregate lending. Given that the overall level of credit in the economy must be subject to control by the monetary authorities, a significant increase in lending by the clearing banks could only mean a smaller market share for some other group or groups of institutions. Even if such a shift in market share towards the clearing banks were thought to be desirable, the banks would be unable to accomplish it as long as they remained subject to the sort of competitive disadvantages described in chapters 17 and 18 (principally the clearing banks' requirement to hold $1\frac{1}{2}$ per cent of eligible liabilities at the Bank of England and the various competitive advantages enjoyed by the building societies). But while the clearing banks will continue to argue against competitive distortions of these kinds, and intend in any case to continue to compete vigorously with other lending institutions, they have no intention of seeking to monopolise the sources of credit in the economy. One of the main strengths of the UK financial system, admired by many other countries including several more economically successful than ourselves, is its diversity of institutions and markets. It is a sign of the system's strength, not of its weakness, that the clearing banks do not seek to meet all the country's borrowing needs. Consequently, they do not feel that the total amount of money they lend is open to attack.

7.34 They are aware, however, of the criticisms expressed from time to time of their allocative record, and would therefore point out the absence of any evidence that bank lending to the financial, personal and overseas sectors has been to the detriment of the banks' industrial and commercial borrowers. As for the amounts that the banks are prepared to lend to individual customers, these depend not only on the overall availability of credit and the financial needs of the various sectors of the economy, as reflected in the demands expressed by individual borrowers, but also on the extent to which the banks can prudently meet those demands. Clearing banks are commercial enterprises which lend money when they are confident that it will eventually be repaid, and when it will produce a return to cover costs and risks and provide a margin of profit. All requests for bank finance therefore require credit analysis to ensure that these criteria can be met. The assessment of a borrower's ability to repay involves many factors (discussed in detail in chapter 8), with the ability of the proprietors to provide the risk capital of the venture being a particularly important consideration.

7.35   The clearing banks' approach to lending, and in particular to the 'gearing' ratios they are prepared to see, has from time to time been attacked for being too conservative. But from the available evidence, the banks seriously doubt whether there is a significant pent-up demand for conventional bank finance on the part of industry which would be given expression if the banks relaxed their lending criteria. Insofar as there is a small element of unsatisfied loan demand from individual customers who fail to meet these criteria, the banks question whether it would necessarily be in the interests of long-term commercial stability for them to accede to it. It is perhaps worth adding that where lending problems do arise the banks deal with them sympathetically whenever possible, but not to the extent of taking unacceptable risks.

7.36   The detailed examination of the terms on which the banks lend which is also contained in chapter 8, is chiefly concerned with three factors: the maturity of the banks' lending; security and similar arrangements; and cost. It is now fairly widely appreciated that a high proportion of the banks' total lending is of a formal medium-term nature, while a substantial though unquantifiable element of their overdrafts is of a 'hard core' nature. However, there are limits beyond which turning short-term deposits into longer-term loans would be unjustifiably imprudent. If there were a significant upturn in industry's demand for medium-term loans – and there is little evidence of this – it might be necessary to consider the possible introduction of official refinance facilities for such loans, to be used in the event of liquidity problems. As for the banks' security requirements, they do not believe that these have proved unduly onerous for borrowers with propositions which are acceptable in all other respects.

7.37   In considering whether the cost of bank finance has been reasonable, a fundamental distinction must be drawn between the basic level of interest rates in the economy, over which the banks have little control, and the margins at which they lend over their full cost of funds, over which they do have control, subject, of course, to the limitations imposed by powerful competitive pressures. When short-term interest rates as a whole rise sharply – as they did, for instance, at the direct instigation of the authorities in November 1973, and September 1976 – the banks are under strong pressure from market forces, and sometimes directly from the authorities, to raise their base rates by similar amounts. They might in effect be defying official policy if they failed to do so. Notwithstanding these pressures, the banks may seek and have sometimes managed to hold their base rates a little below market rates when the latter have been high, with the aim of giving their borrowers a greater degree of stability in the cost of their funds and passing on to them some of the 'endowment effect' which can become significant when rates of interest are high. At the same time, however, in these circumstances the endowment effect itself will tend to be offset to the extent that high interest rates are accompanied by a rise in the proportion of expensive money market deposits on the banks' books and by a higher incidence of bad debts. High interest rates also tend to go hand-in-hand with increases in the banks' operating costs, insofar as both reflect inflationary conditions.

7.38   The clearing banks have no hesitation in saying that the rates at which they lend to industry are reasonable, in that they represent a modest and entirely legitimate margin over the cost of funds to the banks. For various reasons, described in chapter 8, there has been some widening of lending margins in recent years. Nevertheless the banks believe that the cost of the finance they provide still compares extremely favourably with finance from all other sources. They receive very few complaints regarding interest and other lending charges and are aware that after allowing for inflation the cost of bank finance in recent years has been low, if not negative (see diagram 20).

Real cost of bank finance   Diagram 20

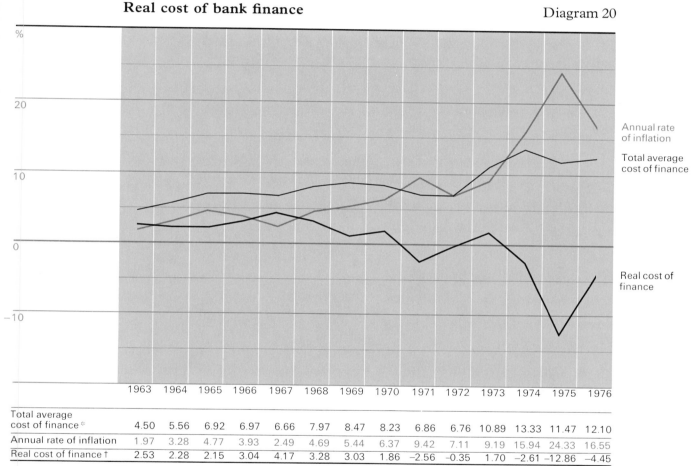

	1963	1964	1965	1966	1967	1968	1969	1970	1971	1972	1973	1974	1975	1976
Total average cost of finance *	4.50	5.56	6.92	6.97	6.66	7.97	8.47	8.23	6.86	6.76	10.89	13.33	11.47	12.10
Annual rate of inflation	1.97	3.28	4.77	3.93	2.49	4.69	5.44	6.37	9.42	7.11	9.19	15.94	24.33	16.55
Real cost of finance †	2.53	2.28	2.15	3.04	4.17	3.28	3.03	1.86	−2.56	−0.35	1.70	−2.61	−12.86	−4.45

* Annual average Bank rate/base rate plus 'blue chip' lending margin.

† Without taking account of tax relief.

Sources: Individual banks and Monthly Digest of Statistics.

7.39   There remains the question of whether the banks do enough to support their customers in other ways. In general, it should be stressed that the only needs to which a banker can respond are those expressed by the customer himself. Although a good banker will occasionally be able to help a customer to perceive opportunities he may not have considered, the decision to pursue a particular path and to seek the necessary finance must be the customer's own. The bank's role as provider of finance and financial services must not be confused with the role of the company's shareholders and management, who alone can determine whether the risks of a particular venture are worth running for the expected rewards.

7.40   Nevertheless it is occasionally suggested that the banks' relationships with industry generally are too passive. It is certainly true that the banks have traditionally not sought to interfere in the management and development of their corporate customers; but the problems that have faced industry in recent years have inevitably brought banks and industry much closer together. In the process, some banks have recruited a limited number of industrial specialists to help senior management appreciate the problems of particular industries, while all have made increasing use of their regional offices as means of providing customers with the support they need. In addition, business advisory services have been established, as described in paragraph 9.5. But beyond a point, a bank's involvement in the affairs of individual companies must run the risk – now widely recognised in Germany – of creating conflicts of interest. The clearing banks do not have an unlimited supply of managerial expertise; to provide greater assistance to their customers would require the further recruitment of highly qualified personnel which would directly increase the cost of bank services. Bank managers, however, do encourage customers to make the fullest use of their accountants and other professional advisers, while in appropriate cases introductions to management consultants can be arranged. But as far as their own involvement with their customers is concerned, the banks must stress that the role of banker is different from the role of proprietor or manager, and that it is dangerous to confuse them.

The effectiveness of the financial system

7.41   It is a general theme of this submission that the role and functioning of the clearing banks can be appreciated only if they are seen in the proper context of the financial system as a whole. Accordingly it seems appropriate to conclude this chapter by making some general judgements on the effectiveness of the financial system as a whole in meeting the needs of the users of finance within the economy.

7.42   Adequate and efficient financial institutions and markets are undoubtedly a necessary pre-condition of a sound economy, but they are not by themselves sufficient. So although Britain's economic performance is universally reckoned to have been less than satisfactory, it is by no means an easy matter to divide the responsibility for this between the financial factors and the various other factors – political, technological, managerial and those connected with labour relations – which are also relevant. With that proviso, the banks greatly doubt whether the degree of effectiveness of the financial system has been a major reason for the country's poor economic record in the post-war period compared with that of other major industrial economies. This is not to deny that the system could be made more effective; nor is it to deny that improvements in the system might work through to economic performance. But it is to deny that defects in the financial system have been anything like as important as defects in the other factors mentioned earlier in the paragraph. To put it another way: even if the financial system had been operating with no defects and gaps at all, the banks doubt whether the country's economic performance would have been significantly better as a result, in view of the serious nature of all the other factors which have been holding the economy back. The onus of responsibility rests with critics of the financial system to show that it has in fact been a major impediment to economic progress; the banks suggest that no such case has yet been made.

7.43   The clearing banks have read such evidence to the Committee as has been published by those representing the users of finance, and have formed the impression from the evidence to date that lack of finance is not reckoned to have been a primary constraint on investment. Industry would no doubt invest more if finance were extremely cheap and plentiful, but the point has already been made that the quantity and cost of finance available to industry is determined chiefly by forces outside the control of the financial system itself. Another way of attempting to assess the effectiveness of the system is to examine whether it appears to be adequate to the needs of particular companies. However, it is extremely important to be satisfied both about the quality of the evidence and about the legitimacy of the conclusions being drawn from it. Hard cases make bad law; and any evidence of ineffectiveness would need to be both accurate and truly representative if it were to be used as the basis of valid policy conclusions. So far, it appears that the main doubts about the overall effectiveness of the system relate to the provision of finance for small companies, a familiar problem which is discussed in chapter 9. With this possible exception, the clearing banks remain confident that the Committee will find from their investigations that the financial system as a whole has been generally effective in meeting the demands of industry and trade for finance on reasonable terms.

Chapter 8
Lending: facilities, terms and conditions

Summary

This chapter surveys the main lending and related financial facilities provided by the clearing banks and the terms and conditions on which they are made available. Overdraft facilities remain very important although companies have latterly been using under half their agreed overdraft facilities. During the early 1970s the banks developed contractual term lending, with loans of up to five or seven years now common: such lending represents 40 per cent of the banks' non-personal lending. Special schemes exist for fixed-rate lending for exports and shipbuilding. Largely through their subsidiaries, the banks offer a range of 'asset finance' services to industry, the chief of them being instalment credit, leasing and factoring. Lending facilities for personal customers include overdraft and bridging finance, personal loans, revolving credit and budget accounts, instalment credit through finance house subsidiaries, and credit card finance. The banks lend mainly at interest rates related to their base rates and to inter-bank rates. Base rates are fixed wholly independently, though they often move together. The increase in lending margins over base rate reflects rising interest and other costs and the need to absorb lending risks. The main purpose of applying lending criteria is to ensure that customers are capable of servicing and repaying their debts; all lending is extended on the assumption that the borrower's business will continue as a going concern, and involves appraising its gearing, liquidity and profitability. This approach is complementary to, and not an alternative to, the so-called 'gone concern' approach. Much bank lending is unsecured, and where security is taken the banks are not unduly restrictive. When companies find themselves in difficulties, the banks do their best to find a solution in concert with the company's directors, advisers and creditors.

Overdrafts and loan accounts

8.1 Over the past 20 years the clearing banks have developed into large, multi-purpose institutions capable of providing a comprehensive range of financial facilities. In addition to the traditional overdraft, a variety of other lending facilities for both corporate and personal customers is now available through the banks' branch networks although several are provided by subsidiary and affiliated companies. In terms of the range of facilities available, from the very short-term advance to the occasional equity investment, the clearing banks are now much closer than they used to be to the traditionally continental concept of the 'universal bank'. But despite this diversification, the corporate customers who account for the majority of the banks' advances still look to them in the first instance to cover their working capital requirements. These fluctuate in amount as a result of seasonal factors, the nature of the production cycle and the pattern of the companies' receipts and payments. The overdraft system was developed to accommodate these fluctuations flexibly and efficiently and it remains to this day the most important of the banks' sterling lending facilities.

It is accordingly with the overdraft that this survey of these facilities begins. (For convenience, corporate and personal lending facilities are considered separately, in that order. Foreign currency lending is covered in chapter 11.)

8.2 An overdraft facility represents an agreed line of credit that may be taken up by a customer through the normal use of his current account. The customer is able to draw on the account as required to meet his day-to-day needs, although he will be expected to keep within the agreed limit. Sympathetic consideration is given to requests for temporary excesses. Originally overdraft arrangements were regarded as 'in-and-out' facilities on which customers borrowed occasionally and temporarily. Nowadays, however, it is quite usual for some accounts to operate permanently in overdraft, though with the overdrawn balance fluctuating from day to day. When a current account constantly operates in debit, a 'hard-core' overdraft exists to the extent of the minimum overdrawn balance. Overdrafts were primarily intended for financing working capital but in many cases they cover all a customer's financing needs, including the purchase of fixed assets. Although lending on overdraft is formally repayable on demand it is not the practice of the clearing banks to call in overdrafts from customers conducting their business in a proper manner; indeed the normal practice is to renew facilities for business customers from year to year.

8.3 Overdraft finance offers the banks' corporate customers a number of advantages. In the first place they can expect to receive a decision on an application for a new or increased facility, if not immediately then usually in no more than a few days. In addition, arrangements are informal and involve a minimum of legal documentation. Most of all, the customer obtains the advantage of flexibility at low cost as interest is charged only on the day-to-day borrowing and not on the full commitment, although in exceptional cases a fee may be charged for standby facilities. In some cases, different interest rates are charged on different tranches of the same overdraft; for instance, customers are sometimes required to pay a higher rate of interest on the 'hard core' element in their overdrafts which represents *de facto* term lending. A particular application of overdraft facilities is in the provision of bridging finance to cover the development phase of a project such as a factory building. Progress payments are financed as required and on completion the advance is normally funded, for instance by a term loan, by mortgage finance or by loan or equity capital.

8.4 The Radcliffe Report recommended that the clearing banks should be ready to offer, within reasonable limits, term loan facilities as an alternative to overdrafts, thus providing smaller companies in particular with a greater degree of certainty on which they could proceed with their investment projects. The clearing banks for their part recognised that such companies generally lacked ready access to the capital markets, and they duly increased the availability of loans which, although technically repayable on demand, were in practice agreed for repayment over a term of years. These loan accounts have advantages to both parties: for the lender the arrangements provide an effective monitoring system which is very useful where an advance has been made for the purchase of capital assets; for the customer the facilities are available without the legal and other formalities of contractual medium-term loans, a feature particularly attractive to smaller businesses with limited internal administrative resources.

8.5 On 18 May 1977, the clearing bank groups' total overdraft commitments (excluding loan accounts) to customers amounted to £18,675 million, but on that date actual borrowing under these facilities was only 48 per cent of the amount available (see diagram 18 on page 89). Because the peak borrowing requirements of individual customers occur at different times, the clearing banks' customers as a whole would never take up all their facilities at the same time. For that reason, percentage utilisation figures are not a perfect indicator of the true level of available credit. Nevertheless, for the past two years borrowing by industry and trade has been sluggish, with overdraft utilisation levels for customers as a whole ranging between 45 and 55 per cent, compared to normal levels of 55–60 per cent. This represents further evidence that there has been no general shortage of finance available to industrial and trading customers recently. Overdraft lending, however, responds quickly to changes in the economic environment, and any move by industry to increase the level of stocks to meet higher output is reflected in greater utilisation. One of the uses of the substantial liquid funds which the clearing banks maintain is to provide a cushion to meet any such upsurge in the demand for overdraft finance.

Contractual term lending

8.6   During much of the 1960s, the clearing banks were subject to lending restrictions which left them little scope to promote medium-term lending, since they felt obliged to reserve most of their lending capacity for meeting the essential working capital requirements of their corporate customers. However, the radical changes of the 1970s brought considerably greater scope for the banks to develop lending in both sterling and foreign currencies. Even before *Competition and Credit Control* the banks' subsidiaries had started to make contractual medium-term loans in a modest way. The ending of quantitative credit restrictions in 1971, and the greater degree of operational flexibility obtained through access to wholesale deposits, provided the opening for the clearing banks themselves to market such loans.

8.7   The contractual medium-term loan is formalised by a specific agreement covering purpose, period, repayment programme and cost, which together with associated conditions are written into a formal contract. The loan will only become immediately repayable if the borrower breaks the terms of the contract. Loans of up to five or seven years are usual, although longer terms of up to ten years or so are increasingly agreed. Interest rates may vary periodically with changes in inter-bank rates, under 'roll-over' agreements, or may be related to the bank's own base rate, or may in a few instances be fixed for the life of the loan. Repayment arrangements are negotiable over the term of the facility and can be tailored to meet the particular circumstances of the borrower, often with a moratorium in the early stages if the project being financed has a development phase. Large medium-term commitments can be syndicated between groups of banks. Over the past four years, advances under contractual term lending arrangements have accounted for an increasing proportion of the clearing bank groups' total advances and, as shown in table 59 on page 276, they now represent 40 per cent of their total lending in sterling and foreign currency to UK residents other than the personal category. If one includes loans under the export finance schemes, which are technically classified as lending to overseas residents, term advances represent 47 per cent of total advances other than to the personal category.

8.8   The clearing banks' foreign currency lending and special ECGD-backed export finance, which are included in the figures in table 59, are described in chapter 11. A similar special scheme was introduced in 1967 to encourage UK shipowners to place orders with domestic shipyards. Under the scheme, the banks provide finance to the extent of 70 per cent of the contract value at a fixed rate of interest (currently $7\frac{1}{2}$ per cent) and for a 7-year period. The Department of

Industry provides the covering guarantee and extends refinancing and interest adjustment facilities similar to those involved in ECGD lending (see appendix B). The amounts outstanding under the scheme are shown in table 17.

Finance for shipbuilding

Table 17

Lending under the special scheme for shipbuilding by London clearing bank groups

November £ million	1972	1973	1974	1975	1976
Gross lending	343	404	450	499	554
Amounts refinanced by the authorities	111	154	198	243	301
Net lending outstanding	**232**	**250**	**252**	**256**	**253**

Source: CLCB Statistical Unit.

8.9 The clearing banks are precluded by considerations of banking prudence from engaging in the provision of long-term debt and equity finance to any great extent. The clearing banks' own term lending rarely extends beyond about 10 years, with the exception of certain lending under the ECGD special schemes. However, there is considerably more that they have been able to achieve through Finance for Industry and the Agricultural Mortgage Corporation, in which they are the majority shareholders. Finance for Industry (FFI) was established in 1973 as the holding company to bring together the Industrial and Commercial Finance Corporation (ICFC) and Finance Corporation for Industry (FCI), both of which had been set up in 1945. The clearing banks hold three-quarters of the shares. The clearing banks have been involved with ICFC since it was established to help plug the so-called 'Macmillan gap' by providing capital to companies too small to make use of the stock market. FCI's main role is the provision of term loans to finance large-scale industrial projects. It was mainly to permit FCI to expand these facilities that steps were taken in 1974 to enlarge the resources of FFI. Demand has not matched original expectations, but loans agreed by FCI in the two years to March 1977 totalled some £203 million. Its lending differs from the clearing banks' own term lending in that FCI is more prepared to lend at fixed rates and for periods beyond ten years. FFI finances its assets partly with debenture and loan stock issues, partly with bank borrowings and partly with deposits sought from the market and from the public. The clearing banks provide it with overdraft and loan finance, and together with the other shareholding banks have extended standby facilities totalling £400 million. As ICFC is primarily concerned with financing smaller businesses, its operations are discussed in chapter 9, as are those of the Agricultural Mortgage Corporation and the subsidiaries and associates established by some of the clearing banks to provide risk capital for industrial and commercial companies.

Instalment credit, leasing and factoring

8.10 While the clearing banks have been actively developing their lending role, they remain largely concerned with financing the current assets of the corporate sector. The circulating nature of these assets limits the banks' capacity to control or oversee the manner in which the funds advanced are deployed, and this can restrict the total amount that the banks are able to advance. To meet the demands of those companies which can nevertheless put additional resources to productive use, the clearing banks have developed services, mainly through specialised subsidiaries, whereby they can safely provide extra finance by exercising greater control over the assets in question. These services rely largely on the customer's ability to generate an acceptable cash flow from holding these assets. The banks for their part need to have a clear understanding of the nature and earning capacity of the assets being financed. The most significant of these 'asset finance' services are instalment credit and leasing; factoring, which is an 'asset finance' of a rather different kind, is also discussed.

8.11   Instalment credit has a major application in the financing of the fixed assets of industrial customers. Industrial instalment credit extended by clearing bank subsidiaries amounted to £540 million at the end of 1976 (see table 18). With industrial hire purchase, as with personal hire purchase, title to the asset is conveyed after an agreed number of regular instalments have been paid. This usually allows companies to obtain finance without the need for security over and above that of the asset itself, and in effect enables those companies to expand by financing capital equipment from the equipment's own earnings – a particular attraction for companies with limited resources. The basic concept of instalment credit has been developed to embrace other financial services, such as contract hire for fleet users of vehicles; aircraft and marine mortgages; facilities for the block discounting of rental and hiring agreements for the retail trade; stocking finance for motor manufacturers and retailers; and facilities for the purchase of small businesses over an extended period.

Industrial instalment credit

Table 18

London clearing bank subsidiaries*

December £ million	1972	1973	1974	1975	1976
	307	402	496	529	540

Mercantile Credit figures are included throughout although the company did not become a clearing bank subsidiary until 1975.

*Including those not classified as banks.

Source: CLCB Statistical Unit.

8.12   Under equipment leasing agreements, the assets in question remain in the ownership of the leasing company, but are effectively hired out to the industrial customer. The aggregate book value of the clearing bank groups' leased assets in December 1976 amounted to £672 million (see table 19); contracted future capital commitments totalled £163 million. Indeed the clearing bank groups have been responsible for the major part of the expansion of leasing in the past three years and together are now the leading UK providers of this service. Leasing falls into two categories: finance leases and operating leases. In a finance lease the lessor fully recovers his costs from the customer during the primary rental period. In an operating lease, this is not so and the lessor aims to engage one customer or a series of customers for a sufficient number of consecutive rental periods to achieve the desired return. The operating lessor therefore assumes the greater risks, since he cannot tell what rental his asset will command when he comes to negotiate his next leasing contract.

Leased assets

Table 19

Assets held for leasing by London clearing bank groups*

December £ million	1971	1972	1973	1974	1975	1976
Individual contracts	84	109	188	288	443	536
Consortium contracts	8	11	61	74	109	136
Total	**92**	**120**	**249**	**362**	**552**	**672**

Capital commitments for leasing contracts amounted to £163 million in December 1976.

*Including subsidiaries not classified as banks.

Source: CLCB Statistical Unit.

8.13   The average value of equipment leased is around £10,000 with most leases falling in the range of £5,000 to £100,000, though assets costing as little as £250 can also be leased. There is practically no restriction on the type of asset which can be financed by leasing. In negotiating the terms of the leasing contract, investment incentives such as grants under the Industry Act and 100 per cent first-year capital allowances are taken into account and are reflected in reduced overall costs to the customer. Leasing is particularly helpful to companies whose UK profit flow is insufficient for them to obtain full advantage from such allowances in their own right, and also in those cases where the effects of inflation on asset replacement costs have exceeded the ability of companies to generate adequate finance internally. Thus the value of investment incentives reaches precisely those for whom the benefit was designed. Large capital projects are commonly financed by leasing consortia in which the subsidiaries of the clearing banks play a dominant role. The most notable are: Airlease International, financing ships and aircraft with a book value of £158 million in December 1976; Computer Leasings, which finances computer equipment manufactured by International Computers Ltd, with a book value of £88 million in December 1976; and Omnium Leasing which is to provide finance to the extent of £70 million for the construction of a new oil refinery which will be completed in 1980.

8.14   Factoring involves a number of closely related services, which may include a financing facility. The essence of factoring is the provision of sales accounting and debt collection services and protection against bad debts. In addition, customers may receive immediate payment of up to about 80 per cent of the trade debts due to them, with the balance (less charges) paid when the factoring company finally collects the debt. The customer's cash flow benefits not only from the initial payment but also from the speedier settlement of the debts themselves which the factoring companies can often achieve. Factoring is particularly appropriate for smaller companies which are spared the burdens of operating a debtors' ledger and controlling and financing their trade credit. The services can be used for export debts, while some factoring companies now operate internationally.

8.15   Before leaving the subject of 'asset finance' it is worth noting that the clearing banks provide additional finance to companies by discounting and 'accepting' bills of exchange. Bill finance is of principal relevance to international trade and accordingly receives its main coverage in chapter 11.

Personal lending

8.16   Conventional overdraft and loan finance has always been available to personal as well as to corporate customers, though the actual amount of personal lending has frequently been subject to official restrictions. An important facility is the provision of bridging loans to those changing home, to finance them during the period between the purchase of the new home and the completion of the sale of the old one. (The clearing banks have traditionally provided housing loans to their own staff, but apart from these and bridging loans their involvement in house purchase finance is relatively modest.)

8.17   Personal loans for fixed periods at fixed rates of interest were introduced in the late 1950s, though they could not be effectively promoted until the 1970s because of lending restrictions. The loans are granted for terms of between six months and three years and for amounts up to about £2,000, repayments being by equal monthly instalments to cover interest (which is fixed at the inception of the loan) and the original sum borrowed. Personal loans are normally unsecured, the principal factor in assessing applications being the customer's capacity to meet the monthly repayment. The loan arrangement is documented in a simple contract, which provides for cancellation of any amount outstanding in the event of the borrower's death during the period of the loan. The clearing banks observe the requirements of minimum deposit and maximum repayment period that are stipulated under terms control regulations. These personal loans are generally regarded as particularly appropriate for the financing of cars, consumer durables and home improvements. Loans may also be provided for longer periods of up to eight years and for larger amounts of up to about £5,000 but in such cases covering security is usually taken.

8.18   Several banks also operate revolving credit loans, which allow the customer to draw up to a given amount whenever he wishes. The scheme is funded by fixed monthly payments, and if the account moves into credit the bank will pay interest on it. Budget accounts – a somewhat similar facility – were introduced during the 1960s and are designed to spread the impact of household and other regular expenses over a 12-month period. The facility is generally unsecured and is made available to creditworthy customers who maintain current accounts. The customer provides an estimate of outgoings for the ensuing 12 months, and signs a banker's order to transfer one twelfth of the total each month from his current account to a special account opened for the purpose. He then uses a special cheque book to pay the outgoings as they are billed to him.

8.19   A more recently developed form of personal credit is that available to holders of the credit cards operated by the clearing banks, Barclaycard and Access. The use of these cards as a means of paying for goods and services is discussed in chapter 3. In the lending context, it is appropriate to mention the extended payment facilities which the cards also offer. When the cardholder receives his monthly bill he may pay it either in full or in part, subject to a minimum monthly payment of 15 per cent of the outstanding debt, or £6, whichever is the greater. (These minimum amounts are higher than those originally adopted by the banks and were imposed at the request of the Chancellor of the Exchequer in 1973. At the same time a £30 limit was imposed on the use of the card to draw cash at a bank. The banks hope that these restrictions will soon be lifted.)

8.20   If a cardholder pays in full by the due date, he will in effect have enjoyed free credit from the moment of purchase to the time of payment. If he makes use of the extended credit facilities he will be charged interest. The true effective cost of the credit will therefore depend on the precise pattern of usage and repayment for each individual customer. Free credit, however, is not available if the card is used for cash withdrawal purposes. It should be noted that it is the individual participating banks which are responsible for marketing the cards, determining cardholders' credit limits and financing any credit resulting from the cardholders' activity. This is true of Access as well as of Barclaycard, although in the former case the administrative and accounting aspects of the operation are handled by the jointly-owned Joint Credit Card Company.

8.21   The clearing banks are also heavily involved in consumer credit indirectly through their instalment credit finance house subsidiaries. Traditionally, the major proportion of business transacted by the finance houses has been introduced by the dealer or vendor of goods sold on extended credit (known as vendor credit), whether by way of a personal loan, conditional sale or hire purchase agreement. The finance houses usually pay commission to the dealers for introductions, though in recent years there has been an increasing tendency for manufacturers or dealers wishing to promote a particular product range to forgo their commission or subsidise in part the interest rate charged to the borrower. Although the relative importance of vendor credit is declining, it is likely to represent a substantial proportion of the finance houses' total personal business for years to come. Increasingly, though, the finance houses have been seeking to attract customers directly to their fixed-term or revolving credit facilities, which are similar to those offered by the clearing banks themselves and described in paragraphs 8.17 and 8.18. The finance houses have used a mixture of branch and money-shop activity and direct mail and media advertising to promote these facilities.

Maturity and cost of lending

8.22 After the preceding survey of the main lending facilities extended by the clearing banks, the remainder of this chapter considers the terms and conditions on which they are made available under four main headings: maturity of lending; cost of lending; lending criteria (by which the banks decide whether, and how much, to lend to particular customers); and security arrangements. Finally, the banks' experience of lending problems and failures is discussed.

8.23 Because of the short-term structure of their deposit base, the clearing banks traditionally sought to employ their deposits in short-term lending and the majority of their advances were provided in the form of overdrafts to meet the revolving working capital requirements of industry and trade. However, the growth in term lending described in paragraphs 8.6–8.8 has changed the structure of the banks' lending portfolio (see table 59 on page 276). Clearly there must be a limit beyond which a clearing bank group cannot commit resources on a term basis, while at the same time maintaining an extensive line of undrawn overdraft commitments available to industry and trade. So whether the recent rate of increase in term lending could be maintained in a period of economic expansion, with demand for overdraft finance rising in parallel, is far from certain. While the banks would themselves not be unhappy to see some of their overdraft commitments removed and replaced by loan arrangements on the American pattern, they very much doubt if industry and trade would willingly sacrifice the flexibility and lower cost of the traditional overdraft arrangement that they have long enjoyed. Also at issue is the extent to which a bank can engage in 'maturity transformation', turning short-term deposits into longer-term advances. Bankers themselves would largely confirm the judgement of the Radcliffe Report, already quoted in paragraph 4.17, about the stability of their current account base, but even clearing banks must guard against liquidity problems.

8.24 The clearing banks lend at interest rates determined in one of three ways: at a margin over base rate; at a margin over the offered rate on the London inter-bank market (LIBOR); or at a fixed rate. Before 1971 the reference point for all bank lending was the Bank rate announced weekly by the Bank of England. One of the consequences of *Competition and Credit Control*, however, was the introduction of a base rate determined independently by each individual bank with regard to the average and marginal cost of its funds. These costs are not confined to the interest-bearing element of its deposits, which as chapter 4 has shown has been an increasing proportion of the total.

They also include the net costs of operating the money transmission system and the branch network through which current account balances are collected. The marginal cost of funds is usually regarded as the cost of short-term deposits on the wholesale money market. It is not possible for a bank's base rate to be seriously out of line with rates on these markets. If it is too high, larger borrowers will switch to borrowing from banks offering facilities linked to market rates; if it is too low, larger customers can engage in so-called 'arbitrage' operations, using their overdraft facilities to borrow from the bank and deposit the funds on the money market at a profit. Substantial sums can shift in this way, causing disruptive movements in a bank's deposits and advances. The main reason why the banks usually move their base rates by the same amount within a day or two of each other is that they are all subject to more or less the same financial pressures. If a bank remained out of line for long, it would be likely to experience a disruptive shift of lending business to or from its competitors. This is because large companies operate accounts at several clearing banks and are highly sensitive to even minor interest rate differentials.

8.25   It was noted in chapter 4 that the margin of base rate over the rate of interest paid on 7-day deposits has increased since January 1975 and has been as wide as $4\frac{1}{2}$ per cent. However, this is not indicative of the change in the overall margin which banks obtain on their lending, not least because 7-day deposits represent only about a third of total sterling deposits. The gap between wholesale deposit rates and base rate has not widened in the same way, while the cost of current account deposits has been rising steadily, regardless of fluctuations in base rate, to the point where the cost in interest terms (net of charges) has exceeded base rate. To that extent the so-called 'endowment effect' has been eliminated. (Movements in Bank rate and its successor, minimum lending rate, together with syndicate base rate since 1971 are shown in diagram 25 on page 231.)

8.26   The relationship between base rate and deposit costs, of course, represents only one part of the picture of the overall margins earned on the banks' base rate-related lending, the other being the banks' lending margins over base rate. When evidence was submitted to the Radcliffe Committee in 1957, the rates charged on clearing bank overdrafts were generally 1 per cent over Bank rate, although 'blue chip' companies were frequently charged a $\frac{1}{2}$ per cent margin. Margins over first Bank rate and latterly base rate have widened since that time: 'blue chip' customers are now normally charged 1 per cent over base rate on their overdrafts, while margins for smaller companies are usually in the range of 2 to 3 per cent, partly because of higher administrative costs, or somewhat more in the case of loan accounts. There are several reasons for this widening of margins. These include the increase in the interest-bearing proportion of the banks' total deposits; the increase in unrecovered operating costs; and the need to reflect more realistically in the rating structure the risks involved in lending.

8.27   A substantial proportion of the clearing banks' term lending is now linked to LIBOR instead of to base rate. Rather than moving daily, however, interest rates charged are adjusted only at the end of specified 'roll-over' periods by reference to the market rate for deposits of the relevant period. The margin over LIBOR is fixed at the outset and would currently be in the range of $\frac{3}{4}-1\frac{1}{4}$ per cent for a medium-term loan to a 'blue chip' customer; margins have recently tended to contract. Where large loans are syndicated between several banks, LIBOR provides a particularly appropriate reference point. It is when participating in such loans that the clearing banks feel most keenly the cost, borne solely by them, of maintaining 1½ per cent of their eligible liabilities as a balance at the Bank of England, since this requirement significantly reduces their profit margin. Competition is particularly intense throughout the banking system for large-volume lending for short periods and clearing banks are among those who offer facilities for their major customers to borrow on variable-rate terms which can represent very fine margins over LIBOR. Many of the commercial sterling loans extended by the clearing banks' finance house subsidiaries are also made on a variable rate basis. The rates are often related to the finance house base rate, which is calculated by the Finance Houses Association by a formula which relates it to the 3-month inter-bank rate over the previous eight weeks. Margins on such lending will typically range from 3 to 5 per cent.

8.28 The banks' fixed-rate lending activities can be divided into two categories. First there is medium and long-term export and shipbuilding finance provided under the 'special schemes' at rates determined by the authorities. These rates involve an element of subsidy which is funded by the exchequer, and the banks receive a return calculated by an agreed formula, which equates closely to what they would earn on a 'blue chip' loan. Secondly there is general fixed-rate lending to industry and trade, most of which is undertaken by the banks' instalment finance subsidiaries. Although some of these subsidiaries advertise for deposits, they generally take the bulk of their funds in large amounts from the wholesale markets, mainly for shorter periods than the duration of the loans they are financing. So although the lending rates are fixed with a view to providing an adequate margin over the expected cost of funds, the profitability of fixed-rate lending is vulnerable to erratic movements in market rates of interest. (Table 20 illustrates typical rates on fixed-rate facilities for industry in the recent past.) In addition, there is a small but increasing tendency for the banks to provide variable rate loans for repayment by fixed instalments, altering the length of the repayment period to compensate for interest rate variations. This helps to insulate the cash flow of the borrower from interest rate variations.

Instalment finance costs   Table 20
Fixed-rate lending by subsidiary companies

Standard interest rates*	1971	1972	1973	1974	1975	1976
Heavy vehicles, average flat rate	7.75	7.75	9.00	11.50	11.50	11.75
(Effective rate for a 3-year loan)	15.02	15.02	17.43	22.24	22.24	22.72
Plant and machinery, average flat rate— loans under £5,000	7.75	7.75	9.00	11.00	11.00	11.25
(Effective rate for a 3-year loan)	15.02	15.02	17.43	21.28	21.28	21.76
Agricultural machinery, average flat rate	8.25	7.75	8.50	10.50	10.50	10.75
(Effective rate for a 3-year loan)	15.98	15.02	16.46	20.32	20.32	20.80
Average finance house base rate	6.83	6.25	10.88	14.04	11.33	11.29
Average bank base rate	5.86	5.76	9.89	12.33	10.47	11.10

*These standard rates are quoted as a general guide but many loans are negotiated at lower rates than those quoted above. Effective rates of interest vary according to the length of the repayment period.
Source: Internal clearing bank figures.

Lending criteria

8.29 The main purpose of applying lending criteria and appraisal techniques is common to all lending institutions: it is to ensure to the best of the lender's ability that its customers are capable of servicing their debts and eventually repaying them. The precise criteria adopted will depend on the type of customer and the type of loan requested; variations in the criteria adopted by different banks accordingly reflect differences in the composition of their lending business rather than any differences in fundamental lending principles. The most fundamental principle of all is that the bank should have confidence in the integrity, competence and continuing creditworthiness of the borrower. How that confidence is gained will depend largely on whether there is an existing customer relationship. Where there is, the bank will already have formed a judgement of the borrower's integrity and competence through personal contacts supported by visits to his place of business. On the other hand, detailed enquiries will be necessary when dealing with a borrower for the first time. It then remains for the bank to establish beyond reasonable doubt that the borrower is creditworthy and likely to stay so throughout the lifetime of the loan, thus remaining able to honour the terms of the loan in the normal course of his business.

8.30   The bank's assessment of the borrower's creditworthiness will be based on past performance, the current financial position and the likely changes in that position in future, not least those resulting from the proposed additional borrowing. A series of audited accounts generally provides an adequate indication of the history of the business, and taken in conjunction with information about the current position serves as a basis for considering its future prospects. Very often, however, the bank will seek further information about particular items in the accounts, especially where there are exceptional items or significant changes in trends: the explanations given for these can be an invaluable guide to the ability of the management of the business to respond to changes in trading conditions.

8.31   Having established a satisfactory opinion of the present state of the business the bank must assess the potential effect of the proposed borrowing, and the activities it is intended to finance, on the business in the future. Various factors are involved in such an assessment and their relative importance varies from case to case. For a company requesting modest additional overdraft facilities for working capital purposes, the bank often relies on the well-established customer relationship and accedes to the request with the minimum of formality, subject to review only when the facilities fall due for re-negotiation. In cases where a substantial loan to enable a large company to undertake a major expansion is under consideration, the company will be asked to produce detailed budgets and cash flow forecasts so as to satisfy the bank that its peak borrowing requirement can be met within the total resources available to it, and that future earnings on completion of the expansion will make an appropriate contribution towards repayment of the loan. If a term loan is to be provided, a facility letter containing specific terms will be drawn up, often setting out covenants on such matters as balance sheet ratios. As a general rule, such practices tend to detract from the traditional simplicity and flexibility of clearing bank lending, but some covenants are essential where the bank has entered into a contractual medium-term commitment. Under such circumstances the bank may require that regular financial information be provided for monitoring purposes. Most large companies do, of course, have highly competent finance departments which produce regular management accounts for internal use, and in many cases clearing banks receive relevant figures drawn from such accounts. The vast majority of the clearing banks' business customers, however, are not large companies, but smaller enterprises, usually with only limited resources, both financial and managerial. It would not be defensible for the clearing banks to deny facilities to the many thousands of their customers with successful businesses but which lack the resources to produce detailed financial forecasts and reports.

8.32 Whatever detailed appraisal techniques are applied in any given case, it must be stressed that all clearing bank lending decisions are made on a 'going concern' basis, in the sense that they are based on the clear understanding that the borrower will remain a viable concern throughout the life of the loan. No loan would be extended if it were evident at the outset that repayment could be achieved only through the forced liquidation of the business. The 'going concern' approach to lending involves three main considerations: gearing, liquidity and profitability.

8.33 Gearing is the term used to describe the relationship between the total borrowing of a business and its proprietorship resources. Current and prospective gearing ratios are of concern to a bank when lending to any company, but particularly so when lending to smaller companies where the risks of overtrading can be acute. The main continuing requirement is that the proprietorship resources of the business should be sufficient to meet the normal trading risks and also to provide a buffer to meet any unexpected problems that could arise. This does not mean that bank lending can be risk-free; but it does seek to ensure that the total risks of a business are appropriately shared between its proprietors and its lenders, bearing in mind that the maximum return to a lender is the net margin between the cost of his funds and his lending rates; as the proprietors stand to benefit most from the success of an enterprise, it is quite reasonable that they should also bear the primary risk of failure. Generally speaking, the proprietorship resources should be at least equal to the level of facilities provided by a company's bankers and any other borrowings, but there will be many occasions when higher gearing ratios can be accepted. In calculating gearing ratios it is important to stress that a borrower's assets are given 'going concern' values based on their future earning potential, rather than the values that they might fetch in liquidation.

8.34 The purpose of assessing the continuing liquidity of a business is to ensure that resources will be available to meet its liabilities as they fall due. In some cases such a judgement can be made with confidence following an examination of the borrower's accounts, though in others the bank will need more detailed and up-to-date information about the borrower's current assets and liabilities in order to assess future cash flow. The maintenance of an appropriate gearing ratio and of an adequate level of liquidity depend in their turn on the future profitability of the enterprise; in the absence of a proven record of profitability, the banker will be particularly anxious to investigate the borrower's prospects.

8.35 The 'going concern' approach described in the preceding paragraphs is usually supplemented by a specialised appraisal technique known as the 'gone concern' or 'liquidation' test. This is designed to establish the extent of the risk to which the bank would be exposed if the assumptions made under the 'going concern' approach proved too optimistic and the borrower ran into difficulties; the results of these tests may well influence the bank's requirement for security. The two approaches are therefore in no sense alternatives to one another; they are complementary, and it is normal to use both. Under no circumstances would a bank make a lending decision solely on the basis of a 'gone concern' assessment, although in certain cases a 'going concern' assessment will be all that is required.

8.36   There is little difference between the techniques employed by clearing banks and other banks when lending to the same type of customer for similar purposes, and there is in fact a considerable degree of similarity in the methods employed in dealing with term loans. The main reason why the clearing banks make proportionately less use of sophisticated appraisal techniques than certain other banks is that a high proportion of the clearing banks' lending is to customers of long standing and to small companies. In the former case there is less need for such techniques, while in the latter case they would often be impracticable.

8.37   The banks are continuously seeking to refine the lending appraisal techniques they employ so as to strike the best possible balance between their need to safeguard their advances and their attempts to provide an improving service to their customers. Responsibility for making the initial assessment still rests with the branch manager, who is the main link between a bank and its customers. By working experience, by professional qualification, and by further formal training during their careers, managers are fitted to negotiate the traditional range of overdraft and loan facilities. The sanctioning and control systems evolved by the banks over many years provide the necessary framework within which individual managers can fulfil their role with confidence. Increasingly, however, as the use of specialised types of finance has been extended, the branch manager has become a general practitioner, identifying particular needs and opportunities and calling on the specialist consultant to complete negotiations. To be used effectively and economically the specialists, with their back-up staff, are often organised in separate departments or subsidiary companies. As the assessment of an application is inevitably partly dependent on subjective considerations, a customer refused by one bank may well be accommodated by another. Customer banking habits are generally stable, so if a bank's failure to lend to a customer does lead the customer to seek accommodation elsewhere, the whole account may be lost for all time. Banks, therefore, do not reject requests for finance without good reason.

8.38   Bank finance is not a commodity of which 'more' invariably means 'better'. This is true for individual companies just as for the economy as a whole. The amount lent to any one borrower must therefore be limited by considerations of creditworthiness, and managers must curb excessive optimism both on their customers' behalf and on their own if they are to avoid a heavy incidence of bad debts. By the very nature of banking, the banks must expect a small proportion of their total loans to prove irrecoverable. But that is very different from extending individual loans knowing at the time that they are likely to turn out as bad debts. It is therefore essential that a lending proposition should be undertaken only on the basis of a well-informed judgement that the entire loan will remain recoverable. If gearing ratios were to be increased substantially, an element of corporate overtrading would undoubtedly ensue and the incidence of business failures would increase. Nor would the resultant losses be confined to the banks; the wider repercussions throughout the economy would be severe.

8.39   The banks would not wish to suggest that purely commercial considerations are the only ones ever taken into account in assessing a lending proposition. They also have regard to other considerations, such as the effect on employment, and in marginal situations these may well tip the balance in the customer's favour. However, the banks do not normally let non-commercial criteria lead them to extend finance to an undertaking which is clearly non-viable and likely to generate a bad debt. Nor do they reject viable applications on non-commercial grounds, unless they are in receipt of guidance from the authorities which requires them to do so.

Security arrangements

8.40 The greater part by amount of the clearing banks' lending is advanced to customers without any security being taken. There are, however, very many situations where the capital resources of a customer are not considered adequate in relation to the level of borrowing requested to warrant lending on a totally unsecured basis, and in these circumstances bankers take as security charges over certain assets, thus minimising their potential losses through bad debts. The basic forms of security taken by clearing banks – such as mortgages, floating charges and guarantees – are of general application throughout the commercial system. Such security ensures the banks a degree of priority (up to the value of the pledged assets) in obtaining repayment in the event of a business failure. The need for security is inevitably greater in the case of smaller companies with modest capital resources and the inability to produce detailed financial information for the banks to monitor. In such cases, security offers a means of offsetting the greater risk of loss.

8.41 Mortgages over land are often taken by a bank providing assistance in a housing development, and a company owning its own premises may use them as security for loans for expansion purposes. In certain circumstances, second mortgages are taken where a prior charge already exists in favour of another lender. However, the most important form of security used by the banks when lending to industry and trade is the floating charge. (Frequently the banks' forms of debenture create both fixed and floating charges.) A floating charge allows the directors of a company freedom of action in the general turnover of the stocks and debtors of the company in the ordinary course of business, but if the need does arise a bank has the right to appoint a receiver and manager. The creation of a floating charge over the total assets of a business need not prevent other borrowings, secured or otherwise, from other sources. Most floating charges permit the creation of specific charges with consent and sometimes there is a succession of floating charges to different lenders whose respective priorities are governed by suitable deeds so that the borrower can enjoy the maximum facilities which the security justifies. If floating charges were not available and security were limited to specific charges, the assets so charged could not be sold or transferred without specific release by the bank, which would result in administrative delays, higher costs, and greater interference by the bank in the borrower's business. If there were no security of any kind available to lenders, either the total amount of lending would be less, particularly in the case of smaller and newly-established businesses, or there would be larger losses to be covered by higher charges.

8.42 The clearing banks' need for security is conditioned by the volume and reliability of the financial information that its customers can produce. To some extent, the banks' ability to monitor such information regularly during the lifetime of a loan is an acceptable substitute for formal security in assuring the banks that their lending is not unduly at risk; that is one reason why lending to large companies capable of producing such information is so often unsecured. To require such information from smaller businesses, however, would in most cases impose undue burdens on their limited administrative resources. In the case of some private limited companies, moreover, the issued capital and reserves may for various reasons be maintained at low levels which do not adequately reflect the responsibility which the proprietors and their management should be assuming for the conduct of the business. It is therefore often necessary to seek guarantees from the directors, which can be supported by charges over their personal assets.

Lending problems and failures

8.43   The clearing banks' appraisal and control systems have proved highly effective in foreseeing problems and averting failures in lending, and the number of accounts which give rise to problems forms a very small percentage of the total loan portfolio. Nevertheless, difficulties do arise and dealing with them can often be very expensive in terms of management time as well as money. The difficulties can be divided into the temporary and the more fundamental. Most temporary problems are of a cash flow nature, and result from delayed deliveries of goods or delayed receipts from debtors. Branch managers deal sympathetically with these short-term problems whenever possible but not to the extent of taking unacceptable risks. More fundamental problems are usually detected from continuing pressure on overdraft limits, with drawings frequently exceeding agreed limits. In such circumstances a detailed investigation will be carried out by the bank to ascertain the nature of the underlying problems. These usually turn out to be either trading losses or excessive investment in fixed assets. Often these problems are exacerbated by inadequate financial information systems. A solution to the problems will be sought in concert with the directors of the company, their professional advisers, and possibly other principal creditors. There has been little research into the causes of company insolvency in this country, but the results of a survey published in *Business Ratios* in 1970 showed that, in the opinion of the official receivers, 71 per cent of the company failures analysed were due to mismanagement, while in 31 per cent of cases insufficient capital was regarded as an important factor.

8.44   The directors of a company have a statutory duty to stop trading when they know their company is insolvent; that is to say, when it is evident to them that they are no longer able to meet their engagements. If a bank holds a floating charge, the directors will usually invite it to appoint a receiver and manager in accordance with the terms of the charge given by the company. but there are occasions when a bank has to make such a decision regardless of the views of the directors. Whether it holds a floating charge or some other form of security, the decision to realise that security is never taken lightly and never without reference to very senior officials of the bank. Such a decision is taken after due consideration of all the circumstances, including in particular the desirability of maintaining continuity of production and employment. The banks much prefer to be able to nurse an ailing company back to good health than to see it fail. Indeed, in their recent submission to the Department of Trade on the reform of insolvency law, the banks recommended that a procedure for the appointment of a manager and a moratorium among creditors, short of winding-up, would be a useful innovation where a company was in temporary cash difficulties. The existing procedure, whereby there can be an informal moratorium among creditors, is unsatisfactory since it can be upset if a dissenting creditor decides to petition for a winding-up order to satisfy his claim.

8.45   If a receiver does have to be appointed, he decides as early as possible how to proceed with his task. Usually he will continue the business while he sees if he can arrange a sale of the whole or a part of it as a going concern: if this is not possible he has to sell the assets piecemeal. In some cases, however, an

growth of the new markets was helped by the positive attitude of the Bank of England, especially its 'open-door' policy towards all reputable banks from overseas who wished to set up in London.

10.14 As a result of these factors, foreign banks set up in London in substantial numbers during the 1960s. Active money markets developed, both in foreign exchange and in eurocurrency deposits, to support the lending business that had evolved. These markets are unrivalled anywhere in the world for breadth and depth, and for the range of currencies traded. Their very existence encouraged more banks to come, and a 'virtuous circle' was set up which ensured London's position as the dominant euromarket centre. By May 1977, 280 foreign banks were directly represented in London by a branch, subsidiary or representative office, compared with 202 in 1972 and only 77 in 1960. The number of foreign banks in London is more than double that in any other financial centre.

10.15 The figures in table 22 on page 124 indicate that some 35 per cent of all eurocurrency business is transacted in London. It is arguable that the figures in a sense understate London's importance, since many of the other euromarket centres are not truly self-supporting, but rely heavily on London to finance their lending. London is in a sense the lynchpin of the whole market, not merely the largest single centre. However, it is clear from the figures that London's share of the total business has been declining. It is noteworthy that the centres which have gained at London's expense are not, by and large, the European centres but rather the newer 'offshore' centres in the Caribbean and Far East. Admittedly, the figures for these relate only to US banks; in the case of the Caribbean especially, some of the business booked there may well be business that would otherwise have been transacted within the United States rather than in other eurocurrency centres. Nevertheless, it is evident that the tax advantages of the offshore centres have caused London to lose business in relative terms. In the foreign exchange market there has also been some decline in London's relative importance; although no statistics are available, it is clear that London's position has been to some extent eroded by the growth of the offshore centres, by the increasing sophistication of many of the continental markets and by the continuing decline of sterling as a trading currency. In the eurobond market too there is a widespread impression that London has lost ground over the past ten years, as the activities of the large continental banks have grown in importance.

10.16 The maintenance of London's status as an international banking centre is important not only for the banks themselves, but for the whole of the UK economy. In the first place, UK industry benefits directly from the high standard of service it receives from the international banking community, which is in part dependent on the status of London. Secondly, the whole economy benefits indirectly, in that the international banks are substantial employers, pay large sums in corporation tax and local authority rates, and make an important contribution to the balance of payments. The figures for the banking sector's 'invisible' earnings as they are officially presented are set out in table 24. The sharply increasing trend is due mainly to London's position as the chief centre of the eurocurrency market, and it is important to stress that these operations in no way impinge on the United Kingdom's official reserves. (A substantial contribution is also made by the return on the banks' overseas investments, including those of the clearing banks; these do not impinge on the reserves either, nor do they divert capital from British industry, as in recent times they have been financed by eurocurrency or overseas

Invisible earnings of UK banking sector   Table 24

£ million		1970	1971	1972	1973	1974	1975	1976
Credits	Financial and allied services	48	59	78	92	109	127	169
	Interest and discount on export credit	60	68	77	105	132	147	172
	Investment income from and services rendered to overseas branches etc	60	58	85	123	104	129	145
	Interest and discount on other lending in sterling	53	38	54	98	141	168	211
	Net interest on borrowing and lending in overseas currencies	16	16	44	18	16	158	266
	Total	**237**	**239**	**338**	**436**	**502**	**729**	**963**
Debits	Investment income due to and services rendered by overseas branches etc	37	58	82	97	142	194	257
	Interest on borrowing in sterling	97	98	126	222	325	331	298
	Total	**134**	**156**	**208**	**319**	**467**	**525**	**555**
Net earnings		**103**	**83**	**130**	**117**	**35**	**204** *	**408**

*In a Parliamentary answer on 2 February 1977 it was reported that the net earnings in 1975 of the London clearing banks were approximately £150 million.

Source: UK Balance of Payments 1966–76.

borrowings, or by their retained earnings to the extent permitted by exchange control.) The banks have also contributed to the balance of payments in ways that do not show up in the 'invisible' figures, for example by harnessing euro-currency funds from abroad to lend to British borrowers including the government, and by supporting the activities of UK exporters.

10.17   Given the importance to the nation of the international banking community, it is in the interests of everybody that nothing be done which needlessly jeopardises London's position as a banking centre. Prominent among the matters which are sources of concern are the restrictive effects of exchange controls. For example, the ban on the sterling finance of third-country trade introduced in 1976 has undoubtedly damaged London's position; it has increased the use of US dollars and German marks for settling transactions, and has enhanced the position of Frankfurt at London's expense. Perhaps as important as anything, though, is the need to maintain a stable political and economic environment so as to preserve the confidence on which banking so crucially depends. The clearing banks hope that the importance of this is fully recognised in official circles.

10.18   The factors affecting the future of London as an international banking centre, the relevance of its role to the UK economy at large, and the measures needed to preserve its position were the subject of evidence to the Committee by the British Bankers' Association, of which the clearing banks are members. The clearing banks endorse this evidence, and its conclusions and recommendations are reprinted in Appendix E.

Chapter 11
International banking: UK-based activities

Summary

This chapter describes the international banking business which the clearing banks transact in this country, both the traditional functions based on the finance of international trade and the banks' more recent involvement in the eurocurrency market. The clearing banks continue to provide traditional forms of bill finance to exporters and importers and have in addition co-operated with the Export Credits Guarantee Department in establishing special schemes for export credit; however, the switch of certain credits from sterling to other currencies may give rise to problems. At the end of 1976 the clearing banks held 12.5 per cent of all foreign currency deposits in the United Kingdom. Eurocurrency deposits are wholesale, and mainly short-term. A substantial proportion of the clearing banks' currency lending is to the UK public sector, primarily to finance the UK balance of payments. The banks also arrange syndicated loans and participate in consortium banks operating in the London market. The clearing banks are among the largest operators in the London foreign exchange market, and provide a number of supporting services to customers engaged in international business.

The finance of international trade

11.1   The clearing banks have always accepted that they have special responsibilities to UK residents engaged in international trade. In particular, the needs of UK exporters have always received the utmost priority. The changes in the international banking environment described in the preceding chapter have altered the relative balance of the clearing banks' international business, mainly because of the growth of their eurocurrency activities, described later in this chapter. But in absolute terms the importance of trade finance and other services to exporters has by no means diminished. Much of the clearing banks' eurocurrency lending is, in any case, directly connected with international trade.

11.2   The greater part of international trade is nowadays conducted on 'open account' terms. This means that no specific arrangements are made to finance the transaction; the exporter simply finds the finance from the resources of his business, either by running down his credit balance or by increasing his overdraft. It is therefore not possible for the clearing banks to identify their total lending for exports. By contrast, in the heyday of the sterling area, bills of exchange were normally used for financing trade, and the bill on London served not only for UK exports and imports, but for much third-country trade as well. Despite the decline in the role of sterling, the clearing banks continue to provide a range of services based on bills of exchange for short-term credit requirements. The period to maturity, or 'tenor', of the bills varies between sight and 180 days, sight and 90 days being the most usual. Typically the purpose is either to bridge the gap between the exporter making shipment and the importer taking delivery, or to provide short-term finance to the buyer pending re-sale of the goods. These services depend on the existence of the clearing banks' overseas networks of correspondent banks and their own overseas branches (see chapter 12).

11.3   There are four main methods whereby bills may be used to finance UK exports. The first is the irrevocable documentary letter of credit. Under this procedure the exporter asks the importer to instruct his bank to set up a credit in favour of the exporter. This will generally be with a clearing bank in London, which undertakes to pay sight bills or to accept 'usance' bills drawn in accordance with the letter of credit and accompanied by the specified documents, such as invoices, insurance certificates and bills of lading. The clearing banks, through their branch networks, are usually the channel whereby such documents are presented. Sterling bills accepted in this way are often discounted in the London money market, in which case the clearing banks may well be indirectly providing the finance through their lending to the discount houses.

11.4   The second method is the London acceptance credit. This is generally established by exporters with accepting houses, whose bill business is regarded by the Bank of England as of the finest quality and whose acceptances, in common with those of the clearing banks and a few other banks, have the accolade of rediscountability at the Bank of England. These credits are broadly similar to irrevocable documentary letters of credit. Again the clearing banks may indirectly provide the finance. The third method is the negotiation of bills under credit or authority to negotiate. Where no letter of credit has been established, the foreign importer may nevertheless arrange for a London bank to negotiate bills drawn by a UK exporter on the foreign importer. The London bank puts the exporter in funds by buying the bill, presenting it later to the importer for settlement. It is not uncommon for such bills to be transmitted to the London bank, generally the London office of an overseas bank, via the exporter's clearing bank. The fourth method is the foreign-domiciled bill. When the foreign importer requests the UK exporter to draw bills on him directly, these will generally be handled through the exporter's clearing bank, which may either buy the bills from him or lend to him against their security. Alternatively, it will simply collect the bills on his behalf without providing any finance.

11.5   As well as these four methods of financing exports, there are parallel procedures for financing imports by bills of exchange. The clearing banks can set up documentary credits on behalf of UK importers, and they also buy inward bills of exchange. Specialised forms of produce lending are available for certain trades (such as furs and timber); these involve pledging the goods to the bank for security, and require specially trained staff to handle the necessary documentation. As well as financing both exporters and importers, the banks also provide them with the means of making international payments, whether in sterling or foreign currency, and can furnish the necessary forward exchange cover. In addition, the banks provide a variety of advisory services to those engaged in international trade, not least to help them ensure that they abide by exchange control regulations (see also paragraph 11.24).

Special schemes for export credit

11.6   Reference has been made in chapter 10 to the increase in world trade, especially in capital goods, during the 1950s and 1960s. In order to meet growing competition in overseas markets, UK exporters found increasingly that there was a need to allow their customers credit for periods of up to five years, or even longer in some cases. A means therefore had to be found whereby financial institutions could give the necessary support to exporters, to enable them to obtain cash on delivery while granting longer credit, and to insulate them from the effects of fluctuating interest rates during the period of the credit. The problem was aired in the Radcliffe Report in 1959, and answers were found soon afterwards with the introduction of special schemes for export credit operated under the aegis of the Export Credits Guarantee Department (ECGD). The schemes are described in detail in appendix B, but their essence is that the banks provide fixed-rate medium and long-term credit for approved UK export contracts against an ECGD guarantee. The scheme was widened in 1961 to include buyer credits. Originally the banks lent for periods of up to five years, while longer-term credit was provided by a consortium of insurance companies. Later, however, the insurance companies withdrew from the scheme. The rate of interest was originally $5\frac{1}{2}$ per cent, but it was later increased and in recent years the rates have been set by ECGD and vary from one contract to another.

11.7   In 1965 it became apparent that there was another gap in the availability of export finance. Medium-term finance was available only for contracts in respect of which the credit period was two years or more, whereas the traditional bank financing of goods 'on the water' was usually limited to six months. Short-term schemes which covered credit periods from sight up to two years were accordingly established, again under ECGD guarantee. Short-term export finance provides 100 per cent advances on presentation of bills or promissory notes for periods up to two years, and 100 per cent of the invoice value of goods sold on open account for periods up to 180 days. A rate of $\frac{1}{2}$ per cent over clearing bank base rate is charged, although this is to be increased to $\frac{5}{8}$ per cent early in 1978. The clearing banks were providing £560 million to UK exporters under this scheme in December 1976. The trends in clearing bank export finance, both short and medium-term, are shown in table 25 and diagram 21. The clearing banks are not only involved in the schemes as providers of funds, they also arrange and manage large credits where the lending is syndicated among many banks. Each clearing bank has its own team of experts in the export finance field who, in suitable cases, accompany exporting customers abroad to help in setting up credit facilities. They are backed up by large departments engaged in the control and administration of all aspects of the various schemes.

Finance for exports
Table 25

Lending under the special scheme for exports by London clearing bank groups

November £ million	1972	1973	1974	1975	1976
Short-term	221	264	381	470	560
Medium and long-term	1,529	1,771	2,165	2,682	3,340
Total (gross)	**1,750**	**2,035**	**2,546**	**3,152**	**3,900**
Amounts refinanced by the authorities	520	704	986	1,355	1,862
Total (net)	**1,230**	**1,331**	**1,560**	**1,797**	**2,038**

Source: CLCB Statistical Unit.

11.8   The clearing banks accept without qualification that export credits are in the national interest, but their participation in the schemes has nonetheless brought problems. The possibility that more extensive participation in medium-term export credits might cause liquidity problems for the banks was officially recognised as early as 1961, when the authorities agreed to provide limited refinancing facilities to aid bank liquidity. The subsequent growth of UK exports and rise in UK interest rates, however, made these arrangements an inadequate support either for liquidity or for profitability. Accordingly, in 1972, the basis of official refinancing was broadened, and it was agreed that all medium-term credits would be refinanced above a ceiling of 18 per cent of each bank's current account credit balances. At the same time the return to the banks on medium-term credits not refinanced was increased to provide a small margin over money-market rates. The borrower continues to pay a fixed rate, and ECGD makes up the difference.

11.9   Concern at the rising volume of public funds required to support export credit led, late in 1976, to proposals for the radical reform of buyer credits. The main change was the decision that certain credits should be provided in foreign currencies rather than in sterling. The existing official refinancing arrangements do not apply to the new currency credits; moreover the clearing banks had already agreed to a progressive increase in the refinance ceiling for sterling credits to 22 per cent of current accounts (or to be more precise non-interest-bearing sterling sight deposits). More recently a review of the fixed-rate sterling schemes has been completed and the clearing banks have agreed to revised refinancing arrangements, which are described in appendix B. New commitments from April 1978 will qualify for refinancing only for that part relating to maturities in excess of a five-year period. At the same time the authorities have allowed access to the schemes to other banks authorised under exchange control and registered in the United Kingdom, but even though this will increase competition, the clearing banks nevertheless expect that the total finance they carry will rise substantially. A slightly improved basis of remuneration has been established for new commitments from April 1978. To the extent that the refinancing facilities are being reduced there will be a reduction in public expenditure, but only because of the rather curious convention that 'expenditure' includes money lent to other sectors of the economy. The other effect of the switch to foreign currency credits, so far as the authorities are concerned, is to increase the official reserves or push up the exchange rate (or both). Under the scheme, the banks raise foreign currency deposits to finance the export credit; the currency is immediately sold to the authorities in exchange for sterling, which is then used to pay the exporter. In effect, foreign exchange accrues to the United Kingdom immediately the goods are exported, instead of when the importer eventually repays the credit. This is of questionable merit, especially since official policy has latterly been to hold the exchange rate down.

11.10   For the clearing banks the new scheme will inevitably mean a forced increase in the proportion of their business in foreign currency. There are, however, limits to how far this proportion can prudently be allowed to rise, and the clearing banks may well have to forgo other profitable opportunities in their euro-currency business in order to continue to play their full part in granting export credits, even though the inclusion of certain other UK banks (including foreign-owned banks) in the scheme will inevitably lead to some reduction in their share of the business. Meanwhile there is little evidence to suggest that the outlook for UK exports has been improved by the change. For the exporter, a new uncertainty has been added to his business, though this may to some extent be covered in the foreign exchange market. On the other hand the foreign buyer may be unable to cover in the market for the necessary period; in the past, cover was less vital because he could usually rely on buying sterling when he needed it at a rate no higher than when he bought the goods. However, the present intention of the authorities appears to be that medium-term supplier

Lending under export schemes Diagram 21
London clearing banks

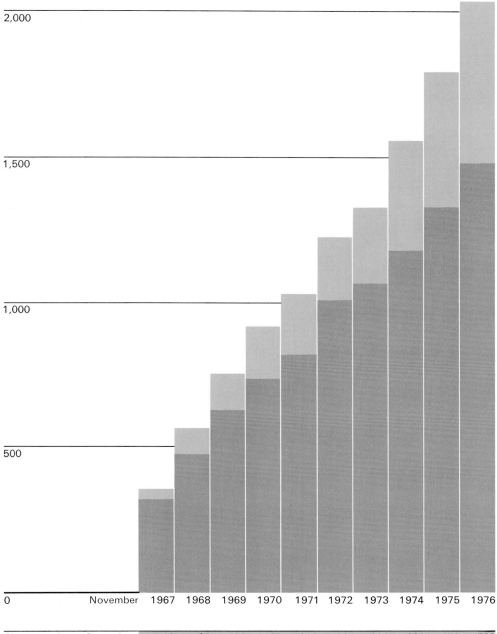

£ million

(net of amounts refinanced by the authorities)

	November	1967	1968	1969	1970	1971	1972	1973	1974	1975	1976
Short term (up to 2 years)		40	90	128	189	213	221	264	381	470	560
Medium term		320	473	628	733	821	1,009	1,067	1,179	1,327	1,478
Total (£ million)		**360**	**563**	**756**	**922**	**1,034**	**1,230**	**1,331**	**1,560**	**1,797**	**2,038**

Source: CLCB Statistical Unit.

credits and short-term export finance will continue to be provided in sterling, at least for the time being.

Eurocurrency business

11.11 The rise of the eurocurrency market, centred on London, has been described in chapter 10. The clearing banks have participated fully in its development, and they regard their substantial share of a competitive market as evidence that they have responded effectively to new opportunities and to the new demands made upon them by customers. A less dynamic response might well have detracted from the effectiveness of UK-based international companies in expanding their overseas markets. Moreover, the clearing banks have had little option but to expand their foreign currency operations, given the official policy of reducing the role of sterling as a trading currency through exchange controls; the frequent periods of weakness and instability of sterling, despite those controls, have also militated against its use.

11.12   By the end of 1976, the foreign currency deposits of the London clearing bank groups had reached 32 per cent of their total deposits; four years earlier they were only 20 per cent. (All the statistics quoted relate solely to the UK offices of the clearing banks: if their overseas activities were included, the foreign currency proportion would of course be higher.) The proportion of the parent banks' deposits in foreign currency is only 17 per cent, however, because several of the clearing banks conduct the greater part of their eurocurrency business in subsidiary companies; indeed, before 1971 it was essential to use a subsidiary since otherwise there would have been an obligation to hold additional sterling liquid assets of 28 per cent of the deposits. The growth in the clearing bank groups' eurocurrency deposits since 1972 is shown in table 54 on page 273, from which it can be seen that they increased threefold in the four years up to the end of 1976. Moreover, when expressed as a proportion of total clearing bank deposits they increased in each of those years. It should be borne in mind, however, that part of the apparent growth is due to the decline in the value of sterling; expressed in US dollars, the clearing banks' foreign currency deposits doubled over the four years. At the end of 1976 the clearing bank groups had 12.5 per cent of the total foreign currency deposits of all banks in the United Kingdom (see table 26 below and table 55 on page 273), their market share having slipped a little since the end of 1972, when it was 14.2 per cent.

Foreign currency deposits and market shares   Table 26

8 December 1976 £ million	Figures in red are percentages	UK banking sector		Other UK residents		Overseas residents		Certificates of deposit		Total	
London clearing banks	Parents	1,156	5.0	544	14.5	2,989	3.8	349	3.5	5,038	4.4
	Subsidiaries	2,093	9.0	446	11.8	5,981	7.7	835	8.5	9,355	8.1
London clearing bank groups		**3,249**	13.9	**990**	26.3	**8,970**	11.5	**1,184**	12.0	**14,392**	12.5
Scottish clearing banks		339	1.5	57	1.5	151	0.2	82	0.8	629	0.5
Northern Ireland banks		24	0.1	–	–	1	–	–	–	24	–
Other British banks (including accepting houses)		1,779	7.6	483	12.8	3,484	4.5	175	1.8	5,921	5.2
Total British banks		**5,391**	23.1	**1,530**	40.6	**12,606**	16.2	**1,441**	14.6	**20,968**	18.2
American banks		5,992	25.7	1,351	35.9	29,609	38.0	5,561	56.4	42,514	37.0
Japanese banks		3,892	16.7	62	1.6	11,175	14.3	897	9.1	16,027	14.0
Other overseas banks		5,311	22.8	779	20.7	20,354	26.1	1,812	18.4	28,256	24.6
Total overseas banks		**15,195**	65.2	**2,192**	58.2	**61,138**	78.5	**8,270**	83.9	**86,797**	75.6
Consortium banks		**2,726**	11.7	**41**	1.1	**4,153**	5.3	**149**	1.5	**7,068**	6.2
Grand total		**23,310**	100.0	**3,764**	100.0	**77,897**	100.0	**9,860**	100.0	**114,831**	100.0

Sources: Bank of England Quarterly Bulletin; CLCB Statistical Unit.

11.13   The majority of the clearing banks' foreign currency deposits are provided by overseas residents, as shown in table 26. These include overseas central and commercial banks as well as other financial institutions, industrial and commercial corporations and a few wealthy individuals. Another important source of funds is banks in the United Kingdom which, together with issues of dollar certificates of deposit, make up most of the balance. Only a small part is held by non-bank UK residents, reflecting exchange control restrictions, but, not surprisingly, the clearing banks have an above-average share of such deposits; further detail on the sources of deposits is given in table 56 on page 273. All eurocurrency deposits are wholesale in character and the rates paid on them reflect market conditions; a substantial proportion of them are obtained through brokers. An analysis by maturity is shown in diagram 22: it can be seen that, like sterling wholesale deposits, they are predominantly short-term, more than three-quarters of the total maturing within six months. However, the market for longer maturities is less narrow than in the case of sterling deposits. The clearing banks' maturity pattern conforms to that of the market generally.

Outstanding maturity of foreign currency deposits Diagram 22
London clearing bank groups

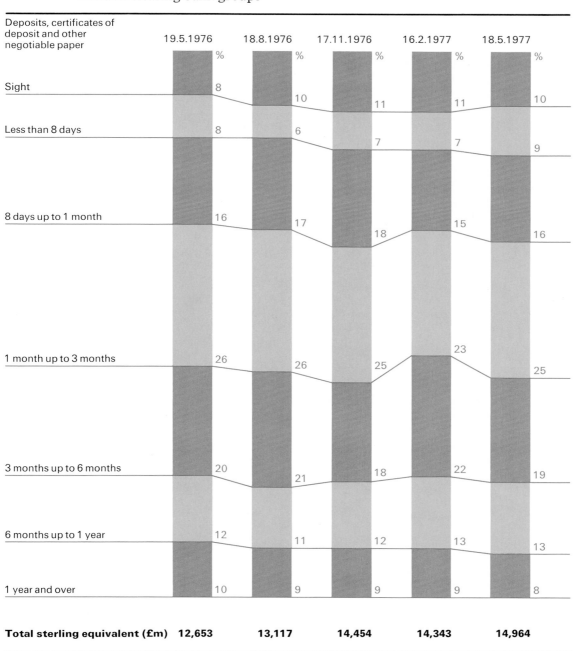

Deposits, certificates of deposit and other negotiable paper	19.5.1976	18.8.1976	17.11.1976	16.2.1977	18.5.1977
	%	%	%	%	%
Sight	8	10	11	11	10
Less than 8 days	8	6	7	7	9
8 days up to 1 month	16	17	18	15	16
1 month up to 3 months	26	26	25	23	25
3 months up to 6 months	20	21	18	22	19
6 months up to 1 year	12	11	12	13	13
1 year and over	10	9	9	9	8
Total sterling equivalent (£m)	**12,653**	**13,117**	**14,454**	**14,343**	**14,964**

Source: CLCB Statistical Unit.

11.14   In their eurocurrency business as in sterling, the clearing banks always maintain an appropriate margin of liquidity, which is held in the form of short-term lending to other banks and holdings of certificates of deposit. Over half of the clearing banks' deposits are in fact deployed in 'market lending', that is to say loans to other banks, whether in the United Kingdom or overseas. By no means all of such lending represents the need for liquidity, however. In the first place, it is not possible for a bank to maintain status in the market if it is seen to be operating on one side of the market only (always a borrower or always a lender). Secondly, in order to ensure a continuing supply of deposits, particularly from non-bank sources, it is necessary not only to offer competitive rates but also to display a willingness to accept deposits even when they are not strictly needed. The surplus funds which thereby arise are placed in the inter-bank market, normally at a small profit, for whatever term seems appropriate in the light of market conditions and of the bank's assessment of its liquidity needs. Most of the banks' market lending is of short maturity, and there are few inter-bank dealings in maturities beyond one year. Some of the lending included in the statistics as market lending is, however, not transacted in the inter-bank market at all, but represents longer-term loans to other banks including, for example, loans to correspondent banks abroad to help them meet the needs of their customers.

11.15   The clearing banks' 'commercial' eurocurrency lending (lending to non-bank customers) mostly takes the form of term loans, either with fixed maturity dates or with agreed repayment schedules. Typically they run for periods of between two and five years, although the banks also engage in some short-term currency lending, often related to trading transactions. Medium-term loans are usually on a 'roll-over' basis, and are charged at a specified margin over the London inter-bank offered rate (LIBOR); this means that the interest rate changes at the end of each roll-over period (normally every six months) in accordance with changes in market interest rates. The bank can then finance the loan with deposits of the same term as the roll-over period, and thereby protect itself against the effects of interest rate fluctuations. Fixed-rate loans are also available, but given the normal term structure of interest rates they are generally more expensive for the borrower.

11.16   Of the clearing banks' commercial currency lending in February 1977 rather more than half was to UK residents. This is in contrast to UK banks generally, for which only about a third was to UK residents. Accordingly, whereas the clearing banks accounted for 18.5 per cent of all commercial lending, they provided 28.5 per cent of lending to UK residents. The clearing banks provided an even higher proportion of currency lending to the UK public sector; the amount outstanding in February 1977 was £1,097 million – 32 per cent of total public sector borrowing, and nearly a fifth of all clearing bank commercial lending. The clearing banks' public sector lending includes their own participation in the two syndicated loans they arranged for the Treasury, the first for $2,500 million in late 1974 and the second for $1,500 million in early 1977. It also includes lending to a variety of public corporations. Such lending serves the same purpose as the Treasury loans, namely that of supporting the balance of payments. The public corporation normally surrenders all the loan proceeds to the official reserves, in exchange for sterling provided by the government through its usual channels; the effect is much the same as if the Treasury had borrowed the foreign currency and the public corporation had borrowed sterling from the National Loans Fund.

11.17 The clearing banks' eurocurrency lending to UK residents in February 1977 is analysed by industrial classification and by the purpose of the loan in table 27. It can be seen that, apart from the public sector lending (mostly included in 'services'), relatively little is for domestic purposes. The greater part is to finance expenditure overseas, whether capital investment, working capital or acquisitions. Lending to investing institutions for portfolio investment abroad is substantial, as is lending connected with North Sea oil and gas (see the next paragraph). If the public sector is excluded, about a third of the total was to the manufacturing sector, rather more than the corresponding proportion for sterling lending. Lending to UK residents grew further in 1977, partly because of the ban imposed in November 1976 on the use of sterling for financing third-country trade. Lending to non-bank overseas residents is of three main types. First, there are loans to overseas-resident corporations for normal commercial purposes. Secondly, there are the clearing banks' contributions to syndicated loans to overseas governments and their agencies; these may be more or less pure 'balance of payments' loans, though more frequently they are specifically intended to finance infrastructure development. Thirdly, there are loans to overseas buyers of British exports. Hitherto these have been mainly confined to cases where the ECGD buyer credit scheme has not been available, for example where 'front-end' finance is required for that proportion of the contract not eligible for ECGD guarantee. From now on, however, there will be an increase in export-related currency lending as a result of the new ECGD scheme (see paragraph 11.9).

Currency lending analysis   Table 27
London clearing bank groups

Industrial classification	Manufacturing		Other production		Financial		Services		Personal		Totals	
16 February 1977 £ million	Facil- ities	Borrow- ing	Facil- ities	Borrow- ing	Facil- ities	Borrow- ing	Facil- ities	Borrow- ing	Facil- ities	Borrow- ing	Facil- ities	Borrow- ing
UK residents (excluding banks) Facilities over £250,000												
Finance for UK exports	58	26	1	1	24	7	7	6	–	–	90	40
Purchase of ships or aircraft	16	10	1	1	–	–	158	116	–	–	175	127
North Sea oil and gas developments	191	124	136	62	9	2	34	25	–	–	370	213
Portfolio finance	4	3	7	6	394	289	15	15	2	2	422	315
Other purposes:												
Overseas capital expenditure	369	300	25	22	233	197	89	70	–	–	716	589
Other overseas expenditure	90	75	36	23	166	131	62	51	–	–	354	280
For use in UK (including all public sector borrowing)	119	77	19	5	104	84	1,257	1,130	2	1	1,501	1,297
Facilities up to £250,000	28	24	2	1	35	32	28	10	4	3	97	70
Total UK residents	**875**	**639**	**227**	**121**	**965**	**742**	**1,650**	**1,423**	**8**	**6**	**3,725**	**2,931**
Overseas residents											**4,413**	**2,723**
Total commercial lending											**8,138**	**5,654**
Market loans (including UK and overseas banks)												8,573
Grand total												**14,227**

Source: CLCB Statistical Unit.

11.18 An important part of eurocurrency lending is project finance, that is to say lending to finance major capital projects where the bank looks largely (or even wholly) to the cash flow from the project to service the loan. Such loans often require sophisticated appraisal techniques in order to cope with the technical, legal and other considerations that may arise. A type of project lending of particular importance to the clearing banks, given its significance for the UK economy, is finance for the development of North Sea oil and gas; as shown in table 27, the clearing banks' outstanding eurocurrency commitments for such developments were £370 million in February 1977. Not all lending to North Sea licensees is in foreign currency, however. Altogether, the cumulative total of loans and commitments extended by August 1977 amounted to £1,201 million, which is estimated to represent about 36 per cent of all North Sea lending. The clearing banks have extended a further £155 million in loans and commitments to non-licensees engaged in offshore activities, such as rig and platform construction yards; they also lend for refineries and chemical plants designed to use North Sea oil. The part played by the clearing banks in financing North Sea oil and gas is set out at length in appendix C.

11.19   In the development of their eurocurrency business the clearing banks are subject to a number of prudential constraints. The need for adequate liquidity has already been mentioned, as has the use of roll-over lending as a means whereby banks limit their exposure to interest rate fluctuations. Just as it is no part of a responsible international banking business to speculate on future movements in interest rates, equally the clearing banks do not engage in exchange rate speculation. This means that, apart from a very small margin of flexibility in their foreign exchange dealing, all foreign currency assets are matched by liabilities in the same currency. Eurocurrency business has important implications for the clearing banks' capital adequacy. In addition to refraining from expanding their business to the point where capital ratios become dangerously low, the clearing banks have to bear in mind that, because their equity is composed of sterling assets, their capital ratios can be jeopardised by falls in the value of sterling. There is therefore a limit to the proportion of total deposits that can prudently be taken in foreign currency. This problem has been mitigated by raising foreign currency loan capital, which amounted to £414 million at the end of 1976, most of it in the form of eurocurrency bonds and notes. It is unfortunate, however, that tax problems should have arisen over currency loan capital. The Inland Revenue has suggested that there may be a liability to tax when sterling falls, because of the increase in the sterling value of eurocurrency assets. This interpretation is being resisted.

11.20   Partly because of the constraints which have inhibited the clearing banks from expanding their own eurocurrency lending, they have increasingly become involved in managing loans for syndication among other banks. The fees from this activity make an important contribution to revenue. In addition, several of the clearing banks are shareholders in consortium banks specialising in eurocurrency business (see table 48 on page 269). Some of these specialise in lending to particular parts of the world, but others are 'multi-purpose'. The latter have the merit of constituting instant syndicates, and can therefore act as a sort of clearing house for loan syndication. All of them, however, are encouraged to develop business of their own, and this can bring them into competition with their clearing bank shareholders. Increasingly, therefore, they tend to specialise in areas where the clearing banks are not especially active, such as international corporate finance and eurobond underwriting. The clearing banks' participation in the eurobond market continues to be inhibited by the fact that their UK customers are effectively prevented from buying eurobonds by exchange control regulations.

Foreign exchange

11.21   The clearing banks are among the largest operators in the London foreign exchange market, and by virtue of their size and international coverage they contribute substantially to its depth. There are, however, no statistics available to pinpoint the clearing banks' share of the business. Like other banks authorised to deal in foreign exchange (of which there are about 280), the clearing banks maintain dealing rooms in London equipped with telephone and telex lines to keep their dealers in touch with the rest of the market. All dealings above a certain size between London banks in the more common currencies are arranged through brokers. Through this telephone market the banks match the transactions which they have entered into with their customers in order to meet the needs of trade. In addition, there are close links between the foreign exchange market and the eurocurrency deposit market, and the same firms of brokers normally operate in both. For example, as an alternative to covering anticipated currency receipts in the forward foreign exchange market it is possible to borrow an equivalent amount in the euro-currency market at the appropriate maturity and sell it in the spot foreign exchange market. Equally, a bank wishing to acquire a deposit in one currency may seek a deposit in a different currency, switch it in the spot foreign exchange market, and cover forward. Accordingly, the growth in the euro-currency market has increased the scope of the foreign exchange market, to the benefit of the banks' UK customers.

11.22 The clearing banks never speculate in foreign exchange. They do, however, execute orders for the purchase and sale of foreign currencies from their customers in the United Kingdom provided these orders conform to exchange control regulations. The financing of 'leads and lags' (as in 1976, when customers earning foreign currency were able to stretch the period before they surrendered it and maintain their sterling cash flow meanwhile by borrowing from the banks) can be neither identified nor controlled by the clearing banks. The banks' own positions are controlled by internal, self-imposed limits, covering currency exposure, maturity mismatching and credit risk. Further-more, under exchange control regulations the Bank of England imposes strict limits on the foreign exchange operations of all authorised banks in the United Kingdom. These limits are designed primarily to prevent speculation against the pound, but take into account the banks' need to maintain a considerable number of foreign currency accounts with correspondent banks abroad in order to ser-vice the requirements of their domestic customers. There is an open position limit for all foreign currencies together, both spot and forward, and, in addition, a spot-against-forward limit, also for all foreign currencies together, on net foreign currency assets held to cover net forward sales.

Supporting services

11.23 The clearing banks have long provided those engaged in international trade with the means of making international payments, such as mail transfers, telegraphic transfers and banker's drafts. These are described in chapter 3. They may or may not be linked to the use of bills of exchange and documentary credits as described at the beginning of this chapter. Another traditional service which, like international money transmission, is heavily dependent on the banks' overseas representation and correspondent banking networks, is the provision of advice on economic and commercial conditions in overseas countries. The banks employ economists and trade promotion experts to assist with this service. Furthermore, specific marketing information can be obtained and followed through by seeking agents and buyers, a service which complements that of the British Overseas Trade Board. Credit informa-tion on agents and buyers can be provided, and advice is given on methods of payment and on the effects of exchange control regulations. As well as giving advice relevant to trading needs, the banks can advise customers wishing to set up their own presence abroad, whether directly or by acquisition or by joint venture. All these advisory services have grown in importance in recent years, especially on account of the increasing involvement of small and medium-sized companies in international activities.

11.24   In order to advise customers on exchange control, the clearing banks maintain central departments staffed with experts whose sole function is to interpret and disseminate the regulations for the benefit of customers. Given the complexity of the rules and the technical nature of the subject this is a vital service, for which the banks receive no payment either from their customers or from the authorities. Much of the routine administration of exchange control is delegated by the Bank of England, and can be handled by the clearing banks themselves, again without payment. It has not been found practicable to calculate the total cost of exchange control to the clearing banks, but the banks note that the costs incurred by the Bank of England are reported to have increased from £1.6 million in 1968 to £8.3 million in 1975. It is thought that the clearing banks' costs have risen proportionately by at least as much over the period. One of the main reasons for the increase was the extension of controls in 1972 to cover transactions in most of the former sterling area.

11.25   In parallel with the growth of the banks' basic support services has been the development of more sophisticated services for large corporations. Of particular importance are those relating to international cash management, foreign exchange exposure and international liquidity management. Companies trading internationally seek to exercise close control over their cash and liquidity positions, particularly in periods of varying interest rates and changing commercial and economic climate. The objectives of cash management services, which are closely linked to remittance services and treasury functions in the banks, are to reduce the period and cost of delays, thus minimising the need to borrow. When exchange rates fluctuate companies are liable to incur losses. The banks are able to help by identifying both the transaction exposure (the pattern of receipts and payments) and the balance sheet conversion exposure (overseas assets less currency loans, allowing for forward commitments). Advice is also given on the implications, costs and benefits of possible exposure policies and techniques. Examples of these techniques include the selection of currencies for commercial and financial contracts, forward cover, matching and hedging. A wide range of factors influence companies' international liquidity management, including interest and exchange rates, availability and flexibility of short and longer-term finance, exchange control regulations and tax considerations. The banks' expertise is relevant to all these factors.

Chapter 12
International banking: overseas activities

Summary

This chapter describes the overseas activities of the clearing banks, stressing the considerable developments that have taken place in recent years. The need for greater representation overseas stems from the growth of foreign trade and from the increasingly international orientation of the banks' UK customers. In earlier times the clearing banks relied on their overseas correspondent banks to meet their customers' requirements; these arrangements remain extremely important, but are no longer adequate in themselves. To supplement them, the clearing banks have extended their own direct representation abroad, and have joined in co-operative ventures with other banks, especially European banks. The co-operative approach has included the formation of European banking 'clubs', which help member banks to offer a flexible service throughout Europe. Those banks which already had overseas branches have tended to make less use of such ventures, and have extended their representation in areas where it was not already adequate by setting up branches, subsidiary companies and representative offices, and by acquiring local banks. Alongside these developments the old-established branch banking business in Africa, the Caribbean and Latin America continues to operate, but has assumed diminished importance.

Introduction

12.1 Each of the clearing banks has, in one form or another, extensive representation abroad. It has already been stressed in chapter 2 that differing approaches have been available for the development of the clearing banks' overseas business, and the strategies adopted by the individual banks in extending their representation have already been described there in outline. In this chapter the different forms that their overseas representation has taken are described in more detail. Because of the marked differences between one clearing bank and another, it has not been possible to discuss their overseas activities in general terms applicable to the banks as a whole; unlike most of the rest of the submission, this chapter therefore deals with the banks individually where it seems appropriate to do so.

12.2 The need for increased overseas representation arises essentially out of the changes in the international environment described in chapter 10. It is important to stress that the development of the clearing banks' overseas business is less a diversification away from their traditional business than a natural development of that business: it is no longer possible to be a major successful domestic bank without also being a major international bank. Twenty years ago the clearing banks' predominantly domestic orientation reflected the similar orientation of their UK customers; today the banks must reflect the worldwide activities of UK-based and other multinational corporations, not least because of the competition they face from international banks based in other countries, which have also been active in developing business all over the world.

12.3   In the 1950s it was enough for the clearing banks to rely on their networks of correspondent banks throughout the world to meet their customers' requirements for international money transmission and for financing international trade. Today these are no longer adequate in themselves either to provide a flexible service to multinational customers or to meet the requirements of a much larger volume of international trade. Nevertheless these correspondent banking relationships have not ceased to be important. Speedy transmission of money to all parts of the world still requires extensive use of overseas banks and their branch systems, despite the clearing banks' extension of their own overseas presence. All the clearing banks therefore continue to maintain a worldwide system of correspondents, and the volume of payments passed through them is enormous. Equally these banks maintain accounts with British banks in London; indeed, meeting the UK needs of foreign correspondents is an important part of the clearing banks' London-based international business. Without this great international network of banks, each supported by its branch system in its own country, international trade would be seriously inhibited.

12.4   Correspondent banking networks are eminently suitable for making international payments, but they have proved less ideal as a means of providing finance for customers, whether for their international trade or for their overseas activities. Therefore the banks have had to expand their capability to offer banking services abroad. Two main approaches were possible to the problem of how to accomplish this. One was for a bank to build up its own direct representation overseas; the other was to improve its indirect representation, building on existing correspondent relationships. The two are not by any means mutually exclusive, but the emphasis adopted has varied considerably from one clearing bank to another. The first approach has the advantage of greater flexibility and, of course, it enables the bank to retain complete control over its own destiny. The second approach involves less outlay and has the merit of not disturbing correspondent relationships, which, as already remarked, continue to be needed and which generate a flow of reciprocal business into London. Those clearing banks which inherited or acquired branch networks overseas by virtue of their links with former British overseas banks naturally emphasised the first approach, while those with especially strong correspondent ties tended to prefer the second.

12.5   Despite these structural differences, the same basic purposes underlie the development of the clearing banks' overseas representation and have, in one form or another, influenced all the clearing banks. A major reason for extending the banks' overseas representation has been to serve widening UK business interests overseas. The changing geographical pattern of UK trading and investment overseas has therefore dictated the pattern of overseas representation. In particular, the much greater importance of European markets has led both to the choice of European banks as partners in the enhanced co-operative relations and to the enlargement of the clearing banks' direct representation in Europe. A second common purpose has been to increase the clearing banks' involvement in the financial markets of other countries, especially in Europe and North America. Although the principal centre for eurocurrency business is London, the market is worldwide and it would not make sense to operate exclusively in one centre. But, whatever the original reasons for expanding overseas, once a bank is represented in a given centre, it will naturally seek to develop as broadly-based a banking business in that centre as it can, dealing with indigenous customers as well as with UK and multinational ones. In this approach, the clearing banks are no different from many of the foreign banks now operating in the United Kingdom. The form and the extent of the clearing banks' expansion into other market centres has, however, varied according to their different strategic attitudes towards direct representation abroad and their varying opportunities for developing business in different countries.

Banking 'clubs' and consortia

12.6   The co-operative approach to overseas representation has involved the grouping of banks from different European countries into 'clubs' based on correspondent ties. Three such clubs involve British banks: Associated Banks of Europe Corporation (ABECOR), European Banks International Company (EBIC) and Inter-Alpha Group. As shown in table 28, each of them has for the most part one member from each of a number of European countries. Their scope varies, but in all cases the basic purpose is to enable member banks to offer an improved service to their customers throughout Europe by means of reciprocal lending arrangements, syndicated lending, and in other ways. These informal arrangements are supported, in the cases of ABECOR and EBIC, by jointly-owned consortium banks serving the whole of Europe, Banque de la Société Financière Européenne in Paris and Banque Européenne de Crédit in Brussels respectively.

Banking 'clubs'   Table 28

Country	ABECOR*	EBIC	Inter-Alpha
United Kingdom	Barclays	Midland	Williams & Glyn's
France	Banque Nationale de Paris	Société Générale	Crédit Commercial
Belgium	Banque Bruxelles Lambert	Société Générale de Banque	Kredietbank
Netherlands	Algemene Bank Nederland	Amsterdam-Rotterdam Bank	Nederlandsche Middenstandsbank
Germany	Dresdner Bank Bayerische Hypotheken- und Wechsel-Bank	Deutsche Bank	Berliner Handels- und Frankfurter Bank
Italy	Banca Nazionale del Lavoro	Banca Commerciale Italiana	Banco Ambrosiano
Austria		Creditanstalt Bankverein	
Denmark			Privatbanken

*Excluding three associate members.

Source: Individual banks.

12.7   The role of these clubs is not limited to Europe, however, since in the cases of EBIC and Inter-Alpha their members have also combined to establish representation outside Europe. This may simply take the form of a joint representative office such as those of Inter-Alpha in Tokyo, Singapore, Teheran and Sao Paulo. More ambitiously, it may mean setting up consortium banks operating in other parts of the world. In the case of EBIC, which is the oldest and most highly developed of the clubs, these ventures include European-American Bancorp, a large commercial banking operation in the United States, and European Asian Bank, which is based in Hamburg but has branches in a number of Asian centres. EBIC banks also have an interest in a finance company in Australia, and Inter-Alpha owns one in Hong Kong. As a more indirect way of transacting business in foreign countries, EBIC has also established consortium banks based in European centres but specialising in other parts of the world, such as European Arab Bank in London and Banque Européenne pour l'Amérique Latine in Brussels, both of which have non-EBIC shareholders as well.

12.8   Both Midland and Williams & Glyn's have opted for limited direct representation abroad, and EBIC and Inter-Alpha are of corresponding importance as a means whereby they pursue their international aspirations. Barclays, on the other hand, relies much more on its own overseas presence, and ABECOR is a somewhat looser form of association. Barclays has, however, like National Westminster, extended its overseas representation in partnership with other banks where cost or other considerations have made it convenient to do so; in some countries it has been found helpful to set up joint ventures with local partners. Both banks also participate in consortium banks based in London but specialising in particular regions, such as Latin America, the Middle East and Eastern Europe. A list of the clearing banks' interests in consortium banks, based both in London and overseas, and including the 'multi-purpose' banks operating in the London eurocurrency market to which reference is made in chapter 11, is given in table 48 on page 269. By contrast Lloyds has tended as a matter of policy to avoid joint operations with other banks. It has, however, established reciprocal lending arrangements with Commerzbank and Crédit Lyonnais in order to supplement its own representation in Europe.

Extending direct representation overseas

12.9   Through their connections with former British overseas banks, described in chapter 2, Barclays and Lloyds both had large long-standing networks of branches overseas. These were mainly based in developing countries in Africa, the Caribbean and Latin America, however, and reflected historical associations rather than the needs of modern international banks. Admittedly both banks also already had, by the early 1970s, branches in New York and some representation in Western Europe, chiefly in France (where there were links extending back to the time of the first world war). But to meet the needs of the 1970s the representation in Europe and North America needed to be greatly extended, and a presence needed to be established in the newer financial centres in the Middle East and Far East. National Westminster did not have the same involvement in developing countries, but it too had an office in New York and a long-standing chain of branches in France and Belgium, which provided the foundations for an extended direct representation to meet modern needs. Midland, on the other hand, had traditionally and as a matter of policy avoided direct representation abroad and had built up a particularly strong network of correspondent banks. As already indicated, Midland has continued in the main to adhere to this policy; so has Williams & Glyn's, whose smaller size places it in a rather different position from the larger banks. Midland's direct representation is limited to a branch in Bahrain, a subsidiary in Toronto and 12 representative offices (Brussels, Frankfurt, Zurich, Madrid, Tokyo, Manila, Teheran, Beirut, Cairo, Johannesburg, Moscow and Sao Paulo). Williams & Glyn's has a branch in Piraeus and representative offices in Oslo and New York.

12.10   In general the three banks which have set up major direct representation abroad – Barclays, Lloyds and National Westminster – have sought to establish a full banking presence in the countries concerned wherever possible. Usually this has entailed opening branches, but in some instances it has been found advantageous to acquire local banks instead (or as well). In countries where foreign banks are not permitted a full presence, or where the business potential does not justify the expense, the banks have set up representative offices. These are not authorised to engage in deposit taking or lending in their own right, but act as marketing outposts to secure business for other offices of the bank. In a few countries (such as Canada and Australia) which are commercially important but which are closed to foreign banks, the clearing banks have established subsidiary finance companies which engage in quasi-banking activities to the extent permitted by local regulations.

clearing banks do, however, participate in the off-shore eurocurrency and investment management centres in the Caribbean.

12.16 Historically, the British overseas banks were set up to finance trade between Britain and distant countries, most of them British colonies. They began with offices in the ports of the countries concerned, and gradually spread inland, developing a local retail banking function as well as a trade financing function. The extent to which this occurred varied from one country to another. On the whole it was more marked in Africa than in Latin America, and it was most marked in those countries where large numbers of British colonists settled, Southern Africa in particular. The overseas banks traditionally traded through branches in the various countries, and looked on their business as a unified whole, not as a collection of distinct banking ventures. Sterling was used to finance almost all the trade in question, and in most of the countries concerned it served as a reserve currency, if not actually as the currency in everyday use. This meant that funds could easily be switched from one country to another, an important feature when the business in any one country tended to be connected with a small range of crops and therefore to display marked seasonal patterns.

12.17 Now most of this flexibility has been lost. The countries concerned are almost all independent and have their own currencies. In Latin America especially, it is the dollar that serves as the international currency. In many African and Caribbean countries the British banks had come to be the leading commercial banks and to play a vital role in their economies. It was not surprising therefore that the newly independent states should have sought a greater degree of control over the operations of the British banks. In a few cases (such as Libya, Sudan and Tanzania) this has been achieved by outright nationalisation. More commonly, governments have required the branches under their jurisdiction to be reorganised into a locally-incorporated subsidiary, subject to local banking regulations and exchange controls. In the majority of cases the governments have themselves taken a shareholding in the local bank, and sometimes the public have also been invited to subscribe for shares. In some countries the bank's own shareholding has been reduced to less than 50 per cent. The most important country where this has occurred is Nigeria, previously one of Barclays' largest operations but now controlled by the government. In May 1977 Barclays gave up control in Trinidad and Tobago, and a few months later its business in Jamaica was nationalised. In Latin America such pressures have been less marked, perhaps because the position of Lloyds in the local banking systems there is generally less dominant. However, its business has been nationalised in Chile and Bolivia, and locally incorporated in Colombia.

12.18 The trend towards local incorporation and greater local control seems likely to continue, and provides the banks concerned with an added incentive to shift the balance of their business away from the traditional areas towards Europe, North America and Asia. It seems possible that the future role of the clearing banks in the developing countries may lie more in specialised activities such as merchant banking and the wholesale money markets, while the basic branch retail banking services are provided mainly by indigenous banks. At present, though, different countries are in different stages of this development, so for the time being the British banks continue to perform a vital function for the economies of those countries which do not yet command the resources or the expertise to provide retail banking services for themselves. They also fulfil a second vital function in helping to provide those developing countries where they operate with access to the international capital markets. This function has assumed a major significance since the rise in oil prices increased the tendency for the investment needs of developing countries to outpace the supply of local savings. By helping to foster economic growth, the banks' activities benefit not only the countries themselves but also the trading and investment interests of their British customers.

12.19   By far the largest of the old-established branch banking networks overseas, and indeed the largest involvement of any clearing bank in any foreign country, is that of Barclays in South Africa. Barclays National Bank is a large commercial bank in its own right, trading through over 800 branches, and with deposits of over £2 billion. A full range of banking services is provided, and there are subsidiary companies engaged in merchant banking, instalment credit and insurance broking. Local incorporation took place in 1971; since then Barclays' percentage shareholding has been progressively reduced by the issue of new shares to the South African public, either for cash or in exchange for acquisitions. The most recent occasion when this was done was in 1975, when the acquisition of Western Bank (an instalment credit specialist) was combined with a rights issue to South African shareholders, thereby reducing Barclays' shareholding to 64 per cent. It is likely to be reduced still further in future, and is expected to reach 50 per cent in a few years' time.

12.20   This chapter has stressed that the clearing banks' overseas representation has been developed primarily to serve British interests. Where, however, the clearing banks have come to be major commercial banks in foreign countries, they have developed a measure of responsibility towards those countries also. In particular, Barclays has obligations to its customers and staff of all races in South Africa; these obligations would not be satisfactorily discharged by withdrawal from the country, as some critics have advocated.

Chapter 13

Other services

Summary   This chapter describes the more important fee-earning services that the clearing banks offer outside the main stream of their banking business. The banks have for many years acted as executors of wills and as trustees of wills, settlements and other trusts. They undertake the management of investment portfolios and in the past decade have entered the unit trust field. They arrange purchases and sales of investments for their customers and provide safe custody facilities. They have developed important insurance broking operations in recent years; in conjunction with their investment and tax advisory services, this enables them to offer a complete range of financial advice to individuals. Through their merchant banking operations, they advise on acquisitions and mergers and on the provision of new capital. Their share registration business has grown rapidly and they act as receiving bankers to new issues. Other computer-based customer services include payrolls, direct debiting, reconciliation and subscription lists, as well as accounting services for commercial customers, retailers and financial institutions. The banks also provide guarantees and performance bonds on behalf of customers.

Executor and trustee services

13.1   The clearing banks' activities as executors of wills and trustees of wills and settlements date from very soon after the passing of the Public Trustee Act in 1906, and are therefore among the oldest of the ancillary services described in this chapter. They are handled in some banks by departments or divisions of the parent bank and in others by specialised subsidiaries, but in all cases there is a national network of trustee branches staffed by specialists in the field. Over the years the trustee divisions have tended to diversify the range of services offered to include advisory services such as investment management and tax planning; these are described along with other advisory services offered by the banks in subsequent sections of this chapter. Statistics relating both to trustee business and to some of the advisory services are given in table 29.

Trust department services   Table 29

31 December 1976	Number under admini-stration or in operation	Capital value £ million
Estates	15,237	397
Trusts *	83,147	3,997
Investment management (ie personal portfolios)	33,895	1,136
Pension funds	359	2,333
Unit trust trusteeships	393	1,610
Unit trusts under management	34	436
Unitholders	542,962	
Insurance-linked managed funds	15	
Bondholders	112,458	
Active personal tax cases	171,535	
Will appointments (ie customers still alive)	801,874	

*Including will trusts, settlements, custodian trusteeships (of wills and settlements), trusteeships for debenture trusts, loan stocks and eurocurrency issues, educational and insurance trusts, minors' legacies.
Source: CLCB Statistical Unit.

13.2   Of the banks' executor and trustee business, narrowly defined, the most important part is that concerned with wills. Banks can act either as executor or as trustee, or both. They do not, however, actually prepare the will itself; this task is at present normally undertaken by the customer's solicitor, although the banks are of course prepared to discuss the provisions of the will with the customer while it is in draft form. When the time comes to deal with the estate the same solicitor normally handles the legal work. The fees charged by the banks are related mainly to the size of the estate, but also to its complexity. No fee is payable until after the testator's death. Although the banks usually act under an appointment in the will, they sometimes act at the request of beneficiaries or next-of-kin in cases of intestacy or where the appointed executor is unable or unwilling to act. The banks can also be appointed attorney to administer the UK assets left by people who have died domiciled abroad, and can act as trustees for legacies to minors.

13.3   The advantages of appointing a bank as executor or trustee are not restricted to the benefits of having trained professionals available to deal with any complications or technicalities that may arise in the course of administering the estate. There is the assurance of continuity: the banks' services are available at all times, whereas individuals may for a variety of reasons be unable to carry out or complete their duties. Moreover, a bank can be relied upon to act impartially and preserve confidentiality, and can ensure that all the documents are safely kept and are readily available when needed. It is, of course, possible for solicitors to act as executors and trustees, but banks often have the advantage of knowing more about their customers' business affairs and are usually better versed in matters such as investment policy, the management of properties and the sale of private businesses or other assets where special expertise is needed. In this way the banks' services complement the legal expertise of solicitors.

13.4   The banks act as trustees for a variety of types of trust not arising from wills. Where individuals place property in trust under marriage, discretionary or voluntary settlements or for charitable purposes, the banks can be appointed trustee at the outset or they can be brought in when an existing trustee dies or wishes to retire. This type of business is, however, on the decline both because of the erosion of capital generally and because of a growing reluctance to tie up funds that might be needed later. The banks also act as custodian trustees where the investments are held by the bank but managed by separate managing trustees; corporate trusts such as pension funds are often dealt with in this way as well as private trusts. A closely related service is that of trustee of authorised unit trusts (other than those managed by the bank itself), and there are a number of other specialised trusteeship services for corporate customers, the most important examples being debenture and loan stock trusteeships and trusteeships under the Insurance Companies Act 1974.

Investment services

13.5   The clearing banks' role as investment managers arose naturally in the course of the management of the trusteeship funds in their care. This function became more important with the passing of the Trustee Investments Act 1961, which permitted trustees to invest in equities, and since then the growing burden of taxation and other legislation has greatly added to the responsibilities of trustees and increased the need for professional investment management. Many of the larger trusts handled by the banks are invested not only in stocks and

Chapter 14
Staff, premises and equipment

Summary This chapter considers the clearing banks' human and physical resources. The number of staff in the parent banks alone has virtually doubled since 1959 to over 200,000, with a further 25,000 or so employed by UK subsidiaries and 50,000 or so employed abroad. Of the total UK employees, over two-thirds work in the branches; a major trend since 1959 has been the increase in the proportion of women in the workforce. Wage and salary differentials, regional factors and changing attitudes to job security have influenced the banks' ability to recruit new staff. With changing educational trends the banks are relying less exclusively on 'O' level school leavers. Training involves a mixture of work experience at the branches and courses at the banks' own residential colleges and training centres. The Institute of Bankers runs a professional examination scheme. Pay and conditions are determined partly by national negotiation and partly within the individual banks. After a period of expansion, the 1970s have seen a net contraction in the number of bank branches, largely as a result of the bank mergers; changes in the role of the branch network are under consideration in some banks. The banks' heavy investment in automation has helped to contain staff and premises growth.

Introduction

14.1   The ability of the clearing banks to fulfil the functions described in this submission depends above all on the qualities of their staff, the nature and location of their premises and the effectiveness of their equipment. While this is true of any financial institution, it is particularly important in the case of the clearing banks' branch banking business. This requires a much higher ratio of staff, premises and equipment to financial assets and liabilities than would be required by, say, a merchant bank or foreign bank in London, operating primarily in the wholesale banking markets without a branch network. The sheer size of the clearing banks' branch operations and the numbers employed in them are inevitably major influences on the pace and direction of change in the clearing banks' role in the financial system. While the clearing banks have consistently proved their ability to adapt to changing circumstances and needs, it is unrealistic to expect them to undergo radical changes in a short space of time.

14.2   Although the banks' staff, premises and equipment are discussed separately in this chapter, all three are highly interdependent. To take an obvious example, the banks' heavy investment in computers and other business machines has both helped to contain the growth in staff numbers and led to important changes in staff functions and working methods.

Staff numbers and functions

14.3   Since 1959, the year of the Radcliffe Report, the number of clearing bank employees has virtually doubled; after reaching a peak of 206,300 in September 1974, the number of employees in the parent banks alone was 203,700 at the end of 1976 (see diagram 23). The total number of clearing bank group employees in the United Kingdom, including those employed in subsidiary companies, was some 25,000 higher than this, with a further 50,000 or so employed wholly or mainly outside the United Kingdom. Nearly one person in four employed in the UK financial service industries works for one of the clearing banks which are clearly, by any standard, major employers. The growth in staff numbers has been necessary to cater for the steady annual growth in the number of accounts held by the banks, the rather faster growth in the number of transactions on these accounts, and the movement by the banks into more diverse areas of activity. Indeed, the growth in staff numbers as a result of these factors would have been very much greater but for the gains in staff productivity that the banks have been able to achieve, partly as a result of automation and partly as a result of greater general business efficiency.

Staff numbers   Diagram 23

Growth of numbers employed in London clearing banks
(parent banks only)

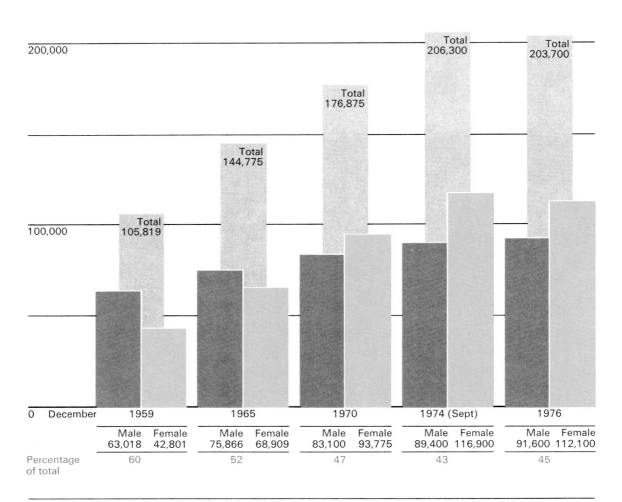

Source : Federation of London Clearing Bank Employers

14.4   Despite the expansion by the clearing banks into non-branch areas of activity about 155,000 of their staff still work in the domestic banking branches; this represents just over two-thirds of their total UK employees, including those in subsidiaries. Of the balance, nearly 35,000 are involved in head office services and support functions such as cheque clearing and computer operations, while some 13,000 work in the banks' various international subsidiaries, departments and branches in the United Kingdom. The trust subsidiaries and divisions employ over 7,000 staff, and slightly under 7,000 are involved in providing leasing, factoring and instalment credit services through the banks' appropriate subsidiary companies. This leaves a balance of nearly 12,000 staff employed in such fields as merchant banking, insurance, travel and credit card operations.

14.5   Of those employed by the parent banks alone, 7 per cent are managers or of equivalent rank and 11 per cent are 'appointed' staff not of managerial status. The remaining staff are divided into clerical (77 per cent) and non-clerical such as bank messengers (5 per cent). The clerical staff are divided into four grades for the purposes of national wage negotiations, and the junior two of these grades in fact account for over half the banks' total employees. This staff structure is reflected in the distribution of bank staff by age range; over a quarter are under 21 and nearly as many again are aged 21–25.

14.6   One of the main changes in the staff structure over the past 20 years has been the increase in the proportion of women in the total workforce, from 40 per cent in 1959 to 55 per cent by the end of 1976. One reason for this trend has been the growth of mechanisation and automation; women account for a particularly high proportion of the junior clerical grades dealing with the 'back office' functions of the banks. In addition, women now predominate in the area of cashier's duties – traditionally a male preserve. The turnover of female staff remains high since many of them look for a short-term career with a bank of not more than about five years. However, a small but increasing number now occupy senior clerical posts. Although less than 2 per cent of all managerial posts are as yet filled by women, the proportion among other 'appointed' staff has risen significantly over the years to its present level of 10 per cent. More women are now studying for professional banking examinations, with the number of female members of the Institute of Bankers having risen from 2.9 to 8.7 per cent of the UK total between 1970 and 1977 (though they still represent only 1.4 per cent of those staff who have achieved the Institute's qualifications).

14.7   An analysis of the banks' staff by geographical area is contained in table 30. All the banks have made determined efforts in recent years to decentralise from London. At first, this was mainly in an attempt to overcome the problems of recruiting an adequate number of suitable staff in the fiercely competitive London job market; more recently, the desire to contain premises costs has

Geographical distribution of staff   Table 30

December 1976	Location	Number of staff
	South East (including the London area)	117,400
	East Anglia	5,400
	South West	15,700
	West Midlands	13,700
	East Midlands	9,700
	Yorkshire and Humberside	9,500
	North West	18,400
	North	6,200
	Wales	7,700

The regions above are as defined for official statistical purposes.

In the London area the number employed was 73,550, of whom 46,320 were employed within 3 miles of Charing Cross. 30,236 were employed in other 'large towns'.

Source: CLCB Statistical Unit.

been an important consideration. Nevertheless, over a third of the banks' staff still work in London, most of them within three miles of Charing Cross. Indeed, the banks account for a significantly higher percentage of the total workforce in London than in the country at large. This reflects both the large number of branches required to service the concentration of business activity in this area and the need to retain a number of key departments of the banks within the City of London, where the head offices of the banks and most other financial institutions are situated.

14.8   Although the precise pattern of employment varies considerably from bank to bank, and from branch to branch or department to department within a bank, it may help to put some of the global employment statistics into perspective by describing the sort of staffing arrangements likely to be found in a typical 'high street' branch in a medium-sized town. An overall staff of 25–30 would be headed by a manager, with overall responsibility for the branch, and an assistant manager; between them they would be primarily responsible for lending and customer relations. There would be a further one or two 'appointed' staff with general responsibilities for the day-to-day administration of the branch. Among the most senior of the clerical staff would be about five securities and foreign clerks, dealing with such matters as the technical aspects of branch lending control, taking and releasing security for advances, safe custody, stock and share purchase, foreign business and exchange control. The branch would have about six cashiers with about eight support staff in the 'back office' handling the money transmission business of the branch. The complement would typically be made up by two secretary-typists, two trainees and a messenger.

Recruitment and training

14.9   The clearing banks' recruitment and promotion practices have been influenced by a number of factors, not least the changing pattern of staff retirement within the banks. This pattern has been somewhat erratic in the post-war period, largely as a result of wartime influences on the age structure of the banks' employees. The early 1960s marked the end of a 30-year period during which retirement levels were low compared with the numbers of staff who were ready for promotion. As a consequence, although promotion was slow, those staff who were promoted were generally well qualified and experienced at each stage in their careers. Throughout the 1960s, however, the numbers of retirements ran at a considerably higher level and opportunities for promotion increased accordingly. More recently, patterns have varied between the banks, partly because of the effects of mergers. The effects of retirements duly worked through to recruitment patterns, with the turnover of junior staff a further important determinant of the banks' recruitment needs. The banks' need for staff has therefore varied from year to year for reasons unconnected with the underlying growth of their business and changes in their labour productivity.

14.10   The supply of labour available to the banks and their ability to retain staff have also been subject to changing influences. For instance, the job security that banks could offer their staff has latterly grown in importance as a consideration in the eyes of applicants, after having diminished since the war. Changing wage and salary differentials between the banks and other competing areas of employment have had particularly marked effects on the ease with which the banks can recruit staff, and these effects have been exacerbated by regional factors, with recruitment particularly difficult from time to time in London. Outside London, the supply of suitable candidates has almost always exceeded

and because, in some countries, banking profits and reserves are not fully disclosed. From such figures as are available, however, there is again no evidence that bank profits are excessive (see table 38).

Profitability of other industries
Table 37

Sample of four leading companies in each sector

Percentages		1969	1970	1971	1972	1973	1974	1975	1976
Profit before taxation **Percentage of end-year shareholders' funds plus minority interests**									
Average for sector sample	Breweries	16.7	19.3	23.5	26.1	21.5	17.1	18.6	21.4
	Building materials	14.1	15.6	27.6	28.9	32.7	17.0	24.2	25.7
	Chemicals	18.6	15.3	14.3	17.0	24.4	33.3	20.2	27.3
	Electricals	16.8	22.7	24.9	30.8	35.5	36.7	35.6	39.6
	Engineering	12.0	12.2	14.0	16.1	21.4	24.6	20.2	25.5
	Food manufacturing	18.5	18.2	21.2	26.2	26.4	27.7	28.1	33.5
	Other industrials	28.9	27.7	30.0	34.8	33.1	38.7	36.8	35.3
	Stores	35.5	36.1	40.2	40.9	38.4	31.0	31.5	35.3
	London clearing banks	17.2	15.6	18.2	21.1	24.1	17.2	14.9	21.3
Profit attributable to shareholders **Percentage of end-year shareholders' funds**									
Average for sector sample	Breweries	9.3	10.5	13.7	15.2	11.5	8.5	9.4	10.2
	Building materials	7.4	8.1	16.7	18.6	18.9	9.4	11.9	13.3
	Chemicals	11.1	8.9	8.6	10.1	13.4	16.8	10.5	13.9
	Electricals	10.4	13.0	14.9	18.7	20.8	18.0	17.6	19.3
	Engineering	6.0	6.6	7.9	9.6	11.1	12.4	10.1	13.7
	Food manufacturing	10.1	10.7	12.7	15.9	14.7	13.5	13.6	16.5
	Other industrials	15.8	15.0	17.0	19.9	18.7	20.4	18.9	17.8
	Stores	18.3	20.3	24.1	24.0	18.3	14.7	14.8	16.1
	London clearing banks	9.2	8.8	10.8	15.3	13.8	8.0	6.7	9.7

Companies sampled:		
	Breweries	Allied Breweries, Bass Charrington, Greenall Whitley, Arthur Guinness.
	Building materials	Associated Portland Cement Manufacturers, London Brick, Marley, Tarmac.
	Chemicals	Croda International, Fisons, Imperial Chemical Industries, Laporte Industries.
	Electricals	BICC, General Electric, Racal Electronics, Thorn Electrical Industries.
	Engineering	Babcock & Wilcox, Guest Keen & Nettlefolds, Hawker Siddeley, Tube Investments.
	Food manufacturing	Associated British Foods, Cadbury Schweppes, Ranks Hovis McDougall, United Biscuits.
	Other industrials	Beecham, Bowater, Metal Box, Reckitt & Colman.
	Stores	Boots, House of Fraser, Marks & Spencer, Mothercare.
	London clearing banks	Barclays Bank, Lloyds Bank, Midland Bank, National Westminster Bank.

Net profits of international banking groups
Table 38

Disclosed net profit after tax as a percentage of shareholders' funds

Percentages	1972	1973	1974	1975	1976
United Kingdom (big four)	15.3	13.8	8.0	6.7	9.7
France (big three)	12.9	13.2	1.7	20.2	15.9
Germany (big three)	7.9	6.9	9.1	9.5	9.0
Japan (big three)	15.2	14.5	12.5	9.1	8.0
United States (big three)	12.5	13.4	13.9	13.4	12.5

For the United Kingdom and the United States consolidated figures are used; for other countries, parent bank figures. The Japanese banks' figures are for the years ended 31 March.
Source: Inter-Bank Research Organisation.

Conclusions

15.24　The clearing banks are among the largest businesses in the United Kingdom, and it is quite proper that they should earn profits compatible in amount with the resources they employ. It is unreasonable to attack the level of bank profits without relating them to the size of the banks' operations and capital base. There is ample evidence that profits have recently not made an adequate contribution to the maintenance of the banks' capital base, and the banks have had to turn to the capital markets merely to maintain their position in real terms. It is unrealistic to expect this process to continue indefinitely, not least because the banks' ability to raise further capital is itself dependent upon their profitability. Unless the banks can earn an adequate return on the resources they employ, their ability to play their role in the economy fully and effectively will be prejudiced.

The Committee of London Clearing Bankers

Summary   This chapter surveys those issues on which the clearing banks co-operate with one another and discusses the role of the Committee of London Clearing Bankers in handling such issues. A major function of the CLCB used to be the administration of a range of agreements, notably on interest rates, but most of these were abandoned in 1971/72. Since then, the CLCB has been primarily concerned with the organisation of the clearing system, the provision of banking services to the public sector and the maintenance of official links between the banks, the Bank of England and Whitehall.

16.1   The Committee of London Clearing Bankers formally consists of the chairmen of the six London clearing banks. More commonly, the Committee is taken to mean the six clearing banks themselves. The CLCB itself is an unincorporated body, but its members jointly own and control a limited company, the Bankers' Clearing House, of which their chairmen constitute the board of directors. The premises at 10 Lombard Street in which the clearing house is situated are owned by the Bankers' Clearing House.

16.2   Until the early 1970s a major part of the function of the CLCB was the management of the series of agreements between the clearing banks, dealing with interest rates and other matters, which are described below. However, in their paper of May 1971 entitled *Competition and Credit Control* (CCC), the Bank of England indicated that one of the essential features of the new proposals was that the London and Scottish clearing banks should abandon their collective agreements on interest rates. These agreements, known more familiarly as the 'cartel', had, until that time, been a central feature of the banking scene. Indeed, for as long as their records exist one of the principal functions of the CLCB had been for its members to meet regularly on Thursdays, the day when changes in Bank rate were customarily announced, in order to agree among themselves the London bankers' deposit rate.

16.3   The discontinuance of the interest rate cartel in September 1971 gave rise to an immediate consideration of other inter-bank agreements. A substantial list of such agreements was examined and by the spring of 1972 it had been decided to abandon a number of them, their original purpose no longer appearing to justify their retention in the new era of CCC. Of the agreements so terminated, one of the most important was that relating to group terms for employees' bank accounts. Under that agreement, the clearing banks provided uniform basic terms (described frequently as 'ICI terms') for conducting employees' accounts under group schemes arranged with employers in those cases where employees' accounts were credited direct with their wage, salary or pension payments. By way of illustration, other agreements abandoned included: charges for encashment of cheques by customers of non-clearing banks; charges for status enquiries by hire purchase companies; commissions on the issue of travellers' cheques; scales of minimum commission for customers abroad; and agreements not to certify cheques, guarantee trade debts or carry on business outside banking premises. In considering these and other collective agreements, the banks were guided by the general principle that their continuance could be justified only where they were necessary to maintain an efficient service and were not contrary to the spirit of restrictive trade practices legislation. Since the implementation of CCC, the banks' lending rates have not been linked directly to Bank rate or minimum lending rate; instead they are generally linked either to the banks' own base rates, which are determined by each individual bank in the light of commercial and market considerations, or directly to market rates of interest, as described in chapter 8. Each bank has also been free to quote its own rate for money at seven days' notice and bid in its own name for deposits of other maturities, as described in chapter 4.

16.4   When the cartel was abandoned it was argued that, as one of the principal justifications for the CLCB no longer existed, the CLCB itself might cease to exist too. This view, however, ignored the many other areas in which the banks had found that a real need existed for co-operation, a need, incidentally, which had frequently arisen as a result of a desire on the part of third parties (notably government) to treat the clearing banks as a single industry, rather than as six individual companies. In responding to this need, the CLCB acts in effect as the trade association of the clearing banking industry. The first obvious area in which the clearing banks co-operate is in the organisation and conduct of the clearing system in England and Wales. It is through this system, which has developed organically since approximately 1770, that an average of nearly 5 million items daily are exchanged between the banks for remittance to the relevant branches so that customers' accounts may be credited or debited. Obviously, for a system which handles each year something in the region of 1,200 million items, the closest possible co-operation on matters of detail is required among the participating banks to achieve the necessary degree of standardisation, while ensuring that the system remains flexible enough to adjust to meet developing needs. The smooth functioning of the system depends on the observance of many detailed operational requirements. These include such matters as the standardisation of vouchers, standard layout of magnetic tape, standard procedures, and the adherence to standard banking practices, to the provisions of the relevant legislation and to timetables and operational rules.

16.5   In addition to the six banks within the CLCB, three other banks – the Bank of England, the Co-operative Bank and the Central Trustee Savings Bank (CTSB) – all have a seat in the clearing house and participate directly in the clearing system. The Bank of England has had its seat since 1864: the Co-operative Bank and the CTSB since 1975, when invitations to become functional members of the clearing house were extended not only to them but also to the three Scottish banks and the Yorkshire Bank. In order to obtain this functional membership, the new members agreed to comply with current clearing procedures and the standards of performance accepted within the clearing departments of the existing clearing banks. An initial payment was made by the new entrants towards the costs incurred in the development of the clearing system; annual contributions are also made towards the running costs of the clearing house. The Yorkshire Bank and the Scottish banks considered that no particular advantage lay in joining the clearing house. The Yorkshire Bank, in declining the invitation, pointed out that it had had access to the clearing house through an agency arrangement with a clearing bank for over 100 years, and that it considered this arrangement entirely satisfactory. Membership of the clearing house would not of itself, in its view, enable it to improve its services to customers.

16.6   The Co-operative Bank and the CTSB were the first new entrants since the District Bank in 1936. There had been no other admissions this century so there was an absence of established criteria for admission to membership. In seeking to establish such criteria in 1974/75 the clearing banks considered four factors to be relevant: first, the existence of a branch network; secondly, a sufficient volume of items entering the clearing system (this being placed at approximately 1 per cent of the total); thirdly, an ability to accept and conform to the functional requirements and timetable of the clearing system, including the establishment of a town clearing branch and a clearing department within a reasonable distance of the clearing house; and fourthly, an acceptance of the costs of participation. The functional membership of the Bank of England, the Co-operative Bank and the CTSB in the clearing house does not extend to membership of the CLCB, nor do they share in the ownership of the Bankers' Clearing House. They are, however, represented on a number of CLCB committees, particularly on those where functional details of the clearing system fall for consideration. The Scottish banks and, for that matter, the four branch banks operating in Northern Ireland are also represented where relevant.

16.7   A further major area in which the banks co-operate is in the provision of banking services to government departments, nationalised industries and public bodies. For the convenience of all the parties concerned, the borrowing requirements of the larger public bodies are dealt with by the banks on a syndicated basis, most frequently under Treasury guarantee. Among those whose banking requirements are dealt with collectively are the Ministry of Defence, the Department of Health and Social Security, Customs and Excise, the Inland Revenue, the Department of Employment, the Department of the Environment, the Crown and County Courts, the National Coal Board, the Electricity Council, British Gas, British Steel, British Rail, the National Freight Corporation, the National Bus Company, London Transport, the Post Office and the British Transport Docks Board.

16.8   The CLCB also exists to provide the official link between the clearing banks, the Bank of England and Whitehall, this being reflected in the formal description of the CLCB as the body through which the Bank of England communicates official policy to the banks and through which the banks may present their views to the Bank of England and the Treasury. This formal description does not, however, do full justice to developments of comparatively recent origin. Over the past five years in particular, the role of the CLCB as the representative body for the clearing banks has been increasingly recognised by the government and the authorities generally so that, more often than not at the instigation of the authorities themselves, it has become the natural channel of communication and consultation between the authorities and the banks on a wide range of issues. This part of the CLCB's role is described more fully in chapter 17. In addition, the authorities deal with a number of other banking associations, including the British Bankers' Association of which the clearing banks are active members. The BBA limits itself to the consideration of issues affecting banks as a whole, notably developments emanating from the EEC.

16.9   As regards methods of organisation within the CLCB, the actual Committee (the chairmen of the banks) is at the top of a pyramid of subordinate committees, some of which are standing committees meeting at regular intervals, others being working parties of an *ad hoc* nature. The Committee meets regularly every month and also has a monthly meeting with the Governor of the Bank of England. Immediately below them on the pyramid is the Chief Executive Officers' Committee, also meeting every month. This Committee has its own regular contacts with the Chief Cashier at the Bank of England. The chairmanship and deputy chairmanship of the CLCB and the chairmanship of the Chief Executive Officers' Committee revolve around the four largest banks on a biennial basis in such a way that the chairman of the CLCB and the chairman of the Chief Executive Officers' Committee never come from the same bank. Below these two committees are over 70 subordinate committees or working parties dealing with a host of diverse subjects. It is normal for each bank to provide a representative for each committee, but the smaller banks sometimes decide not to be represented on sub-committees. Representatives of the Bank of England, the Co-operative Bank, the CTSB and the Scottish and Irish banks are co-opted in appropriate cases.

16.10   All CLCB committees work in a similar fashion. No formal rules govern their procedure and there are no arrangements for the taking of votes. All their proceedings are based on the principle of achieving a consensus: if that proves impossible, each bank is free to act as it thinks fit in the circumstances. Decisions of the committees are not binding on any individual bank, although should any bank decide to abandon a previous understanding, it would as a matter of courtesy notify the other banks. The committees of the CLCB are supported by a secretariat of about a dozen, most of whom are permanent staff, although the Secretary-General is a secondee from one of the clearing banks. Various other inter-bank units also operate under the auspices of the CLCB. These include the Statistical Unit, the Banking Information Service and the Inter-Bank Research Organisation, which also serve the Scottish banks.

16.11   Finally, it should be stressed that in the majority of their deposit-taking, lending and other services the banks now compete strongly against one another, and against outside institutions, without any recourse to collective or co-operative agreements. The activities of the CLCB are limited to those issues where co-operation is clearly in the interests of the banks' own customers or is required of the banks by the actions of government.

Chapter 17

The banks and government

Summary

This chapter examines the changing nature of the clearing banks' relations with government and the Bank of England over the past 20 years. Increasingly the banks have dealt directly with government departments rather than through the Bank of England, though the banks still deal continuously with the Bank of England on operational matters such as prudential regulation, exchange control, monetary policy and the provision of statistics. In its capacity as 'bankers' bank', the Bank of England provides the banks with current account facilities, assists in the arrangements for clearing cheques and provides facilities for the withdrawal and return of banknotes. The banks argue that the requirement that they alone should hold balances of $1\frac{1}{2}$ per cent of their eligible liabilities as current accounts at the Bank is onerous and discriminatory. Unnecessary costs are also incurred by the banks in handling banknotes because of the way the present cash distribution system is organised.

Consultative relationships

17.1   The clearing banks' relationship with government has changed and developed very considerably in the 20 years since the banks gave evidence to the Radcliffe Committee. The process of government has become more complex and intrusive so that the banks' involvement has necessarily become greater. As government has become more and more active in a growing number of areas of business life, so the banks have been drawn increasingly into a dialogue with the Treasury and other government departments, such as the Inland Revenue, the Department of Trade, the Department of Prices and Consumer Protection and the Office of Fair Trading. Like other institutions and interest groups, the banks have recognised the need to become constructively involved in a complex relationship with government as the public and private sectors have become more intimately related. Indeed they have been encouraged by government to become so involved.

17.2   The most striking aspect of the change in relationships which has occurred during the past 20 years relates to the position of the Bank of England as intermediary between the banks and government. The banks' attitude had long been that lines of communication between themselves and Whitehall and Westminster should run via the Bank of England. The Governor of the Bank was seen as acting both as the government's representative in the City and as the City's ambassador to Whitehall. The clearing banks' evidence to the Radcliffe Committee made clear (notably in paragraph 103 of the written evidence and in questions 3794 to 3837) that they were then very firmly wedded to the view that they should have little contact with government other than their traditional relations with the Bank of England. For example, in answer to a suggestion by Lord Radcliffe that there would be advantage in the banks having wider and more regular contact with the Treasury, one of the clearing bank representatives replied:

is not required until the notes are actually in circulation with the public. Scottish banks can therefore hold notes in their tills at no incremental cost. The position in England could be brought into line with that in Scotland, and the need for unproductive transhipment of notes avoided, if Bank of England notes held by the banks were regarded as 'in bond', and no payment made to the Bank of England for them until they actually crossed the counter. There would be difficulties of supervision, but presumably no more than are already involved in policing the Scottish arrangements. A possible compromise would be to allow the 'bonding' arrangements to apply to notes held in the banks' cash centres (whence they are distributed to branches), but not to those actually in branch tills. Indeed, a pilot scheme which would have this effect has latterly been under consideration by the Bank of England and the banks. As a general principle, however, the Bank of England has always stated that it is unable to accept any arrangement which either increases its costs or reduces its note issue.

Chapter 18
The banks and other financial institutions

Summary

This chapter examines the changing nature of the competitive and other relationships between the clearing banks and other financial institutions. The erosion of the traditional demarcation lines between institutions has enhanced competition, thereby providing customers with wider choice and stimulating efficiency. The clearing banks welcome the increased competition, but stress the need for it to be fair. At present, savings banks and building societies enjoy various fiscal advantages and are exempt from monetary controls. Different standards of capital adequacy, and different types of commercial objective, also apply. In the case of building societies, the banks stress the need to rationalise official attempts to encourage the flow of resources to different sectors. The main example of the inter-dependence of financial institutions is their participation in the money markets, where the position of the discount houses remains pivotal. The essence of the banks' relationship with the houses has not changed, but the way it works in practice has, notably because call money now ranks as a reserve asset and has thereby lost much of its effective liquidity.

Changing patterns of competition

18.1   As major institutions in the financial system providing a wide range of services, the clearing banks are engaged in competition not only with one another but also with most other types of financial institution. The past 20 years have seen a progressive erosion of the traditional lines of demarcation separating the activities of the various sectors of the financial system. The result has been a more competitive environment which has provided customers with wider choice and has stimulated efficiency and innovation.

18.2   The wider choice available to customers has come about despite the effect of mergers and takeovers (and the failure of some fringe enterprises) on the number of individual independent businesses offering their services in the financial markets. This decline in numbers has been offset partly by the establishment in London of a large number of foreign banks, and partly by the efforts of institutions in all parts of the financial system to diversify the range of their services and thereby encroach on the traditional preserves of other types of institution.

18.3   Few institutions have been as active in this process of diversification as the clearing banks. The steps taken by the clearing banks to broaden their range of services have been described in chapter 2, and the new services they have introduced have been covered in the appropriate contexts, especially in chapters 8 and 13. In diversifying their services the banks have responded to the perceived needs of their customers. They are aware that their extensive branch networks place them in a favourable position to meet the needs of their customers for a growing range of financial services, and they believe that an increasing number of customers welcome the opportunity of satisfying their various requirements within a single financial institution.

18.4   Diversification, whether by the clearing banks or by other institutions, has been achieved both by takeovers of existing companies in other parts of the financial spectrum and by the 'in-house' development of services formerly regarded as the province of a different part of the financial system. The breakdown of the boundaries between the different sectors has also been assisted by the emergence of wholly new services which, although perhaps originating in one part of the system, have rapidly spread to other types of institution. The evolution of the wholesale money markets during the 1960s is a case in point, and likewise the great expansion in medium-term lending has been common to clearing banks, merchant banks, and finance houses alike. Leasing is another example. The concept was originally developed by finance houses, and before long all the major banks and finance houses had specialist leasing subsidiaries. The clearing bank groups now account for about 60 per cent of the total business of members of the Equipment Leasing Association.

18.5   As explained in chapter 2 all the clearing banks have either acquired finance house subsidiaries or made major investments in the sector. Other banks have done the same, with the result that six of the eight leading companies are now bank-controlled. The clearing banks compete with the independent finance houses not only through their own finance house and leasing subsidiaries but also through the activities of the parent banks themselves. The development of personal loan schemes by the banks, particularly since 1971, is one such area of overlap, especially as finance house personal lending has increasingly taken the form of personal loans as well as hire purchase and credit sale agreements. The banks' credit card activities also effectively compete with finance houses' personal lending. Although it remains broadly true that the banks' personal lending tends to be marketed directly to customers while the finance houses market at the point of sale, the old idea that banks and finance houses served quite different types of customers is now obsolete. Some finance houses have also been active in seeking deposits from the personal sector, while in the corporate market the development by the finance houses of straight lending, as opposed to industrial hire purchase and leasing, has similarly increased the overlap with the activities of the banks.

18.6   The demarcation lines between clearing banks and merchant banks have similarly been eroded by the development of corporate finance, investment management and other merchant banking services within the clearing bank groups, and, in the case of one clearing bank, by the acquisition of an accepting house. The clearing banks' merchant banking subsidiaries are now among the largest merchant banks in the country, and their combined deposits at their latest accounting dates amounted to almost £2 billion (the corresponding figure for the 16 independent accepting houses was a little over £6 billion). Although the accepting houses continue to transact the lion's share of the acceptance business (£1,144 million in May 1977, against £357 million for the clearing bank groups, out of a total for all banks of £2,471 million) there is virtually no activity in which the accepting houses engage where the clearing banks are not also involved. Likewise the division of function between the clearing banks and the British overseas banks has disappeared. Even in the case of the Scottish and Irish banks, where the geographical demarcation largely remains, that demarcation has been increasingly blurred by competition for the accounts of large customers whose activities span the whole of the United Kingdom.

18.7   In many ways the most important competitive development in the financial system of the past 20 years has been the increase in both the numbers and the market share of the foreign banks in London. There are now more than 280 foreign banks directly represented in London, four times as many as there were 20 years ago, and there are another 90 represented indirectly through their participation in consortium banks. All of these banks are in London primarily in order to engage in international banking activities and some of them do exclusively international business; their presence reflects the status of London as the world's foremost international banking centre. Yet their impact on the domestic market has been very considerable. This can be seen from the fact that the total sterling deposits of foreign and consortium banks of £8.9 billion at the end of 1976 amounted to 18 per cent of the total for all statistical banks, and their sterling lending to 16 per cent of the total.

18.8   The competition offered by the foreign banks in the domestic market is especially strong in the provision of finance for the UK business of overseas companies and for multinational and other large UK companies, fields where the larger American banks are particularly active. The liberation of many foreign banks from very restrictive lending ceilings in 1971 soon led to a sharp increase in their lending. By contrast not many foreign banks have built up a substantial customer deposit base in sterling, and they mostly rely heavily on the money market to finance their lending. A few foreign banks, however, have set up 'money shop' operations aimed at personal customers, and there are a number of foreign banks operating in various parts of the country which provide retail banking facilities to expatriate communities.

18.9   The developments described in the preceding paragraphs have involved mainly the commercial part of the financial system. But there has also been an increase in the competition the clearing banks face for retail deposits from mutual and public sector institutions. The building societies have greatly expanded their branch networks, and their savings facilities are increasingly regarded as alternatives to a bank account rather than as outlets for longer-term saving, as the secular increase in withdrawals as a percentage of the societies' gross receipts suggests. Indeed the amount of the societies' shares and deposits, which 20 years ago was of the same order as the clearing banks' 7-day deposit accounts, is now three times as big. Competition for money transmission business has come from the entry of the Trustee Savings Banks into the current account field in 1965 and from the establishment of the National Giro. In the case of the latter institution the competitive impact has actually been more marked in the corporate market than in the personal, contrary to the intentions expressed by the government when the Giro was set up.

18.10   Nor is the overlap in lending services between these institutions and the banks by any means unimportant. Although the clearing banks do little mortgage lending of the type offered by the building societies (except to their own staff), the fact that both types of institution lend to the same people means that they are indirectly in competition: a person who takes out a large building society mortgage may thereby have less need to borrow from a bank. Moreover building society 'further advances' compete directly with the short-term housing loans offered by the banks. Direct competition for the banks' personal lending will also come from the development of TSB and Giro lending over the next few years.

The need for fair competition

18.11 The clearing banks welcome the increased competition in financial markets because it fosters efficiency and benefits customers. In order for competition to be effective, however, it is of paramount importance that all institutions compete on fair terms. This principle underlay the reform of the credit control arrangements in 1971, described in chapter 6, as a result of which all commercial banks were placed on more or less the same footing. But it remains the case that many of the mutual and public sector institutions with which the banks are in competition are endowed with artificial competitive advantages. Examples include the fiscal advantages enjoyed by the building societies, savings banks and national savings in the payment of interest on savings, the totally inadequate capital base on which the Giro is being allowed to expand its range of banking services and the unequal application of monetary and credit controls. The clearing banks strongly believe that these competitive advantages should be terminated. They lead to a misallocation of resources in financial markets and distort the market shares of different types of institution. Any subsidies which the government wishes to provide should relate to particular financial functions, not to particular financial institutions.

18.12 In gathering 'ordinary department' deposits both the TSBs and the National Savings Bank have the advantage that the first £70 of interest earned by a depositor is free of income tax, although it has been agreed that for the TSBs this concession will be phased out. In addition, the various national savings instruments enjoy favourable fiscal treatment: the returns on national savings certificates, premium bonds and SAYE deposits are free from income tax, as is the bonus on British savings bonds. These fiscal advantages inevitably lead to distortions in the savings market and the clearing banks believe they should be abolished or else extended in some common form to all retail savings instruments. Their removal would presumably lead to the payment of higher rates of interest on national savings but the resulting situation would have the advantage of making the true cost of government borrowing more apparent.

18.13 The building societies have a less direct but important fiscal advantage in the arrangements whereby the societies are allowed to pay income tax on behalf of their depositors at the agreed 'composite rate'. This acts as an inducement to those paying income tax to place their funds with building societies rather than with banks; the societies benefit from the fact that tax-paying investors are evidently more sensitive to interest differentials than non-taxpayers. Building societies also have the advantage of a special low rate of corporation tax (40 per cent); moreover neither building societies nor savings banks are liable to corporation tax on gains arising on the sale of government securities, provided they have held them for more than twelve months.

18.14 The building societies, savings banks and Giro are all exempt from the monetary controls imposed on banks, though it is intended in due course to bring the TSBs and Giro within the system. Building societies do have portfolio constraints of their own; but these are in force for prudential purposes rather than to limit the growth of the societies' liquid liabilities. Thus the building societies are not obliged to hold $12\frac{1}{2}$ per cent of their liabilities in the form of reserve assets. Much more important, however, has been the building societies' exemption from credit ceilings in the period up to 1971, and more recently from the 'corset' controls on interest-bearing deposits described in chapter 6. In addition the clearing banks were subjected between September 1973 and

February 1975 to a restriction on their deposit rates in order to limit their ability to compete with building societies.

18.15   The prudential constraints which these institutions are expected to observe in order to ensure their capital adequacy are also less onerous than those observed by commercial banks. Again, it is intended eventually to bring the TSBs within the same framework as the banks, although it is not yet clear how they will be furnished with the necessary capital resources. The inadequate capitalisation of the Giro has been defended by a government spokesman with the observation that the resources of the Post Office stand behind it*. Clearly this involves subsidisation of the Giro by other parts of the Post Office. The clearing banks believe that a formal separation of the Giro from the rest of the Post Office would make it much easier for the Giro to be treated in the same way as other institutions.

18.16   The nature of the competition between the banks and the building societies and TSBs is also affected by these institutions' mutual form of organisation. Not only does this mean that they are able to add to their capital resources sums which a commercial bank would have distributed in dividends, but it may also affect their attitude to new investment in their businesses and to the rates of interest they charge and pay. Provided that they are earning a sufficient surplus to maintain suitable prudential ratios, they have no clear incentive to ensure that new ventures are profitable. In this respect the position of the building societies and TSBs is quite different from that of mutual insurance companies, where the benefits of profitable management are enjoyed by the policyholders in the form of bonuses. Where institutions are not effectively owned by anyone, there can sometimes arise in an especially acute form the problems of the separation of ownership from control. In the case of the TSBs no such problems appear to have arisen hitherto; but this has been largely because their discretion has been severely limited by government controls and they have been unable either to earn worthwhile surpluses or to expand and diversify their business. Now that these controls are to be relaxed it remains to be seen how far the TSBs will feel constrained by commercial disciplines.

18.17   In the case of the building societies the clearing banks recognise that the advantages bestowed on them reflect an official commitment to support the ideal of home ownership. The banks do not disagree with the importance of this ideal but they consider that there is a need for some rationalisation of the authorities' sometimes inconsistent attempts to encourage the flow of resources to a multitude of sectors (such as industry, housing, exports and the government itself). The building societies are now of such size and importance that fuller consideration than hitherto should be given to the effects of their activities on other financial institutions and markets so as to avoid undesired distortions in the allocation of savings and credit. In particular, the banks consider that there is a strong case for providing any subsidy to home owner- ship which the authorities deem appropriate directly to home buyers and letting the building societies compete with other institutions on equal terms.

18.18   In the first place this would reduce the present distortion in the distribution of intermediation between the building societies and other institutions and might encourage other institutions to compete with the building societies in the home mortgage market. How far they would wish to do so is hard to say, but the extra flexibility so created could only be beneficial. Secondly, the present

*Official Report, Standing Committee B, 29 January 1976, Q 91–2.

privileged financial circuit would cease to exist and the way would be open for the building societies to become more integrated with the rest of the financial system. On this subject the clearing banks note with interest two suggestions in the government's recent consultative document on housing policy. These were that building societies should be prepared to raise short-term loans on the money market and that consideration should be given to the possibility of channelling funds from the investing institutions into housing finance. Thirdly, the cost of the subsidy would be known and subject to public scrutiny and it would be met by the exchequer rather than distributed arbitrarily among a range of participants in the financial markets.

The money markets

18.19 Despite the increasing competition between different financial institutions and the diminishing precision with which their roles are defined, they remain interdependent in a variety of ways. Numerous instances could be cited of co-operation between different institutions. Some, like syndicated lending to large borrowers, are of relatively recent origin. The formation of banking consortia and clubs in the international field, described in chapter 12, is another example of increasing co-operation between banks. Interdependence between the clearing banks and other financial institutions is also apparent in the use these institutions make of the banks' money transmission services.

18.20 The most important respect in which banks are interdependent is their partici- pation in the money markets; yet paradoxically it is the rapid development of the money markets that has done so much to permit the increased competition described earlier in this chapter. The growth of the inter-bank and certificate of deposit markets in particular has enabled banks to finance their lending by borrowing from other banks when their own deposit base has generated insufficient funds, and hence to respond more flexibly to their customers' bor- rowing needs. These newer 'parallel' markets flourish alongside the traditional markets in Treasury bills and call money, and the discount houses retain their distinctive position in the system. Because of the importance of their position it is worth describing their relationship with the clearing banks in some detail.

18.21 For a long time the essence of this relationship has been that the clearing banks lend money at call to the discount market, which enables it to carry on its specialised business of investing and trading in various money-market instru- ments. From the banks' standpoint, such lending traditionally has provided part of their second line of liquidity behind the cash in their tills and their current account balance with the Bank of England. Money lent to the market is not only available on demand whenever required, but also is fully secured by holdings of Treasury bills, commercial bills, certificates of deposit and other short-term paper.

18.22 The importance of the relationship stems traditionally from the fact that the discount houses are the vehicles whereby the Bank of England smooths out day-to-day shortages and surpluses in the money market. On some days the balance of factors such as government tax receipts and disbursements, official transactions in government stock, intervention in the foreign exchange market and fluctuations in the note circulation results in a net outflow from the commercial banking system as a whole to the Bank of England. The banks can then call in loans to the discount market to meet their shortage, and the market looks to the Bank of England to rectify its position. Likewise on days of surplus the Bank of England can supply Treasury bills or other assets, through the discount houses, to mop up the unwanted cash. In particular, the facility of last-resort lending, which all central banks provide, is given only to the discount houses and not to the banks directly.

18.23 The essence of the relationship between the banks and the discount market has remained unchanged, but the details of the relationship, and the way it works in practice, have changed radically. First, the range of assets held by discount houses has been enlarged. In addition to their traditional holdings of Treasury bills and gilt-edged securities, the houses have greatly expanded their holdings of commercial bills and local authority debt over the past 20 years and have become substantial holders of the newer money-market assets. Secondly, as well as their traditional secured call money, the houses now take unsecured deposits from the inter-bank market and from outside the banking system, which brings them into more direct competition with banks. Some of them are also active in the eurocurrency markets. Thirdly, and most important, are the changes to the discount market made when *Competition and Credit Control* was introduced. Those which chiefly affected the clearing banks were the placing of dealings between the banks and the market on a more competitive footing and the decision that call money with the market, which until 1971 had counted towards the liquidity ratios imposed only on the clearing banks, would become a reserve asset for all banks.

18.24 As part of the reforms of 1971 the clearing banks formally abandoned the old agreement under which they refrained from bidding at the weekly tender for Treasury bills for their own portfolios but bought bills from the discount market after the first week of their lives. They also dismantled the agreements between themselves on the rates charged on call loans to discount houses. Under the old arrangements the banks had made available to the houses very large lines of 'basic money' at the agreed (and very cheap) rate of $1\frac{5}{8}$ per cent below Bank rate. Although nominally at call these lines normally remained in existence more or less permanently. Only the marginal money which ebbed and flowed from day to day was at market rates. 'Privilege money' lent by the banks under individual stand-by arrangements to enable the houses to balance their books at the end of the day was also charged at an agreed rate. Since 1971 all money is charged at rates freely negotiated between the lender and the borrower. For their part the houses abandoned their syndicated bid at the Treasury bill tender; each house now puts in a competitive bid for as many bills as it requires, though the collective obligation to underwrite the whole issue remains.

18.25 The designation of call money as a reserve asset had far-reaching consequences. Because of their privileged status, reserve assets often yield less than competing instruments that lack reserve asset status. This confers an advantage on the houses; their borrowing costs are artificially held down, and they enjoy part of the profit that in most countries is retained by the central bank itself. But because the yield on reserve assets tends to be inferior, banks have an incentive to keep their holdings at as low a level as they can. (The clearing banks tend to maintain their reserve ratios at around $13\frac{1}{2}$ per cent, the $12\frac{1}{2}$ per cent minimum plus 1 per cent for contingencies.) This means that the banks' call money is not available to meet any but minor outflows of funds. Instead of being the next most liquid asset after cash, it has become in practice almost completely illiquid.

18.26 The liquidity buffer function that call money used to fulfil has been taken over by the 'parallel' markets, especially the inter-bank and certificate of deposit markets. Most of the daily ebbs and flows in the system are between one bank and another. A bank may experience a withdrawal of deposits, or an increase in its lending as customers draw on their agreed facilities. These movements will in general have equal and opposite counterparts elsewhere in the system. Since 1971, the necessary reconciliation has increasingly been achieved directly through the inter-bank market rather than via the discount houses. Where the discount market retains its liquidity buffer function is for movements between the banks as a whole and the Bank of England, where (as described earlier) the special relationship between the Bank and the houses comes into play. These are, however, but a small part of the overall movements. Moreover the mechanism does not always work satisfactorily, essentially because the relief of a shortage via the discount market replaces the cash lost by the banking system but not the lost reserve assets.

18.27   Banks as a whole have essentially three ways of dealing with a shortage: they can call in loans to the discount market; they can sell reserve assets (chiefly Treasury bills) to the discount market or (at the authorities' initiative) directly to the authorities; or they can sell non-reserve assets (chiefly certificates of deposit) to the discount market. The first two methods will tend to result in a loss of reserve assets. The third will not, but because discount houses are limited in the amount of 'undefined assets' they are allowed to hold this method is not always available. At times therefore money-market shortages have led to severe temporary reserve asset squeezes, even where this is not the intention of official monetary policy. This is unnecessary and undesirable. The problem mentioned is especially acute for the clearing banks. As well as the three methods already mentioned for coping with a shortage, non-clearing banks as a whole have two further options: they can draw on their 'stand-by' lines of credit with their clearing banks, or they can allow market lending to non-banks (chiefly local authorities) to run off, thus forcing the borrowers to use their clearing bank lines instead. Both methods effectively pass the shortage on to the clearing banks, who may thus be called upon to find the missing reserve assets for the whole banking system.

18.28   The Bank of England has at times relieved a reserve asset squeeze by lending in the local authority market. This is a device it has resorted to only sparingly. But there is a simple and obvious alternative: the Bank could lend in the inter-bank market. The banks suspect this might be unwelcome to the discount houses, since it would call into question their present role in smoothing out day-to-day movements. But the present system does not work altogether to the advantage of the houses either. In particular it forces them to buy substantial amounts of Treasury bills at rates they may not themselves think appropriate. On such occasions the Bank has sometimes brought influence to bear on the houses in an attempt to forestall unwanted movements in rates which in the event took place anyway. No doubt the houses will themselves develop this point in their own evidence to the Committee. On the other hand (almost as if by way of compensation) the Bank of England gives weekly guidance to the discount market as to the government's wishes regarding the immediate path of interest rates. In short, the banks do not regard the present situation as altogether satisfactory. They believe that, without in any way threatening the discount market's existence, it would be in the interests of all parties to explore ways of alleviating the problems that can arise.

Chapter 19
Banking systems abroad

Summary

This chapter contains the main findings of a survey undertaken by the clearing banks of banking and financial systems in the United Kingdom and eight other industrialised countries. Deposit-taking institutions (including those not formally termed 'banks') occupy a dominant position in all countries, the degree of strength depending mainly on the roles played by investing institutions and capital markets. Common characteristics of the commercial banks include their involvement in an increasingly wide range of financial activities ('universal banking'); the largely short-term nature of their deposits; the recent growth of term lending; their increasing reliance on interest-bearing deposits; and the fairly extensive prudential, monetary and other controls to which they are still subject. Germany apart, direct participation in industry is not widespread. The tendency for the systems to converge is apparent in the increasing institutionalisation and internationalisation of financial markets.

Introduction

19.1 The main purpose of this submission is to describe the clearing banks' own operations and position in the UK financial system. The banks are aware, however, of the increasing importance attached to international comparisons in the continuing debate about the overall effectiveness of the UK financial system, and they therefore commissioned their own survey of the systems in Germany, France, Italy, the Netherlands, Switzerland, Sweden, Japan and the United States, with particular reference to the position of the leading deposit banks in each country; comparisons are made with the United Kingdom where appropriate. The survey was undertaken by the Inter-Bank Research Organisation and was based partly on its own research work and partly on evidence collected by the clearing banks through their branches and correspondent networks abroad. The survey is being published as a separate volume but the salient features of the banking and financial systems of the eight countries are identified in this chapter, thus illustrating some of the themes which emerge from the full survey.

19.2 The principal themes which are apparent are:

a. the 'role and functioning' of banks in the various countries can be properly judged only if the banking systems are seen in the context of their individual financial systems; otherwise, many of the differences between banking systems will seem inexplicable;

b. when due allowance is made for the differences in the individual financial systems, the major commercial banks of the various countries are marked more by their basic similarities than by their differences;

c. the differences in the financial systems themselves are explained largely by historical factors which in many cases are of diminishing present-day significance;

countries in which subsidiary operations are particularly important. (By omitting subsidiaries in the other six cases, market shares are inevitably understated, but only in Italy is the extent of the understatement thought to be significant.) The table shows that the leading banks all account for large shares of their national banking markets, though the degree of concentration ranges from a very high level in Sweden, the Netherlands and Switzerland to a more moderate level in Italy, the United States and Japan. In some of the continental countries, the concentration factor would be somewhat greater if one included with the leading commercial banks certain large institutions (such as savings and co-operative banks) which also operate as general-purpose banks and therefore compete with the commercial banks in both deposit-taking and lending, even though they are not formally designated as commercial banks. Often, indeed, their formal position is that of a collection of regional institutions, though in any particular place only one such institution will be represented. An example would be the French Crédits Agricoles, which operate in most major respects as if they were a single commercial bank.

Major banks abroad

Table 40

Market shares in deposits and other liabilities to non-financial
sectors, end 1975

Percentages		Commercial banks	Deposit-taking institutions	All financial institutions
Germany	big three banks*	51	13	11
France	big three banks	61	25	18
Italy	big five banks	43	23	19
Netherlands	big three banks*	80	35	15
Switzerland	big three banks	77	32	17
Sweden	big four banks	87	51	24
Japan	12 city banks	61	30	21
United States	176 money-centre banks	43	27	15
United Kingdom	London clearing banks*	68	38	20

*Based on group figures.

The banks included are as follows:
Germany: Deutsche Bank, Dresdner Bank, Commerzbank;
France: Banque Nationale de Paris, Crédit Lyonnais, Société Générale;
Italy: Banca Nazionale del Lavoro, Banca Commerciale Italiana, Credito Italiano, Banco di Roma, Banco di Napoli;
Netherlands: Algemene Bank Nederland, Amsterdam-Rotterdam Bank, Nederlandsche Middenstandsbank;
Switzerland: Swiss Bank Corporation, Union Bank of Switzerland, Swiss Credit Bank;
Sweden: PK Banken, Svenska Handelsbanken, Skandinaviska Enskilda Banken, Götabanken.

Source: Inter-Bank Research Organisation.

19.14   With such large shares of total financial intermediation in the various countries, it is not surprising that the banks have shown a general tendency to expand their activities beyond the traditional confines of short-term deposit taking and lending. 'Universal banking' in one form or another is now prevalent in all the countries – especially if one takes account of the activities of the subsidiary companies within the major banking groups. The concept of universal banking has a number of different connotations, but it has two main characteristics as far as the major commercial banks are concerned: these are the banks' involvement in medium or long-term lending and in what the Americans would refer to as investment banking. Involvement in the provision of medium and long-term finance to industry is now fairly commonplace, while banks in several of the countries are also involved directly or indirectly in the provision of mortgage finance to houseowners. (The United Kingdom is in the minority in having separate, independent building societies to discharge this function.) Even in a country such as Italy, where the banks are prohibited by law from engaging in long-term business, they are allowed to operate autonomous term credit divisions and to participate in special credit institutions which do engage in such lending.

19.15   As for investment banking, this term implies close involvement in the stock market, the provision of advice on corporate finance, the management of issues of shares and bonds, the preparation of mergers and takeovers and other related activities. The major banks in most of the countries engage in such investment banking activities to a certain extent, mainly through specialist subsidiaries. The chief exception is the United States where commercial and investment banking are still legally separated. However, this separation applies in effect to domestic business only and the leading US commercial banks are heavily involved in investment banking activities through overseas subsidiaries in London and elsewhere. Investment banking can also imply equity participations and direct involvement in industrial management. However, formal involvement by the banks in the ownership and control of non-financial enterprises is not common. Of the countries reviewed, only in Germany do the banks have large participations in industrial companies. In the Netherlands, Italy, Sweden and the United States there are major restrictions on the permissible extent of a bank's equity investments.

19.16   Similarly, the close involvement of banks in the affairs of industry is not as common or extensive as is widely believed: even the influence of the big German banks over industry stems not from a large concentration of lending and investing power but from a limited number of equity holdings, augmented by the exercise of proxy votes for other shareholders and by the tradition of bank representation on company boards. (In fact the 'big three' German banks account on a group basis – including their mortgage banking and other subsidiaries – for only 12.5 per cent of total loans, investments and other claims on the non-financial sector.) In Japan, the city banks have close ties with the big trading and industrial conglomerates, but these are largely informal. In other countries, big banks generally keep an arms-length relationship with their customers, though co-operation with them can still be extremely important.

19.17   Deposits from companies and individuals are by far the most important source of funds for the banks in all countries. Deposits from other banks play a much smaller role, though a not insignificant one in Switzerland, the Netherlands, France and Germany. As for the capital markets, equity and bond issues tend to be employed for strengthening the banks' capital bases rather than as a means of raising funds for on-lending. Only the mortgage bank subsidiaries of the leading German banks raise substantial funds on the bond markets for direct lending purposes. The great majority of customer deposits are short-term. In some countries deposits of between six months and two years are of some importance, but the majority of funds are notionally held for shorter periods than that. Nevertheless, customer deposits with large banks are fairly stable irrespective of their maturity. However, in all countries there has been a decline in the proportion of non-interest-bearing sight deposits with a corresponding increase in the banks' reliance on interest-bearing deposits in general. Customer reaction to the high level of interest rates experienced in recent years is the main reason for this trend, although in several of the countries the banks have actively attempted to increase their share of the retail deposit market by offering savings accounts and other facilities geared to the needs of the small saver. It is worth noting that in some continental countries interest is paid on sight deposits. However, such deposits are generally subject to restrictions on withdrawals and cheque usage. The question of whether to allow banks to pay interest on demand deposits is currently a live issue in the United States.

19.18   In few countries do the leading banks play so important a role in the nation's money transmission system as the clearing banks in the United Kingdom, partly because of the importance of postal giros on the continent and partly because in several countries (notably the United States) the banks are precluded from operating the necessary large national branch networks. However, in other countries (notably the Netherlands, France and Germany) the leading banks have greatly expanded their branches in recent years and now provide national coverage much more closely akin to that of the clearing banks.

19.19   Comparing how the leading banks employ their funds is complicated by differences in reporting and accounting practices and by the high level of inter-bank lending in countries such as Switzerland, the Netherlands, France and Germany. Nevertheless, loans to non-bank customers and holdings of bills and other securities account for the majority of the assets of the leading banks in all the countries. Overdrafts are the most common type of corporate loan in the Netherlands, Switzerland, Italy and the United Kingdom and are used fairly extensively in Sweden, Germany and France, but they are almost non-existent in the United States and Japan. In France and Italy, the discounting of bills is still extensively used, particularly as a means of financing small and medium-sized firms, and it is also popular for different reasons in Japan. Term loans for short periods are the chief form of short-term finance in the United States and Japan, usually accompanied by requirements for compensating balances. Revolving credits are growing in popularity in several countries, notably Sweden and the Netherlands.

19.20   The maturity structure of the banks' loan portfolios differs less between the various countries than is usually assumed. Medium-term loans of one form or another account for about 40 per cent of total lending in Germany, France, the United Kingdom and the United States, rather less in Japan, Switzerland and the Netherlands, and under 10 per cent in Italy. (Data for Sweden are unavailable.) The tendency for overdrafts and short-term credits to be renewed over fairly long periods, and indeed to be used for financing capital investment, is apparent in all the countries. A sectoral analysis of bank lending is more difficult to make; data in a form which permits meaningful comparisons are only available for Germany, Italy, Japan, the United Kingdom and the United States. The generally higher proportion of bank lending to manufacturing industry in the first three of these countries reflects not only the greater reliance of the corporate sector on banks as a source of finance but also the larger share of manufacturing in the gross domestic product of the three countries.

19.21   Interest rates on loans and deposits differ substantially between the countries, largely reflecting differing rates of inflation. Up to the mid-1960s, interest rates in most countries were closely regulated by the monetary authorities, or by agreement between the banks themselves, so as to protect the position of mutual institutions such as savings banks and generally to limit the amount of competition for funds between banks. Since the mid-1960s, interest rate controls have been completely or partially removed and the informal cartels relinquished in several of the countries (notably France, Germany, the United Kingdom and the United States). However, formal controls on deposit interest rates, including a ban on the payment of interest on demand deposits, persist in some countries, while in most cases there are informal understandings from time to time between the authorities and the banks as to the appropriate level of interest rates. Interest rates on loans are free from formal controls in all major countries, though inevitably they are strongly influenced by the operation of monetary and credit controls. In Italy, the banks are required to invest a substantial proportion of their funds in certain low-yielding securities and are therefore forced to charge particularly high lending rates to redress the balance. Because of recent wide fluctuations in interest rates there has been a tendency in all the countries to move from fixed to variable rate lending and to link lending rates directly or indirectly to the cost of funds on the money markets.

19.22   The large commercial banks in all the countries have always been engaged extensively in financing international trade, and the importance of such activities has increased in recent years. To fulfil their role effectively many banks have established direct representation in the leading financial centres in the world. Several have had offices in London for a very long time, but with the development of the eurocurrency markets in the 1960s all the Japanese and European banks covered in table 40 on page 199 (except some from Sweden) are now established there. The larger US banks are particularly active in the London eurocurrency market; moreover, the largest US banks have been the most aggressive in expanding their international representation, and a few now cover almost every country in the world. Certain banks from some European countries, notably the United Kingdom and France, also have long-standing interests overseas in developing countries, especially in Africa. A number of European banks have formed themselves into banking 'clubs' as a means of developing international business (see paragraph 12.6).

19.23   Banks in all the countries are subject to close regulation designed to ensure both their solvency (prudential controls) and their compliance with economic policy objectives (monetary controls). Prudential controls have traditionally been the less formalised of the two, but increasingly they are now being enshrined in legislation, with the emphasis switching from generalised controls on capital/deposit ratios to more specific controls on liquidity requirements and on the capital backing for different types of banking asset. Comprehensive controls imposed by law are already to be found in five of the countries. Of the other four, the United Kingdom will have its own legislation in due course, while in France, Italy and Japan various requirements exist regarding such matters as medium-term loan ratios in France, loan limits for individual customers in Italy and Japan, and the financing of bank premises in France and Japan. The fact that the leading banks in France and Italy are state-owned may explain why formalised prudential controls are considered less necessary than elsewhere. As for monetary controls, the United States and Germany have consistently relied on measures such as reserve requirements and open-market operations, which do not impede competition, for controlling the growth of credit and the money stock. Direct credit controls have been used to a greater or lesser extent in all the other countries. While there was a move in the earlier 1970s away from direct controls in certain countries such as France, the Netherlands and the United Kingdom, this has subsequently been reversed in certain respects. There are also differences in the extent to which monetary and credit controls are used to influence the allocation of credit within the economy. The selective element in credit policy is of particular significance in France, Italy and Sweden and, in a less formalised way, in the United Kingdom and Japan. In the other countries, especially the Netherlands and Germany, it is of only minor importance.

19.24   In addition to enforcing prudential and monetary controls, the authorities intervene in the affairs of banks in many other ways, though the general tendency over the past two decades has been one of gradual liberalisation, with restrictions and controls being removed in a number of areas. In France and Italy, where the leading commercial banks are state-owned, the governments still appoint their senior management, while the Swedish authorities have the right to appoint directors even to the privately-owned commercial banks. However, such intervention in the appointment of bank management is found nowhere else. Formal restrictions on equity investments are still in force in six of the countries, the exceptions being Germany, Switzerland and the United Kingdom, while the opening of branches is controlled in the United States, Japan, Italy and Sweden. Taking an overall view, banks in Germany and Switzerland enjoy the greatest freedom from regulation and intervention, though certain agreements among the Swiss banks mean that this freedom does not necessarily result in as much competition as is to be found, say, in the United Kingdom or the United States. Banks are most closely controlled in France, Italy and Sweden, where the governments' interventionist tendencies are strongest.

19.25 Any attempt at an analysis of the level and pattern of bank profits in the various countries comes up against major problems of comparability, mainly arising from differences in accounting practices governing such matters as transfers to inner reserves, bad debt provisions, asset valuation and the treatment of depreciation. However, some comparative data are set out in table 38 on page 173. Reported figures indicate that for most countries net profits have latterly represented 0.3–0.4 per cent of total assets, shareholders' funds 3–4 per cent of total assets and net profits 9–12 per cent of shareholders' funds. The main exceptions are banks in France and Italy, where a low level of capitalisation is reflected in a low ratio of profits to total assets; and American and British banks, where relatively high levels of capitalisation are reflected in higher than average ratios of net profits to total assets. The cyclical nature of bank profits described in chapter 15 is fairly universal, although this is concealed in some countries by transfers to and from undisclosed reserves.

Differences and similarities: the changing pattern

19.26 Although the basic features of the financial and banking systems of the major industrialised countries are less diverse than is sometimes assumed, this chapter has shown that some significant differences persist in such matters as the relative importance of investing institutions and special credit institutions. Before concluding, it is worth trying to show why some of these differences have arisen and whether they are tending to become more or less pronounced. As a general rule, most of the differences on which attention is usually focused have their roots in the social, economic or political history of the countries concerned; it is relatively rare for them to reflect contemporary influences. Although such historical factors become less relevant with the passage of time, their effects on national attitudes and practices can persist. Nevertheless, financial systems are characterised by considerable flexibility and responsiveness and their ability to adapt continuously to changing circumstances and needs must not be underestimated. History abounds in examples of that ability, from the development of capital markets for industrial equities in the United States and the United Kingdom to the more recent rise of the eurocurrency and eurobond markets.

19.27 Even so, some of the historical factors which underlie the differences in institutional structure have had pervasive and self-reinforcing effects on the various financial systems. An institution or market may have developed to fill a particular need at a particular point of time; but once it has established itself, it may well prove hard to dislodge from its position in the system. Thus the present strength of the leading German banks, and their particularly close relations with industry, can be traced back to the early years of industrialisation, when a shortage of risk capital and the absence of organised markets for industrial securities forced the banks to take an active interest in the provision of longer-term industrial finance, some of which subsequently had to be converted into equity. This orientation of the leading commercial banks towards large companies created in its turn a gap in the facilities for financing small traders, farmers, and the professions, which was largely filled by the development of credit co-operatives. These historical factors probably represent the main reason why the German banking system differs from those of, say, the United Kingdom and the United States, where active capital markets allowed the commercial banks to concentrate more on the shorter-term needs of large and small companies alike, thereby leaving less scope for the development of general-purpose co-operative banks.

19.28   Many of the institutional differences can be traced back to the different circumstances in which the leading countries became industrialised in the first place. In the United States, the wave of technological innovation and the growth of big businesses which occurred towards the end of the last century coincided with a concentration of private wealth and a willingness to take financial risks which permitted the rapid emergence of a large and highly sophisticated market for industrial equities. In the United Kingdom the earlier stages of industrialisation had been financed largely on internally-generated funds and short-term credit; surplus private wealth had tended initially to go into government debt and railway bonds at home and overseas. The market for industrial equities developed rather later when many industrial companies merged to form larger units and began to sell equities to the public, providing an investment vehicle for the large available supply of risk capital.

19.29   By contrast, in Japan and the continental countries companies have had to rely on self-financing and bank debt for much longer periods of their history, partly because industrialisation generally came later when institutional structures were already more firmly established, and partly because the ultimate sources of finance were dispersed among a generally risk-averse public who favoured holding their wealth in liquid form as cash or bank deposits. Thus even in those continental countries where investing institutions such as insurance companies subsequently became more important, the lending tradition was so strong that they too tended to finance companies with debt rather than with equity. This tendency was often reinforced by tight restrictions on many of the institutions' investment activities and by a reluctance on the part of the proprietors of the small, family-controlled companies prevalent in many of the continental countries to surrender control of their equity. It is historical factors such as these which need to be borne in mind when attempting to compare gearing ratios in different countries: they are a far more important explanation of the high debt/equity ratios prevalent in countries like Japan, Italy and France than any differences in the willingness of bankers to lend.

19.30   Important though many of these historical influences and the resultant institutional differences still are, there has been a clear tendency in the past 10 or 15 years for the banking and financial systems of the various countries to converge towards structures with fewer marked national characteristics. This tendency is to a large extent explained by the fact that none of the systems is wholly free from institutional gaps and defects. New financial and economic problems are constantly arising, and increasingly they are taking common forms in all of the major countries. It is hardly surprising, therefore, that the solutions to these problems also have a great deal in common.

19.31   The tendency for financial systems to converge has had a number of distinctive features. For instance, in every country institutions have been playing an increasingly important role in the capital markets in particular and the financial systems in general, because of both the decline of the private investor and the increasingly large surpluses and deficits experienced by the various sectors of the economy. The forces behind these trends are unlikely to be reversed. The financial markets of all the major countries have also been increasingly 'internationalised': the growth of the euromarkets and the expansion in the foreign operations of American banks in particular have led to a rapid acceleration in what might be termed the transfer of financial technology. The dismantling of barriers to trade and other international trans-actions has led to a general increase in business undertaken by institutions for non-residents and has contributed greatly to the reduction in the importance of distinctive national attitudes and practices. On the domestic front, there has been a general decline in the number of institutions operating in the main financial markets, largely through mergers, and as a result the size and market share of the largest institutions have increased. The widespread expansion of universal banking described already in this chapter is another instance of convergence, while perhaps the most interesting example of all is the tendency for corporate debt/equity ratios in different countries to move more closely in line: for while companies in the United Kingdom and the United States recently increased their gearing ratios, as bank finance filled the gap left by the decline in company profits and new issues, attempts were being made in most other countries to reduce gearing ratios by fostering a shift from debt to equity finance. However, these attempts have not been notably successful, largely because weak equity markets tend to perpetuate their own weaknesses.

19.32   How far the process of convergence has still to go is impossible to say, but it has probably not run its full course yet. While some of the differences in financial and banking systems will doubtless persist indefinitely as a result of historical and other factors, the similarities are becoming increasingly evident and important. The ability of financial institutions to learn from the experience of other countries has long been among their major strengths, but that does not mean that they should be expected to imitate other countries' systems uncritically. It certainly does not mean that there must be a causal connection between the particular financial system that has developed within a country and that country's economic record. The financial systems of the countries surveyed in this chapter differ as much one from another as they do from that of the United Kingdom and there is no evidence that any one of those systems is likely to be more conducive to economic success than any other.

Chapter 20
Public ownership

Summary

This chapter begins with an historical survey of proposals for bank nationalisation, and then examines the main arguments for and against it. The banks recognise their importance in the economy but deny that their power is excessive or abused. Their market shares in deposit taking and lending are frequently exaggerated. Competition is intense, both between the banks and with other institutions, especially in lending to industry. Bank profits are not excessive and the profit discipline helps ensure the banks' responsiveness to their customers' needs. Banks are already closely regulated, and nationalisation is not necessary to achieve effective control over their activities. The banks do not believe that the availability and cost of bank finance have been significant factors in holding back investment. The banks' property lending has not been at the expense of other sectors and their general lending terms and conditions have been reasonable. Nationalisation could well reduce standards of customer service. The chapter concludes by refuting the suggestions that public ownership is the norm abroad, that banking is unduly concentrated in the United Kingdom and that differences in economic performance can be attributed to differences in financial structures.

Introduction

20.1 Since the terms of reference of the Committee include consideration of "the possible extension of the public sector", the clearing banks consider it appropriate to draw together in this chapter their general observations on this issue. However, they would point out that many of the matters most relevant to the issue have already been covered elsewhere in the submission. They believe that the activities and achievements described in the course of their submission represent the most relevant evidence in the debate on public ownership.

20.2 The clearing banks believe that the present competitive banking system has served Britain well, and they are convinced that any large-scale extension of public ownership in banking would have adverse consequences for British industry and for the British people. Nevertheless, in stating the case for the present competitive system the banks do not wish to appear complacent: in any system there is always room for improvement. Indeed one of the strongest arguments for competition is that it leads to a constant search for new ways of providing better services to industry and the public. Merely to show that the present system has its faults does not prove the case for public ownership. To prove their case, the advocates of nationalisation must also show that public ownership would rectify those faults, while avoiding the creation of even greater problems than those it sought to solve.

Historical survey

20.3 The origins of the proposals for the public ownership of the banks can be traced back to the writings of Karl Marx. According to his analysis, the capitalist system, in which the provision of credit played a key role, was bound to move inexorably towards monopoly and towards the exploitation of the working man:

> "To begin with, the credit system appears furtively, as it were, in the form of a modest helper of accumulation, drawing into the hands of individual or associated capitalists the monetary resources scattered over the surface of society, and doing this by means of invisible hands. Ere long, however, it becomes a new and formidable weapon in the competitive struggle; and in the end it manifests itself as a gigantic mechanism for the centralisation of capital. Competition and credit, the two mightiest levers of centralisation, develop concomitantly with capitalist production and accumulation. . . . The expansion of capitalist production creates . . . the technical means for the inauguration of those tremendous industrial undertakings which can only arise as the outcome of the centralisation of capital."

K Marx, *Das Kapital*, translated by E & C Paul, 1928.

20.4   The socialist movement in Britain, largely based on the work of the early Fabians in the 1880s, rejected Marxist revolution in favour of state control of certain key industries. The banks have been included in the list of such industries at certain times (one of the earliest was in 1883) and excluded at others: no very consistent reasons related to the nature of banking appear to explain this alternation of socialist policies. In 1918 the Labour Party adopted a constitution which included a commitment to "the common ownership of the means of production, distribution and exchange and the best obtainable system of popular administration and control of each industry or service". The 1920 and 1921 Labour Conferences urged measures for state and municipal banking; these proposals were largely inspired by the work of Beatrice and Sidney Webb, who had suggested that it was not right permanently to tolerate "any of the waste and inefficiency involved in the abandonment of British industry to a jostling crowd of separate employers with their minds bent not on service to the community but, by the very law of their being, only on the utmost profiteering" (*Labour and the New Social Order*, 1918). Thus the emphasis was beginning to shift from the control of monopoly exploitation to the desire to rationalise the competitive scene. The Communist Party in Britain has consistently argued for nationalisation without compensation as a means of expropriating the capitalists, but this policy has never been accepted by the Labour Party or by the Trades Union Congress. For example, at the 1932 Congress the criticism that nationalisation with compensation paid in government securities would only serve to guarantee the income of the former owners was rejected on the grounds that this disadvantage could be counteracted by taxation.

20.5   The depression of the inter-war years led to increasing emphasis on the need for public ownership of a wide range of industries, including the banks, on the grounds that the capitalist system had produced mass unemployment and that, as a Labour Party policy document approved by the 1934 Conference put it, "the only sane alternative which is left is a policy of full and rapid socialist planning". Indeed it was reaction against the restrictive economic policies of the inter-war years which formed the background to the decision to bring the Bank of England into public ownership. The Bank of England Act 1946 gave the Bank of England power to issue directives to banks, and although this power has never been formally used, it exists as the ultimate legal authority for the system of controls and requests that the Bank has operated since the war in the furtherance of official monetary policy and in its attempts to ensure the general stability of the banking system.

20.6   Little more was heard about public ownership of the banks until 1971, when the Labour Party Conference, against the advice of its National Executive, passed two resolutions advocating nationalisation of all banking and insurance companies. A study group under the chairmanship of Mr Ian Mikardo was set up and published its report in August 1973. The report criticised the banks for lack of competition and for maintaining too many branches on expensive High Street sites. It recommended that a single publicly-owned banking corporation should be set up and that this should include the London clearing banks, the Scottish banks and all British overseas banks. This proposal did not meet with universal approval within the Labour Party, and during the subsequent years there was some discussion of the case for extending public ownership to one bank only.

20.7   In 1975 the Labour Party National Executive Committee published a document entitled *Labour and Industry: the Next Steps*. This suggested that one of the main causes of the country's economic difficulties lay in the failure of the financial institutions to direct sufficient funds to manufacturing industry. It proposed the target of doubling investment in manufacturing industry over the following decade; the creation of "a substantial publicly-owned sector in banking—whilst, as in France, retaining a large measure of consumer choice"; the creation within the government machine of a specialist planning unit which would give "advice on the allocation of investment funds between firms, sectors and regions"; and a major role for the National Enterprise Board, whose capital funds should be increased to at least £1 billion a year over the following five years. It was recognised that if funds were to be diverted into manufacturing investment this would inevitably limit the growth of consumer spending and "mean increasing taxation over the years relative to public expenditure".

20.8   The then Prime Minister (Sir Harold Wilson) made it clear (in a letter to Sir Charles Villiers, published on 24 January 1976) that these proposals did not represent official government policy. This was confirmed in a debate in the House of Commons on 19 May 1976, when Mr Harold Lever stated that:

> "The government have no intention of nationalising any company in the banking industry . . . In fact, it is the government's view that our banks are a very efficient sector of our private enterprise. They are competitive. Our branch banking system is unrivalled throughout the world, and our banks adjusted to Britain's changing position in the world with remarkable advantage to our country. They continue to make a major contribution to invisible earnings. . . . In our society profitability is not a perfect yardstick for allocating resources although, in general, it is pretty good, as its results show whenever it has been applied. It is certainly better than the combination of whim, intuition and prejudice which will replace it unless one sets clear criteria for the control of funds. Where one wishes the funds to be allocated otherwise than because of profitability, then the obligation is upon us to give clear alternative criteria. . . . The problem is not how to control the banks with government policies but rather to ensure that the government policies they are asked to carry out are wise. . . ."

20.9   Nevertheless, in August 1976 the Labour Party National Executive Committee adopted and published a further document entitled *Banking and Finance*. It reiterated the thesis that Britain's low rate of growth was the result of insufficient investment. The document, which was approved by the Labour Party Conference in September 1976, included the following recommendations:

    a. the establishment of an investment reserve fund into which companies should be encouraged to place a proportion of their funds and "releases from which would be supervised by a reformed Bank of England and conditional upon being devoted to productive investment";

    b. the merger of the National Giro, National Savings Bank and the Paymaster General's Office to "form a major state bank" – possibly with the inclusion of the Trustee Savings Banks;

    c. public ownership of the big four clearing banks (Barclays, Lloyds, Midland and National Westminster), the top seven insurance companies (Commercial Union, Royal, Prudential, Guardian Royal Exchange, General Accident, Sun Alliance and London, and Legal and General) and one merchant bank.

Thus the argument has turned 180 degrees from the Marxist analysis of the banks playing too powerful a role in the creation of industrial enterprise to the current criticism that they do not do enough in this respect.

Possible methods of public ownership

20.10   The arguments about public ownership have recently focused on the specific proposals of the Labour Party for nationalising the four major clearing banks. However, this is by no means the only method that has been suggested over the years for extending public ownership into banking. In all, four major variants can be identified and these are commented upon briefly below.

20.11   If public ownership of the banks were to follow the pattern of the coal, gas, electricity, steel, rail, airline, aircraft or shipbuilding industries, then one might envisage a single publicly-owned banking corporation being established with a single board of management. This would appeal to those whose main aim was to use the provision of finance to facilitate the detailed operation of economic planning, or to those who were anxious to carry out extensive rationalisation through the closure of bank branches. Indeed as noted above, this was a structure recommended some four years ago by the committee under the chairmanship of Mr Mikardo. This approach, however, has few proponents today. It is generally recognised that the ending of competition might well lead to a decline in service to bank customers, and the creation of a monopoly banking organisation might well lead to an excessive increase in the power of government.

20.12   Another proposal is that the National Giro and the National Savings Bank (together perhaps with the Paymaster General's Office) should be amalgamated to create a single publicly-owned banking organisation. This subject is known to be under official consideration at the time of writing. (It is sometimes suggested that the Trustee Savings Banks should also be included; no doubt they will themselves be submitting evidence on this point.) It is not for the banks to comment on any possible reorganisation of activities which are already within the public sector. It is, however, necessary to emphasise the importance of ensuring fair competition. Any new banking structure created within the public sector should be subject to the same (or equivalent) rules about such matters as reserve assets and prudential ratios as apply to banks in the private sector, and should not enjoy artificial fiscal advantages. To allow a public sector bank to expand its services by undercutting the commercial banks on the basis of an implied guarantee from the exchequer would not only represent an uneconomic diversion of resources but would also be to court the risk of substantial loss, the cost of which would have to be borne by the taxpayer.

20.13   It has also been suggested that public ownership should be extended to one clearing bank only. The argument is presumably that this would increase competition and widen consumer choice. However, the banks would maintain that adequate competition and choice exists already. Clearly this solution would not be as effective for pursuing detailed planning objectives as complete public ownership. If it were known that the publicly-owned bank was using non-commercial criteria there would be a natural tendency for some depositors to prefer not to be associated with that bank. Moreover there would be the practical problem of deciding which bank should be selected, and ensuring that individual shareholders and depositors were not discriminated against – a problem that is reflected in parliamentary terms by the need for complicated 'hybrid' legislation. It is for these and other reasons that the 'one bank' solution appears to have lost favour within the Labour Party.

20.14   Most recent discussion has centred on the proposal in *Banking and Finance* that the four main clearing banks should be taken into public ownership but retain their individual identities. Presumably this would be brought about by legislation to acquire the shares of the banks concerned, with the payment of appropriate compensation. The cost to the exchequer of acquiring the shares of the four banks and the seven insurance companies also named in the document would, at September 1977 prices, be of the order of £5,000 million. This would cause a corresponding increase in the public sector borrowing requirement. There is no reason to suppose that the members of the public who have chosen to invest their savings in bank shares would be content in exchange to hold fixed-interest government stock; therefore, the transaction might well cause problems in the management of the national debt. If this course were to be followed it would have to be decided whether the acquisition should include the entire operations of the four companies – including their very substantial overseas activities – or only their domestic clearing banking activities. In their concern with the latter activities, the proponents of nationalisation appear to have given little consideration to the implications of their proposals for the rest of the banks' business at home and overseas, and that of their subsidiaries.

20.15   Almost certainly, nationalisation would present an opportunity for the 300 or so other domestic or foreign banks to gain business at the nationalised clearing banks' expense. In such circumstances, there is a serious risk that the nationalised banks would be officially permitted, or even encouraged, to meet this competition by operating on non-commercial criteria. If each of the four publicly-owned banks were subject to direction by some central agency, and if they had no real motive to maximise their profits or minimise their losses, it is hard to see how the competition between them could be as effective as it is at present.

The main arguments

20.16   The remainder of this chapter considers the main arguments for and against bank nationalisation. Most attention will be paid to the arguments contained in *Banking and Finance*, but various other arguments are also used from time to time by the supporters of nationalisation and some of these are also considered. The arguments for bank nationalisation are extremely diffuse; between them they touch on almost every aspect of domestic clearing banking activities, though latterly the emphasis has been on lending. Many of the arguments take the form of criticism of the banks' record without any indication of whether, or how, nationalisation would improve it. It should not be necessary for the banks to have to defend every last particular of their record in order to refute the case for nationalisation. Rather it is up to the supporters of nationalisation to show that their various criticisms of the banks are not only valid but also directly relevant to their case.

20.17 The main arguments for and against nationalisation can be divided into two groups. The first group relates to the economic power of the banks and covers such matters as their profit record, their market share and the amount of competition between them. The second group relates to the actual performance of the banks and covers such matters as their lending record and their customer relations. Both sets of arguments can be further divided into those concerned solely with UK banking experience and those which draw on comparisons with banking structures and activities abroad. In this chapter, all the arguments based on international comparison will be considered together.

The banks' economic importance

20.18 The banks would not deny that they occupy a pivotal position in the economy and the services they provide are clearly essential ones. However, the banks would deny that their economic power is either excessive or subject to abuse. In practice, the extent of their power and their freedom to wield it are strictly limited by a number of factors; the chief of these are the competition to which the banks are subject across the entire range of their activities and the regulations and controls imposed on them by the authorities.

20.19 There is a danger that these safeguards would not apply to the same extent in the case of a nationalised banking industry, which would enjoy both more real economic power and more scope to abuse it. Significantly, those countries which have nationalised their major commercial banks have almost always retained a substantial buffer (in the form of a semi-autonomous central bank or other regulatory authority) between the machinery of the state and the banking system, to ensure that the banks remain free from excessive political influence. The supporters of nationalisation in this country have failed to provide assurances that they would guarantee a comparable degree of independence for the nationalised British banks.

The banks' market share

20.20 A central plank of the case for nationalisation contained in *Banking and Finance* is that the clearing banks account for an excessively large share of the banking market. In support of this claim it is usually stated that the 'big four' banks control over two thirds of all (sterling) bank deposits. What this argument fails to recognise is that bank deposits (as defined by the official statisticians) themselves represent less than half of all the funds held by UK residents in liquid form. If one includes funds held with the savings banks, the Giro, the finance houses and above all the building societies, as well as funds held by the public in the form of Treasury bills and local authority loans, the clearing banks' share falls to less than a third of the total. This is a much fairer indication of their true market share (see table 57 on page 274). Less attention has been paid to the clearing banks' share of the lending market. Here too, what might seem to be a large share of bank lending is a very much more modest share – certainly under 20 per cent – of total lending, including loans extended by the building societies and the government.

20.21   In fact the only market which the clearing banks might be said to dominate is the market in cheque clearing and related forms of money transmission. Their share of the total number of accounts which can be immediately used for making payments (that is, all bank current accounts, all TSB current accounts and all Giro accounts) is well over 80 per cent. This, however, is neither surprising nor sinister. The clearing banks, TSBs and Giro are the only organisations with the branch networks to support a money transmission business of any size; and the relatively small market shares enjoyed by the TSBs and Giro largely reflect the restrictions imposed in the past on the banking services that they could offer – restrictions which are now gradually being removed.

20.22   One of the most important consequences of nationalising the major clearing banks would be to ensure that the public sector totally dominated the market in money transmission services in England and Wales, with the mutual and private sectors confined to the fringes. The public sector would also control a disturbingly large percentage of the deposit-taking and lending markets – especially in view of the fact that the lending activities of certain mutual and private sector institutions (such as the savings banks and building societies) are also subject to rigorous official control.

Competition and choice

20.23   In virtually every aspect of their business the clearing banks compete not only with one another but also with many different types of institution. The public at large benefits from this competition, not only in terms of the range and variety of services available to it, but also through the effects of competition on the quality and cost of those services. It is hard to see how nationalisation could fail to impair this competition and reduce the amount of real choice available to the public.

20.24   The specific competition faced by the clearing banks in their principal activities has already been described in the appropriate chapters. As far as the banks themselves are concerned, competition between them is intense and very few of their activities are now governed by collective agreements. Those agreements which remain (for instance, on lending rates for nationalised industries and on reciprocal cash withdrawal facilities) have survived mainly because they are judged appropriate to the needs of the banks' customers. Indeed, even while the so-called 'cartel' was in force until 1971, the banks competed aggressively in the standards of service they offered; moves to dismantle the 'cartel' in the early 1960s were blocked by the government, who feared that an unwelcome increase in industry's borrowing costs would result.

20.25   It should not be assumed that competition is weak simply because the services the banks provide, and the rates they charge, are broadly similar. It is a characteristic of an efficient and competitive industry that product and pricing policies implemented successfully by one firm will tend to be matched by its rivals as they seek to close the competitive gap that has opened up. Nowhere is this more true than in the setting of interest rates. The banks all operate in the same economic environment, and if it makes economic sense for one bank to raise its base rate or change its interest margins it will probably make equal sense for its rivals to do so too. Even when the banks' circumstances and policies are not entirely identical, the nature of banking is such that banks' interest rates are bound to stay more or less in line in response to market forces.

A bank which failed to raise its rates when its rivals had done so would be vulnerable to a heavy increase in advances and loss of deposits.

20.26 Nevertheless, there are differences in the banks' interest rates – notably those applicable to personal customers – and even more marked differences in their account charges; a customer paying several pounds of annual bank charges at one bank may well be eligible for free banking at another. Differences between the banks are also apparent when it comes to comparing the full range of services that they provide, directly or through subsidiaries. Thus the range and nature of the banks' business advisory and merchant banking operations vary considerably, as does the extent of their involvement in term lending, equity investment and international banking. The banks' own customers certainly do not regard them as identical institutions. Market research in the past has illustrated significant differences in public attitudes towards the individual clearing banks. Most of the larger corporate customers have accounts at more than one bank and a significant proportion of personal customers have seen fit to move their accounts from one bank to another in search of better service.

20.27 Obviously the clearing banks do not conform to the textbook model of pure market competition; but then no major industries do. Unless there are geographical restrictions (as in the United States) or other artificial impediments, it is probably inevitable that a country's branch banking industry will be concentrated in a relatively few hands. But this does not mean that customers' choice is restricted to those major branch banks. It has already been pointed out that in each of the three main aspects of their business – deposit taking, lending and money transmission – the banks are in competition with different institutions as well as with one another. Many of these institutions, notably the building societies, enjoy fiscal and other competitive advantages which have helped them to gain an increasing share of the total available business (a point developed in chapter 18).

20.28 The aspect of banking in which competition is undoubtedly fiercest is precisely that on which the banks' critics have chosen to concentrate their attention – namely, the provision of finance to industry. Much more than money transmission, this is an activity in which small units can compete successfully with large ones; it is also one in which individual corporate customers will often wish to use the services of several banks. The clearing banks ignore at their peril the competition, especially for large-volume lending business, posed by other institutions and markets. Particularly worthy of mention are the lending activities of the American banks in London who now account for some 20 per cent of all bank lending to UK manufacturing industry. Nor are the direct lending activities of other banks and financial institutions the only competitive threat: for instance, bill finance and inter-company lending are also of importance.

20.29 It is also necessary to consider the charge made by some advocates of nationalisation that the banks actually compete too much – notably in the number of branches they operate. Branch rationalisation has been advanced in the past as the main argument for merging all the clearing banks into a single state-owned banking corporation. Although this proposal has not been retained in *Banking and Finance*, the charge of wasteful competition at branch level can still be heard. It is true that in a competitive banking system, the branches of different banks will tend to gravitate towards shopping centres and other commercially attractive sites. But while in theory a single monopolistic bank might wish to adopt a different branching policy, in practice it would remain circumscribed by the impossibility of closing or moving more than a small proportion of the branches which already exist (see chapter 14).

Bank profits

20.30   Two separate arguments about clearing bank profits have found their way into the debate about bank nationalisation. The first is that bank profits are too high ('obscene' being the favourite epithet). The second is the more sophisticated argument that bank profits are largely 'non-functional', in the sense that they depend heavily on factors outside the banks' own control. The banks' full response to the first argument has already been provided in chapter 15. The main points to stress here are that bank profits are inevitably highly cyclical; that, taking one year with another, they represent no more than a reasonable return on the resources the banks employ; and that in recent years a major proportion of reported bank profits has been necessary simply to offset the erosion through inflation of the real value of those resources.

20.31   It is true that in any one year the banks' profits will tend to be more heavily influenced by changes in monetary conditions, loan demand and other external factors than by actions initiated within the banks themselves. These external influences, however, are reflected primarily in short-term changes in the level of bank profits rather than in their absolute level or in their long-term growth trend. In the longer term it is unquestionably possible for one bank to perform better than another, particularly through the ancillary services it chooses to develop at home and abroad. And while in the short term external factors may limit a bank's capacity to make profits, they are less able to limit its capacity to make losses, as the contrasting bad debt experiences of different banks showed all too clearly in 1974. More important, the profit discipline helps ensure that the banks provide efficiently and effectively a range of services that the public actually want.

Bank supervision and regulation

20.32   Throughout the world it is generally recognised that the public interest requires a country's banking system to be sound, effective and responsible. This is reflected in the extensive supervision and regulation to which banks are subject: indeed, it is unusual for any other sector of a country's economy to be as closely controlled as its banks. The controls to which banks are subject can be divided into three closely related groups. First there are those which ensure that their actions are consistent with the government's overall economic policy objectives. Then there are those designed to influence the detailed allocation and cost of bank credit or the extent of the banks' competition with other institutions. Finally there are those which seek to ensure the health and solvency of the banking system and the protection of bank depositors.

20.33   In the first category fall reserve requirements and other instruments of monetary policy, discussed in chapter 6, together with exchange control regulations. In the second category fall detailed lending guidelines and 'suasion' as well as any direct controls that may be applied to the interest rates paid and received by the banks, also discussed in chapter 6. In the third category fall prudential controls on the capital adequacy and liquidity of the banking system, discussed in chapter 5. In the case of the British banking system, many of the prudential controls currently exercised in a relatively informal manner will be made explicit and formal with the passage of legislation on the licensing and supervision of banks and deposit-taking institutions. If closer controls over the banks were thought to be necessary in other contexts, it would always be possible to invoke the powers of direction extended to the Bank of England in 1946 but never yet used.

20.34   *Banking and Finance* began with a quotation from *The Banker* about the crisis in the City in 1974, and there were enough references to this subject elsewhere in the document to imply a clear association between the health of the banking system and the case for state ownership, even though this association was never formally spelt out. It is therefore necessary to emphasise that the four clearing banks which it has been proposed to nationalise have never been other than fully solvent and capable of meeting all their obligations. Such losses on individual loans as they did incur were well contained within their own resources. Many of these losses arose in any case from the banks' involvement, in the public interest, in the 'lifeboat operation' and the rescue of the Scottish Co-operative Society's banking department. State ownership is no guarantee against financial difficulties. The answer to the problems of 1974 lies rather in the closer supervision of all banks and deposit-taking institutions, which the Bank of England has already undertaken and which will in due course be given formal expression in law.

20.35   An important point about the panoply of controls is that the authorities already enjoy – actually or potentially – most of the powers to influence the course of banking activity that the proponents of nationalisation appear to be advocating. It is simply not necessary to nationalise the banks in order to achieve a greater degree of official control over the direction of bank credit. Indeed, the lesson of foreign banking systems seems to be that there is little correlation between the formal ownership of a country's major banks and their responsiveness to official controls and directives. Thus the nationalised French banks may well enjoy greater independence in their lending activities than the privately-owned Japanese banks.

20.36   If the advocates of nationalisation intend not only to nationalise the banks but also to increase the range and severity of controls to which the banks are subject, then they are proposing to place in the hands of the state an instrument of massive economic power. As long as the banks are private sector institutions whose activities are closely controlled by the public sector, and as long as they are not owned by a single shareholder, there will always be a reasonable assurance that their power will not be abused. Nationalisation as envisaged by the authors of *Banking and Finance* would largely remove that safeguard.

The banks' lending record

20.37   It is on the alleged deficiencies in the clearing banks' lending record that the case for nationalisation has been chiefly based. The more important allegations are considered in the contexts of the financing of industrial investment, property lending and lending terms and conditions. But first, it should be reiterated that the total amount that the banks have available to lend to their customers is largely a function of the savings habits of the community and of official monetary policy. The actual amount that they lend at any one time is determined primarily by their customers. (Manufacturing companies have latterly been borrowing less than half the amounts that the banks have agreed to lend them.) The banks believe it would be neither appropriate nor prudent for them to 'force-feed' their customers by pressing them to borrow funds which they had not themselves requested, or to lend to customers who would otherwise be turned down on grounds of creditworthiness.

20.38   The clearing banks play a major role in financing Britain's industrial investment. Many of the financing facilities which they have developed in recent years, such as term lending and leasing, make an important direct contribution to fixed investment, while a high proportion of their conventional overdrafts is applied to industry's need to invest in stocks and work in progress. (These various financing activities are described in detail in chapter 8.) Given the extent of this involvement, the banks naturally share the widespread concern about the quality and effectiveness of Britain's capital stock and the level of new investment. However, they believe that the evidence does not suggest that the availability of bank finance has been a remotely significant factor in holding investment back. As argued in chapter 7, they believe that the poor and uncertain rates of return anticipated from new investments have been the major inhibition. They also endorse the view of the Bank of England, expressed recently to the National Economic Development Council, that the financial system is capable of accommodating a considerable upturn in industry's demand for investment finance. Certainly the banks do not envisage any problems arising as far as the provision of short and medium-term finance is concerned under even the most optimistic assumptions about possible future investment levels. As for long-term debt and equity finance, the banks believe that the institutions and markets involved in providing such funds will also be equal to the demands of industry, although certain suggestions for improvements are made in chapter 1. However, this is a field in which the banks themselves have only a minor role to play, given the structure of their deposits and the extent of their existing lending activities and commitments.

20.39   Those who criticise the banks for lending too little for industrial investment usually also criticise them for lending too much to property companies and other financial institutions. It must therefore be stressed that there is no evidence to suggest that clearing bank lending to property companies, or any other borrowers, has ever been at the expense of manufacturing industry; the only period in recent years in which the banks' lending to property companies increased significantly (1972–74) was also the period when the officially-inspired growth in the monetary resources of the banking system greatly outstripped manufacturing industry's demand for finance. Inevitably the money found its way elsewhere, as described in appendix D. Yet even in its peak years of 1973–75, lending to the property sector never exceeded 9 per cent of the clearing bank groups' total advances to UK residents (see table 61 on page 277). Most of this was in any case non-speculative and served important economic and social purposes. Latterly the figure has been held below 8 per cent, in compliance with official requests for restraint in lending to the financial sector. It is hard to see how nationalisation as such would make any difference to the quality of a bank's lending decisions. Indeed it is salutary to remember that some ill-judged lending has been undertaken in the past by financial institutions in the public and mutual sectors as well as in the private sector.

20.40   A further element of the case for nationalising the clearing banks is that the terms on which they lend are said to be inappropriate to the needs of their customers. Three charges in particular are made: that bank interest rates are too high; that the banks lend too little on medium term; and that they are unwilling to accept high enough gearing ratios on the part of their customers. On the first charge, the banks would reiterate that the general level of interest rates in the economy is determined primarily by the actions of the monetary authorities and by market forces. The narrowness of their net lending margins over the cost of funds to them has been described in chapter 8. The banks believe that they have adequately answered the second charge by showing that by the end of 1976 term lending accounted for 40 per cent of their total UK non-personal lending, or 47 per cent if lending under the special export finance schemes is included (see table 59 on page 276). Though the absolute volume of term lending may continue to grow, it is hard to see how this percentage could increase much further without unduly straining the liquidity of the banking system, given that the overwhelming majority of the banks' deposits are repayable on demand or short notice. If a need for more term lending is felt, it may be necessary to consider introducing some form of refinance facility as a safeguard against liquidity problems; it will certainly not be necessary to nationalise the banks.

20.41 The argument about gearing ratios is rather more complicated. Obviously there is no single figure below which it is perfectly safe to lend to a company and above which it is wholly imprudent. Yet in practice a line must be drawn somewhere if banks and their borrowers alike are to remain solvent. (The financial crisis of 1974 was a graphic illustration of the dangers of over-gearing.) The real question is therefore whether the gearing ratios which borrowers are expected to observe are reasonable and appropriate. This question cannot be answered by drawing superficial comparisons with gearing ratios in other countries of the kind contained in *Banking and Finance*. Comparisons such as these tend to ignore the major differences in the various countries' financial institutions and markets discussed in chapter 19, and in particular the extent to which companies in different countries have enjoyed access to equity finance: high gearing ratios are largely a reflection of underdeveloped equity markets. The comparisons also ignore major differences in accounting conventions – notably those relating to the valuation of a company's assets. Thus a further explanation of the apparently high gearing ratios in several other countries is the fact that the companies in question have not valued their assets fully and have therefore understated the real value of their capital and reserves.

20.42 In any case, comparisons have tended to concentrate on historical gearing ratios. More relevant, perhaps, are the incremental gearing ratios of companies in different countries – that is, the ratios between the debt and equity elements in the additional finance they raise in any one year. The evidence suggests that Britain has been far less out of line with other countries on the basis of these ratios than *Banking and Finance* would lead one to believe. Indeed the differences between the various major countries are probably less important nowadays than the difference from one year to another. Thus most major countries shared in the tendency for incremental gearing ratios to increase substantially in the face of the exceptional financial circumstances of 1974.

20.43 The banks believe that the gearing ratios which they are prepared to accept when lending to industry are in general no more restrictive – and often less so – than those which industry imposes on itself. There will inevitably always be some companies which are anxious to borrow more than their bankers are prepared to lend. But they constitute a tiny minority of the banks' total corporate customers. In most cases the banks would willingly lend more if their customers felt it made commercial sense for them to borrow more. Nationalisation of the banks would do nothing to encourage customers to seek additional finance. Nor would it affect the considerations of prudence which lead companies and their bankers to set limits to the amounts borrowed. It might increase the number of occasions when those considerations were overruled for non-commercial reasons. But the banks submit that this would be in nobody's long-term interest, least of all that of the borrowers themselves.

Standards of customer service

20.44   The advocates of nationalisation rarely go so far as to say that standards of service would actually be improved by state ownership; but they frequently imply that present standards are poor. This is a subjective matter on which only the banks' own customers can pass valid judgement. It is therefore relevant to note that a research study conducted in 1976* showed that over 80 per cent of the clearing banks' own customers, and over 70 per cent of the public at large, expressed favourable opinions and impressions of the banking industry as against 5 per cent or less whose views were unfavourable. Of the 13 industries on which views were sought, no other did so well. The banks were also the most highly-rated industry in terms of the standards of their customer service, though respondents generally believed that those standards would fall if the banks were nationalised. Also relevant are the results of a survey of industrial companies conducted by the Confederation of British Industries, quoted in its evidence to the Committee (paragraph 92), which showed that 78 per cent of respondents assessed the clearing banks' services as 'good' and only 1 per cent as 'bad'.

20.45   While bank staff could be expected to do everything possible to maintain standards of service after nationalisation, the banks share their customers' ap-prehension that standards would fall nevertheless. At best there would be a general dulling of the banks' competitive edge which has helped to ensure a high degree of customer satisfaction in the past. At worst there would be the danger that a nationalised bank would prove to be less punctilious in its protection of confidential information about its customers' affairs when dealing with other parts of the public sector. The banks' customers include, of course, a substantial proportion of overseas companies, institutions and individuals, who perhaps enjoy even more opportunities than the UK customers to take their banking business elsewhere. It is to be feared that nationalisation would alienate many of them.

Extent of public ownership abroad

20.46   The case for nationalisation as stated in *Banking and Finance* is based to a considerable extent on a report presented by the Labour Party's research department in 1975 under the title *Comparison of Banking Systems in the EEC: the Policy Implications*. The central arguments of this report were that, with the exception of the Irish Republic, the United Kingdom has the least degree of public or co-operative ownership of banks of any member of the EEC; and that there was less real competition and consumer choice in the United Kingdom than there was among financial institutions on the continent. The first of these assertions is highly debatable, depending as it does on the precise definition of a bank. The reason why the public and co-operative sector in UK banking appears so small is that most of the public and co-operative institutions involved in providing banking and related services in the United Kingdom are not officially defined as banks at all. These include the National Savings Bank, the Trustee Savings Banks, the National Giro, the building

---

Public Attitudes to Nationalisation, 1976. (A research study conducted for the Committee of London Clearing Bankers by Market and Opinion Research International.)

societies and (in the case of lending activities) public bodies such as the National Enterprise Board and central and local government.

20.47 In a report commissioned by the clearing banks in 1976 from the Inter-Bank Research Organisation *, all the deposit-taking institutions in 10 major countries were divided into three groups – private, mutual/municipal and public. A similar three-way division was made between all institutions engaged in lending in the seven countries for which adequate data were available. The results showed that in only one respect was the Labour Party research department's judgement even partly fair. It was true that the public sector share in deposit taking was smaller in the United Kingdom than in most other EEC countries, though not as low as in Denmark and only a little lower than in Germany and the Netherlands. However, the share of the mutual/municipal sector was towards the top of the EEC range. So was the share of the private sector, though this was exceeded by the private sector figures for Denmark and the Netherlands. The private sector share in Japan, a country also mentioned frequently in the Labour Party papers, was of identical size to the United Kingdom. The private sector share in the United States, a country hardly mentioned at all, was much larger.

20.48 If one turns from deposit taking to lending, one finds the Labour Party research department's claim to be even less valid. The public sector accounts for a significantly larger share of lending in the United Kingdom than in countries such as Germany and Japan, though the share is smaller than in France and Italy. (In France, significantly, up to 25 per cent of the shares in the 'big three' nationalised banks are now in the process of being sold by the state.) The UK private sector share is correspondingly smaller than in Germany and Japan, and larger than in France and Italy. (Of the seven countries reviewed, the private sector was largest and the public sector smallest in the United States.) Nationalising the four major London clearing banks would inflate the public sector share in both deposit-taking and lending to the point where it would be among the largest of any of the industrialised countries. The United Kingdom would be moving out of line with the generality of other developed countries, not into line with them.

Concentration of banking power

20.49 The claim that banking power in the United Kingdom is far more concentrated than in any other member of the EEC can be challenged on several scores. In the first place, this claim also ignores the wide variety of institutions which may not be termed 'banks' but which offer deposit-taking or lending services. Indeed at one point in the Labour Party paper it is stated that the four main clearing banks have over 95 per cent of the deposits of London clearing banks – an irrelevant fact, presumably intended to convey an impression of undue concentration. However, even the less extreme claim that the clearing banks as a whole have over 70 per cent of all bank deposits misses the point that the banking sector itself accounts for only about half of total domestic deposits. The impression of greater concentration in the United Kingdom than elsewhere is also partly due to the regional factors which prevent banks from operating on a national basis in many other countries, a point discussed in chapter 19.

20.50 Taking all these factors into account, there is no evidence that banking power is more highly concentrated in the United Kingdom than elsewhere. The

Banking Comparisons: a study of public ownership and banking activities in major industrial countries.

clearing banks' share of all deposits is higher than the share of the corresponding large deposit banks in some countries (notably Germany, Japan and the United States), not much different from certain others (such as France and Italy) and lower than others (notably Belgium and the Netherlands). Yet however great the concentration of power in the hands of the big four clearing banks, nationalisation would certainly do nothing to reduce it, unless of course the result was a shift of business away from the nationalised banks towards the smaller, non-nationalised banks, which is hardly what would be intended. The only way in which the balance of banking power is likely to be seriously altered in the future will be through the development of existing institutions such as the foreign banks in London, the Giro and the savings banks. As the clearing banks have frequently stated, they have no objection to vigorous competition for market share from any quarter, provided it is on fair terms.

Banking structures and economic performance

20.51   The true nature of the relationship between a country's banking system and its economic performance is central not only to the question of bank nationalisation but also to the more general debate about the role of banks in the economy with which this submission is concerned. At issue is whether the ownership and control of a country's banks, the ways in which they are organised and the terms on which they lend have a significant influence on the country's rate of growth, level of investment and other aspects of its economic performance. The clearing banks do not deny that the organisation and activities of a country's financial institutions are relevant to its economic performance. But they do repudiate strongly the crude assumption that differences in national economic performance can be attributed directly to financial differences, and that changes in financial arrangements would therefore have predictable and beneficial economic effects.

20.52   In fact, the various combinations of financial system and economic record to be found abroad differ widely to the point where the connection between the two may seem almost random. Thus countries with financial systems as relatively similar as France and Italy can show totally contrasting economic records, while countries with relatively successful post-war economic records (such as France and Germany) may have totally contrasting financial systems. Critics of the UK system seem not to recognise that there are as many differences between the systems of most other major countries as there are between the systems of any one of them and the United Kingdom. Certainly there is nothing to suggest a causal connection between the public ownership of banks and a national record of economic success. Italy is a good example of a country where the major banks are publicly owned and where the economic record has been a poor one; Japan and Germany – though often mentioned by the advocates of nationalisation – are in fact economically successful countries where the public sector in banking is relatively small.

20.53   The belief that nationalising the banks would be an aid to economic performance is not only misconceived but also counterproductive, since it serves to divert attention from the real problems which underlie the poor economic performance of the United Kingdom. The banks hope that in future more effort will be devoted to solving these problems and less to passing the blame for them.

Chronology of events affecting banking 1957–1977

This appendix presents a chronology of the more important events relating to the banking and financial environment and the activities of the clearing banks between 1957 and 1977. Four main types of event are covered: major economic events; banking and financial controls; developments in the clearing banks; and various other institutional developments. In general, the events listed follow this order, rather than the order in which they occurred during the year.

The economic developments covered include specific events, such as the introduction of incomes policies and major tax changes, and landmarks in the performance of the economy, such as peaks and troughs in the current account of the balance of payments, the rate of unemployment and (later in the period) the rate of inflation. In the case of banking and financial controls, attention is focused primarily on those measures which have affected a wide range of institutions or have been of particular concern to the clearing banks. However, the more important changes in controls over other groups of institutions are also covered. Developments in the clearing banks include major changes in their organisation and structure and the introduction of important new services. Of course, there have been many instances where a particular development has occurred within the different clearing banks at different times; in order to prevent the chronology from becoming unnecessarily long, only the first innovation by a clearing bank in a particular field is normally mentioned. Interest rate movements over the period are shown in diagram 25 on page 231 rather than described in the following text.

Many of the developments listed are described fully in the main body of the submission. It has therefore been felt unnecessary to go into any great detail when covering them here.

1957

The Treaty of Rome was signed, establishing the European Economic Community.

The Radcliffe Committee to enquire into the workings of the monetary system was formed.

Quantitative lending controls were introduced for the London and Scottish clearing banks; medium-term export credits guaranteed by the ECGD were excluded.

The Cheques Act was passed.

1958

The external convertibility of sterling was restored.

The special deposit scheme for the London and Scottish clearing banks was announced.

Companies were allowed to borrow up to £50,000 (previously £10,000) without obtaining official consent.

Credit ceilings were suspended.

Official restrictions on hire purchase and rental terms were removed.

Most of the clearing banks made substantial investments in the finance house sector. Midland acquired Forward Trust, National Provincial acquired North Central Wagon and Finance and a number of other clearing banks took minority interests in the sector.

Most of the clearing banks introduced personal loan facilities.

1959

The cyclical peak in the rate of unemployment was reached.

The report of the Radcliffe Committee was published.

Control of borrowing and of new capital issues was suspended.

The National Bank of Scotland, a subsidiary of Lloyds, merged with the Commercial Bank of Scotland, with Lloyds having a substantial minority stake in the resulting institution, National Commercial Bank of Scotland.

1960

The current account balance moved sharply into deficit.

The European Free Trade Association was established.

Special deposits were called for the first time.

Hire purchase terms control was reintroduced.

The Payment of Wages Act was passed, facilitating the use of cheques for this purpose.

The clearing banks established the centralised credit clearing.

1961

The cyclical trough in the rate of unemployment was reached.

A pay pause was introduced and remained in operation until the spring of 1962. It was followed by 'guiding lights' for the next two years.

There was a further call for special deposits, the impact of which was intended to fall on advances. The banks were asked to restrain personal and property lending.

Refinancing facilities were introduced for the clearing banks' medium-term export credits guaranteed by the ECGD.

The clearing banks began to establish computer centres and introduced magnetic ink coding for cheque clearing.

The Trustee Investments Act, which widened the investment powers of the pension funds in particular, was passed.

1962

The current account balance moved into surplus.

Outstanding special deposits were repaid.

Formal selective restrictions on bank lending were withdrawn though the banks were asked to favour exports and regional development.

The clearing banks began to extend certain medium-term export credits at fixed rates of interest.

National Provincial acquired District Bank.

The Building Societies Act was passed.

1963

The cyclical peak in the rate of unemployment was reached.

The minimum liquidity ratio for the clearing banks was reduced from 30 to 28 per cent.

The Protection of Depositors Act laid down restrictions on advertising for deposits.

Midland joined in the establishment of the European Advisory Committee (later EBIC), an association of leading European banks and the first of the 'banking clubs'.

1964

In conditions of a substantial balance of payments deficit and rising inflation, an import surcharge was imposed on manufactured and semi-manufactured goods. This was in operation until 1966.

The clearing banks were asked to reduce the rate of increase in their lending. Selective lending guidance was reintroduced and the banks were asked to give priority to exports, manufacturing investment and regional development. Lending for property development, hire purchase and professional and personal needs was to be restrained.

Midland participated in the establishment of Midland and International Banks, the first London-based consortium bank. Subsequently other clearing banks made similar investments.

Clearing banks introduced industrial leasing facilities.

1965

The government laid down a $3-3\frac{1}{2}$ per cent norm for the average annual rate of increase in money incomes and established the National Board for Prices and Incomes (PIB).

Special deposits were reintroduced.

Credit ceilings were reintroduced and, for the first time, acceptance facilities and purchases of bills were included. Later in the year the banks were asked to restrain the provision of finance for imports as well as favouring exports.

The clearing banks agreed to extend the range of export transactions for which they would provide fixed-rate credits.

Midland acquired Northern Bank, a Northern Irish bank; in 1970 it was merged with the Belfast Banking Company, another Midland subsidiary.

The clearing banks began to introduce cheque cards.

The Trustee Savings Banks (TSBs) introduced a current account facility.

1966

The cyclical trough in the rate of unemployment was reached; a small surplus was recorded on the current account balance.

Following the sterling crisis, a statutory freeze on prices and incomes was introduced for six months from July. This was followed by a further six months of 'severe restraint' and then by a series of guidelines.

Selective employment tax was introduced.

The Bank of England stressed to the clearing banks the need for early and substantial reductions in non-priority lending. Two further priority lending categories were announced – productive investment in agriculture and temporary bridging finance for house purchase.

The clearing banks agreed to provide short-term export credits (up to two years) guaranteed by the ECGD at Bank rate.

Barclays launched the Barclaycard credit card operation.

Lloyds Bank Unit Trust Managers was established, the first of a number of moves by clearing banks into the unit trust field.

National Commercial Bank of Scotland acquired the English business of the National Bank: its Irish business was acquired by the Bank of Ireland.

Lloyds acquired the National Bank of New Zealand.

Dollar certificates of deposit were first issued in London.

The Post Office Savings Bank (National Savings Bank) introduced investment accounts.

The PIB report on building societies rejected the claim that the societies needed higher interest margins.

1967

The current account balance moved into substantial deficit. This, together with heavy speculative selling of sterling, culminated in a devaluation of 14.3 per cent.

The clearing banks agreed to provide additional lending facilities for projects in development areas; lending for housebuilding was named as a further priority category.

Credit ceilings for the clearing banks were suspended (April) and then re-introduced (November). Export and medium-term shipbuilding credits were excluded from the ceilings.

The clearing banks agreed to provide fixed-rate medium-term credits to domestic shipowners buying ships in the United Kingdom.

The Companies Act established the categories of section 123 banks exempted from the provisions of the Moneylenders Acts and section 127 banks exempted from the Protection of Depositors Act.

The PIB report on clearing bank charges recommended the termination of the interest rate agreements, and indicated that the authorities would not object to further clearing bank mergers.

A number of clearing banks established 'bidding' subsidiaries to take deposits and make loans outside the banks' interest rate agreements around this time.

The clearing banks began to introduce cash dispensers.

1968

After rising rapidly for two years, the rate of unemployment stabilised.

The import deposits scheme was introduced. This was in operation until 1970.

Export and shipbuilding credits were brought within the credit ceilings (May) but subsequently excluded again (November).

Barclays and Lloyds announced that they intended to merge and bid for Martins. The Monopolies Commission reported that a merger between Barclays and Lloyds would be against the public interest, but did not object to Martins joining with either of the other banks. Subsequently Martins was acquired by Barclays and in the following year the businesses were merged.

National Westminster was established with the merger of District, National Provincial and Westminster.

Royal Bank of Scotland and National Commercial Bank of Scotland combined to form National and Commercial Banking Group. The business of National Commercial Bank was merged with that of Royal Bank.

The clearing banks set up the Inter-Bank Computer Bureau (IBCB) for the exchange of bank and customer tapes. Also bank branches began to be linked to computer centres. (In 1972 the IBCB operation was incorporated as Bankers' Automated Clearing Services.)

Sterling certificates of deposit were first issued.

The National Giro opened for business.

1969

The current account balance moved into substantial surplus.

The Chancellor laid down a ceiling for domestic credit expansion in his 'letter of intent' to the IMF.

Following a marked increase in advances, the Bank of England imposed a 'fine' on the clearing banks by halving the rate of interest paid on special deposits until 1970.

New arrangements for refinancing fixed-rate export and shipbuilding credits were introduced.

The PIB report on pay in the London clearing banks was published.

Barclays sold British Linen Bank to the Bank of Scotland in exchange for a 35 per cent shareholding in the latter.

The London clearing banks ceased to open on Saturdays.

A standard reciprocal cheque card was introduced by the clearing banks (except Barclays) and certain other banks.

Save As You Earn was introduced.

1970

The banks were asked to direct any increased lending towards the finance of exports and of production and investment which would contribute to the balance of payments.

The PIB report on overtime in the London clearing banks was published.

The authorities gave their approval for the Eurocheque scheme.

The National and Commercial Banking Group merged Williams Deacon's, Glyn Mills and the National Bank to form Williams & Glyn's.

National Westminster acquired Lombard Banking, which it subsequently integrated with North Central Finance to form Lombard North Central.

The clearing banks disclosed full profits for the first time.

The clearing banks began to expand their medium-term lending to industry at about this time.

The National Giro introduced a personal loans facility in co-operation with Mercantile Credit.

1971

There was a marked increase in the rate of inflation.

Against a background of a substantial inflow of funds, sterling was floated. A new fixed parity was established later in the year.

The system of monetary and credit controls was completely overhauled with the introduction of *Competition and Credit Control* (CCC).

Decimal currency was introduced.

Hire purchase terms control was suspended.

The discount houses were permitted to act both as principals and brokers in foreign currency deposits.

The banks were prohibited from paying interest on additional sterling deposits from outside the sterling area between August and December.

The report of the Crowther Committee recommended extensive changes in the law governing consumer credit.

The clearing banks terminated most of their interest rate agreements.

The clearing banks introduced new personal lending facilities.

Barclays DCO became a wholly-owned subsidiary of Barclays and its name was changed to Barclays Bank International.

Lloyds Bank Europe was merged with the Bank of London and South America (BOLSA) with Lloyds having a controlling interest in the resulting institution, Lloyds and Bolsa International.

Barclays established its business advisory service for small firms, and subsequently other clearing banks introduced similar services.

The Page Committee to review national savings was formed.

The government decided to retain the National Giro but to reshape the service and to increase charges.

The government announced that the tax reserve certificate scheme was to be withdrawn by stages.

The report of the Bolton Committee on small firms concluded that there was no institutional deficiency in the sources of funds for small firms but that many firms had insufficient knowledge of the sources of funds available to them.

1972

After reaching a new post-war peak, the rate of unemployment started to decline.

Sterling joined the EEC's new system of linked exchange rates ('the snake') in May but left it in June and was allowed to float. Exchange controls were extended to the overseas sterling area.

The government introduced a 90-day statutory standstill on most increases in pay, prices, rents and dividends, which was followed by further statutory controls. (Controls on pay increases were abandoned in 1974.)

Qualitative guidance on bank lending was reintroduced. The Bank of England asked banks to restrain lending to property companies and for financial transactions not associated with the maintenance and expansion of industry. (In 1973 restraint was extended to personal lending.)

Bank rate was replaced by minimum lending rate (MLR) determined by a formula calculated from Treasury bill rate.

The Bank of England made its first call for special deposits since the introduction of CCC.

New refinancing facilities for export and shipbuilding credits allowed the clearing banks to refinance lending in excess of 18 per cent of their current accounts, and to receive a return broadly in line with market rates.

The Bank of England relaxed the conditions under which other institutions could take participations in accepting houses.

Midland took a controlling interest in Thomas Cook (now wholly owned).

Lloyds, Midland, National Westminster and Williams & Glyn's launched the Access credit card, through the Joint Credit Card Company established in the previous year.

Lloyds introduced the first on-line cash dispensers.

Some of the larger finance houses were recognised as banks by the Bank of England.

The amalgamation of the London and main provincial stock exchanges was announced.

1973

After falling rapidly, the rate of unemployment reached a trough towards the end of the year and started to rise sharply; the current account balance moved into deficit.

The United Kingdom joined the EEC.

The government established the Pay Board and the Price Commission.

Value added tax and the unified system of income tax were introduced. Purchase tax and selective employment tax were abolished.

Many commodity prices increased sharply. In particular the first in the series of major increases in oil prices was posted.

Instead of having to hold at least 50 per cent of borrowed funds in defined assets, the discount houses were obliged henceforth to limit holdings of non-defined assets to a maximum of 20 times their own funds.

The banks were asked to limit the interest paid on deposits of less than £10,000 to 9½ per cent in order to protect the building societies.

It was announced that during the third stage of the counter-inflation policy no interest would be paid on a portion of the banks' special deposits.

For the first time the Bank of England suspended temporarily the formula by which MLR is calculated and raised the rate to 13 per cent. At the same time the Bank 'encouraged' the clearing banks to raise their base rates.

Hire purchase terms control was reintroduced, and restrictions were imposed on the clearing banks' credit card operations.

The Bank of England introduced the supplementary special deposits scheme (the 'corset').

The EEC directive on freedom of establishment and freedom to supply services for banks and other financial institutions was passed.

Midland acquired the outstanding capital of Montagu Trust, thus making the accepting house Samuel Montagu a wholly-owned subsidiary.

Lloyds and Bolsa International became a wholly-owned subsidiary of Lloyds and its name was changed in 1974 to Lloyds Bank International.

A rescue operation was launched for the Scottish Co-operative Society banking department.

The secondary banking crisis began and the lifeboat operation was launched.

Finance for Industry was established as the holding company for Finance Corporation for Industry and the Industrial and Commercial Finance Corporation, and new capital was subscribed by the shareholders.

The building societies received an £18 million bridging grant from the government to enable them to limit the increase in mortgage rates, and the government and the building societies established a joint advisory committee.

The Page Committee Report recommended extensive changes in the organisation of national savings and greater freedom for the TSBs.

A number of TSBs introduced a personal loan facility in co-operation with a finance house; the Central Trustee Savings Bank was set up.

A Labour Party report recommended that a single publicly-owned banking corporation should take over the London and Scottish clearing banks and the British overseas banks.

The British Bankers' Association was reorganised and its membership extended following entry into the EEC.

1974

There was a sharp increase in the rate of inflation, a record deficit on current account and a fall in real gross domestic product (GDP).

The miners' strike led, temporarily, to a three-day working week.

Corporation tax relief on increases in stocks was introduced.

The Consumer Credit Act was passed.

The Bank of England set up the Banking and Money Market Division, thus strengthening its supervisory role.

Barclays and Lloyds both acquired commercial banks in the United States.

The clearing banks arranged a $2,500 million eurocurrency loan for the government. (A further $1,500 million was arranged in 1977.)

The clearing banks and Bank of England, together with certain other institutions, agreed to enable Finance for Industry to make up to £1 billion available in medium-term loans for productive investment.

The government broadly accepted the Page Committee's recommendations for the TSBs which began the process of merging into large regional units.

The Co-operative Bank and the Central Trustee Savings Bank became functional members of the Bankers' Clearing House.

1975

There was a further acceleration in the rate of inflation, a very large rise in the rate of unemployment and a further fall in real GDP.

The Industry Act provided for planning agreements and established the National Enterprise Board to set up industrial enterprises, assist existing ones and extend public ownership into profitable manufacturing industry.

Pay guidelines were reintroduced, supported by sanctions.

The 'corset' was suspended and the limitation on deposit rates was removed.

The Bank of England published the text of a paper agreed with the London and Scottish clearing banks on liquidity and capital adequacy.

Mercantile Credit became a wholly-owned subsidiary of Barclays.

A White Paper on the development of the National Giro outlined plans to allow the Giro to provide a wider range of banking services, and the Giro started to provide personal loans from its own resources.

The TSBs established a central board.

In response to an initiative by the Bank of England, a working party was set up by the investing institutions to study finance for industry.

Index-linked national savings certificates for people of retirement age and index-linked SAYE facilities were introduced.

1976

Unemployment rose further but there was a fall in the rate of inflation.

Tax cuts in the budget were made contingent on TUC agreement to the government's pay policy.

Ceilings for domestic credit expansion and the public sector borrowing requirement were set out in the 'letter of intent' to the IMF. The Chancellor also announced a target for the growth of the money supply (M3): this practice was continued in 1977.

The first North Sea oil flowed ashore.

A White Paper foreshadowed arrangements for the licensing and supervision of deposit-taking institutions and a deposit protection fund.

The clearing banks agreed to raise the threshold at which they could refinance their export and shipbuilding credits. (There have since been further increases.)

The 'corset' was reintroduced.

The sterling financing of third-country trade by UK banks was prohibited.

Restrictive trade practices legislation was extended to banking services.

Equity Capital for Industry was established.

The Trustee Savings Bank Act and The Post Office (Banking Services) Act prepared the way for the TSBs and the Giro to offer fuller banking services.

The Labour Party's National Executive Committee published *Banking and Finance*, calling for the public ownership of the four largest London clearing banks, seven insurance companies and a merchant bank. This proposal was endorsed by the Labour Party conference.

The Treasury began to study the possibility of a merger between the National Giro and the National Savings Bank.

It was announced that a committee would be formed to study the role and functioning of financial institutions.

1977 (to November)

The current account balance moved into surplus and there was a further fall in the rate of inflation.

The system of price controls was overhauled and the Price Commission began an enquiry into bank charges.

Arrangements were made for more ECGD lending to be undertaken in foreign currency rather than in sterling.

The 'corset' was suspended.

The TSBs began to provide personal loans from their own resources.

The government issued a stock to be paid for in instalments and a floating-rate stock, both for the first time. Floating-rate stocks were also issued by local authorities and companies.

The government's consultative document on housing policy recommended that the building societies should increase their stabilisation funds, be more flexible in their interest-rate policy and be prepared to raise money-market loans.

Bank rate/minimum lending rate 1957–1977   Diagram 25

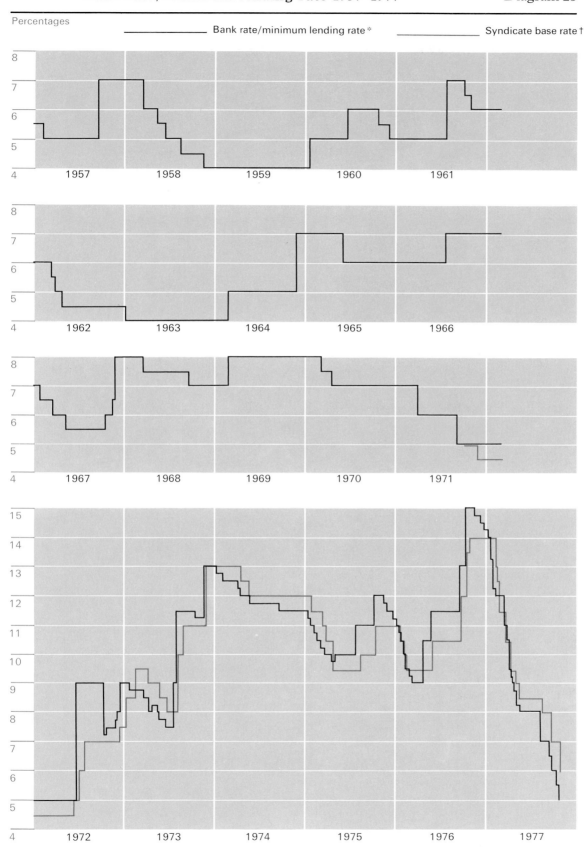

*Following the introduction of Competition and Credit Control in 1971, Bank rate ceased to be the base for the interest rate structure of the clearing banks, and it was replaced by base rate. This rate is altered only when and to the extent that each individual bank decides and does not necessarily change with MLR (formerly Bank rate).

†Because there have been periods when individual banks' base rates have been temporarily out of line, this chart shows the syndicate base rate which is applied to borrowing from the London clearing banks by nationalised industries and certain other customers.

Appendix B
Special export finance schemes

B.1 The clearing banks provide for UK exporters a series of special facilities, which are covered by guarantees given by the Export Credits Guarantee Department (ECGD) for customers who have arranged covering insurance with the department. The schemes, which are continually reviewed and amended to meet the changing needs of exporters, can be classified under two broad headings: export credit facilities and export support services.

Export credit facilities

B.2 Finance is provided either directly to the exporter, which enables him to contract with his overseas buyer on credit terms (supplier credit); or, for major capital contracts, to the overseas buyer or other approved borrower in the buyer's country (buyer credit). Short-term supplier credit is provided by either:

a. the bills or notes scheme covering credit periods of less than two years: the bank provides 100 per cent of the value of the relevant transaction; or

b. the open account scheme where the exporter supplies goods on terms from cash against documents to six months credit: the bank provides 100 per cent value against the exporter's promissory note and invoice.

An interest rate of $\frac{1}{2}$ per cent over base rate, with a minimum of $4\frac{1}{2}$ per cent, is charged to the exporter plus the normal bill collection charges, or, under the open account scheme, a charge of 50 pence per promissory note handled. Refinance arrangements do not extend to short-term schemes. An increase in the interest margin to $\frac{5}{8}$ per cent will be implemented early in 1978, and the revision of other charges is under consideration.

B.3 Medium-term supplier credit is provided to UK exporters of capital goods and services for contracts involving credit terms of two years or over. Usually 80 to 85 per cent of the contract value can be covered by credit terms (70 per cent for new ships), against a series of accepted bills of exchange or promissory notes maturing over the period involved. The interest rate is fixed at the outset by ECGD, the basic range at present being $7\frac{1}{4}$ per cent to 8 per cent depending on the overseas market and whether the term is up to or over five years. In addition a commitment fee of 1 per cent and a negotiation fee of between 1 and 2 per mille of the total credit amount are charged, supplemented in exceptional cases by a management fee of $\frac{1}{2}$ per mille per annum.

B.4 Medium and long-term buyer credit is provided directly to an overseas buyer of UK capital goods or services in two forms:

a. for single contracts of £1 million or over by finance of 80–85 per cent of the value over terms of up to five years, or possibly longer if the contract sum is in excess of £2 million;

b. lines of credit either for individual projects involving several UK suppliers, or general purpose lines for contracts between several buyers in the same country and several UK suppliers.

The interest terms and charges for sterling buyer credit are the same as for supplier credit as set out in paragraph B.3 above, but the management fee is charged in all cases. One advantage to UK exporters of buyer credit is that in approved cases progress payments at various stages of manufacture can be arranged, subject to agreement with the buyer.

B.5 Refinancing facilities for medium and long-term sterling credits are made available to the clearing banks by ECGD. Under the arrangements each clearing bank refinances fixed-rate export lending in excess of an agreed percentage of its non-interest-bearing sterling sight deposits. The percentage was fixed at 18 per cent in March 1972; subsequently it was increased to 21 per cent and more recently the banks have agreed to an increase to 24 per cent by March 1978. The ratio of a bank's unrefinanced lending to its total lending under the scheme will be established in March 1978 and this ratio will thereafter be maintained in respect of the bank's lending under the present scheme. New commitments from April 1978 will, however, qualify for re-financing only for that part relating to maturities in excess of a five-year period. The authorities have allowed access to the new scheme to other banks authorised under the Exchange Control Act and registered in the United Kingdom, but the clearing banks nevertheless expect that the total finance they carry will rise substantially.

B.6 The clearing banks receive an interest adjustment payment from ECGD when the income they receive under the fixed terms applicable to medium and long-term loans falls below current market rates, or make an interest adjustment payment to the authorities if market rates are lower than the fixed rates. The agreed formula is currently related to the average of Treasury bill rate and the banks' base rates. A variable margin is added, tapered so that smaller margins apply when the general level of interest rates is high. Under the new scheme the formula will be related to the London inter-bank offered rates for sterling.

B.7 Arrangements were introduced in 1976 for medium and long-term buyer credits to be financed in foreign currencies, predominantly US dollars and German marks, as an alternative to sterling at the discretion of ECGD. Refinance arrangements will not be available for these facilities, and while the clearing banks have indicated that they expect little difficulty in meeting requirements as forecast for the first two years, the extent of their commitment is inevitably limited by balance-sheet constraints. This scheme has also been opened to other banks in the United Kingdom as well as the clearing banks.

Export support services

B.8 Contract bonds are provided by the clearing banks, indemnified by ECGD, for overseas contracts of £1 million or over (less in the case of consultancy contracts) when the contract is on cash or near cash terms. These facilities are complementary to commercial contract bonds referred to in paragraph 13.18. Pre-shipment finance can now be provided with ECGD guarantees to approved customers in respect of overseas contracts for capital goods of £1 million or over where the manufacturing period is one year or more. In addition to direct participation in the schemes mentioned above, the specialist staffs of the clearing banks provide an advisory service to exporters. An important feature of this service is to communicate changes in regulations in overseas countries, documentation and new ECGD facilities, which in the last two years have included cover against cost escalation and the insolvency of a participant in a project.

Appendix C
North Sea oil and gas

C.1   This appendix surveys the role played by bank credit in financing North Sea development, and the contribution made by the clearing banks. It begins by giving estimates of capital expenditure in the UK sector of the North Sea, goes on to outline the oil companies' approach to finance, and concludes by describing the lending activities of the clearing banks in relation to the companies' total bank borrowing. Some indication is also given of the factors influencing the future demand for bank finance in the North Sea, and of the willingness of the banks to meet this demand. In considering the part played by the clearing banks their links of ownership with the Scottish banks should be borne in mind, since the two have in practice worked closely together in financing North Sea investment, both offshore and onshore.

C.2   One of the most widely-quoted estimates of North Sea capital expenditure is given in table 41. It shows a total for the period from 1972 to 1987 of £22.3 billion, of which £15.1 billion is in the United Kingdom and £7.2 billion in the Norwegian sector. Of the UK expenditure, £10.1 billion is being incurred on the 18 fields now under development, including the Brent gas field, and the UK part of the Frigg, Murchison and Statfjord fields, which are all on the

North Sea oil capital expenditure   Table 41
Estimated figures for fields currently under development

Figures in millions in 1977 dollar terms	1972–74	1975	1976	1977	1978	1979	1980	1981	1982	1983–87	Total	£m*
Argyll	59	23	6	5	–	–	8	–	–	–	101	
Auk	55	35	20	15	5	2	2	1	–	–	135	
Beryl	110	210	145	55	20	20	–	–	–	–	560	
Brent—oil	260	480	520	780	590	570	200	200	200	–	3,800	
—gas	–	10	30	350	490	320	200	–	–	–	1,400	
Buchan	–	23	5	10	95	47	–	–	–	–	180	
Claymore	–	90	285	145	70	30	–	–	–	–	620	
Cormorant	–	55	60	155	110	65	65	40	–	–	550	
Dunlin	–	180	180	140	80	30	60	290	–	–	960	
Forties	695	540	225	135	65	–	–	–	–	–	1,660	
Frigg	124	450	398	150	28	10	–	–	–	–	1,160	
Heather	–	20	150	145	30	65	40	–	–	–	450	
Montrose	40	105	60	45	–	–	–	–	–	–	250	
Murchison	–	27	29	70	192	220	64	72	48	20	742	
Ninian	–	350	440	650	590	370	150	100	50	–	2,700	
Piper	160	315	180	85	10	–	–	–	–	–	750	
Statfjord	–	17	36	45	23	10	12	7	–	–	150	
Tartan	–	–	–	40	185	265	130	30	–	–	650	
Thistle	–	205	305	230	110	85	65	–	–	–	1,000	
Sub-Total (UK)	**1,503**	**3,135**	**3,074**	**3,250**	**2,693**	**2,109**	**996**	**740**	**298**	**20**	**17,818 =**	**10,067**
Probable finds	–	–	–	5	465	1,275	2,500	2,390	1,030	1,195	8,860 =	5,005
Total UK	**1,503**	**3,135**	**3,074**	**3,255**	**3,158**	**3,384**	**3,496**	**3,130**	**1,328**	**1,215**	**26,678 =**	**15,072**
Ekofisk area—oil	760	885	830	580	395	160	60	35	25	140	3,870	
—gas	160	340	400	135	65	20	–	15	15	240	1,390	
Frigg	186	675	597	225	42	15	–	–	–	–	1,740	
Murchison	–	–	–	34	48	55	16	18	12	5	188	
Statfjord	–	138	284	355	182	85	98	58	–	–	1,200	
Sub-Total (Norway)	**1,106**	**2,038**	**2,111**	**1,329**	**732**	**335**	**174**	**126**	**52**	**385**	**8,388 =**	**4,739**
Probable finds	–	–	–	10	635	1,080	1,045	725	555	340	4,390 =	2,480
Total Norwegian	**1,106**	**2,038**	**2,111**	**1,339**	**1,367**	**1,415**	**1,219**	**851**	**607**	**725**	**12,778 =**	**7,219**
Total North Sea	**2,609**	**5,173**	**5,185**	**4,594**	**4,525**	**4,799**	**4,715**	**3,981**	**1,935**	**1,940**	**39,456 =**	**22,291**

Source: Wood Mackenzie.   * £1 = $1.77

Anglo-Norwegian median line. Nearly 45 per cent of this sum had already been spent by the end of 1976, and nearly 80 per cent, or £7.7 billion, was due to have been spent by the end of 1978. Since most of the post-1978 capital expenditure on these fields will be financed out of internal cash flow, this figure of £7.7 billion may be taken as a rough estimate of the capital expenditure to which bank borrowing to date can be specifically related. Development costs vary considerably according to the size of a field, its distance from the shore, and the depth of the water and the oil. The most expensive fields among those already being developed are Ekofisk and Brent (nearly £3 billion each); four others are expected to cost over £800 million each (Statfjord, Frigg, Ninian and Forties). About half the total capital expenditure is on the construction, equipment and installation of production platforms, one-third on pipelines, and one-sixth on development drilling.

C.3 Capital expenditure on UK fields under development is analysed by company in table 42. North American (nearly all US) companies account for 45 per cent of the total; if Shell is counted as 40 per cent UK and 60 per cent European then UK companies account for 34 per cent and European companies for 21 per cent. Nearly 40 per cent of all capital expenditure, or £3.7 billion, is accounted for by Shell and Esso, operating as equal partners in Auk, Brent, Cormorant and Dunlin. BP, operating mainly in Forties, accounts for another eighth, or £1.1 billion; other major UK operators are the new British National Oil Corporation, with £0.7 billion of capital expenditure committed so far, and ICI, with £277 million. (The capital expenditure total in table 42 differs from table 41, since it dates from some months earlier.) The large international oil companies have traditionally financed most of their exploration and development costs out of internally generated cash flow. Although this pattern could change in the future if project costs rise sharply, they have financed a large part of their North Sea operations in this way. BP has been an exception to this rule, borrowing almost all the originally estimated capital expenditure for Forties from the banks; but this can be explained by its exceptional need for finance for Alaska and its other world-wide operations at about the same time. In general, the smaller the company, the less it has been able to finance North Sea development out of its own cash resources.

C.4 American oil companies, and sometimes the larger non-American ones, are accustomed to supplementing their own cash flow by means of long-term bond issues, of up to 25 years, on the New York bond market. It is impossible, in view of the world-wide nature of these companies' operations, to say how much of the proceeds of such bond issues go to pay for capital expenditure in the North Sea, and how much to other oil-producing areas. In some other cases, oil companies may borrow from their banks with the intention that the funds will be used for North Sea development, but with no specific and binding commitment linking the loan to a particular oilfield. It is clear, however, that banks have been the main source of outside finance for the North Sea, apart from the US bond market and a handful of equity issues. The clearing banks and Scottish banks have played an important part, as will be explained below. The large US and Canadian international banks have also been prominent, often operating through their London branches, as have a number of smaller Texan banks with special oil experience. The American companies have, as might have been expected, made extensive use of American banks for North Sea finance. In many cases US and UK banks have joined in syndicated loans for either a US company or a UK company, or a combination of the two.

North Sea oil capital expenditure and known borrowings   Table 42

August 1977 Figures in red are percentages		Capital expenditure $ million	Known borrowings $ million	£ million	Total known borrowings in $ million treating £1 =$1.70
1. The majors	BP	1,999	486	180	792
	Shell	3,276	250	—	250
	Exxon	3,276	—	—	—
	Texaco	22	—	—	—
	Socal	454	—	—	—
	Mobil	280	—	—	—
	Gulf	523	—	—	—
	Total	**9,830** 57.2	**736**	**180**	**1,042**
2. The large US 'independents'	Amoco	77	—	—	—
	Conoco	523	—	—	—
	Amerada	170	—	—	—
	Oxy	465	325	—	325
	Getty/Skelly	438	—	—	—
	Union Oil	141	—	—	—
	Tenneco	141	—	—	—
	Allied Chemical	254	—	—	—
	Texas Eastern	150	80	—	80
	Ashland	54	—	—	—
	Total	**2,413** 14.1	**405**	—	**405**
3. Smaller US and Canadian companies	Murphy	189	50	—	50
	Odeco	189	50	—	50
	Santa Fe	163	30	—	30
	Hamilton	33	—	—	—
	Ranger	162	120	—	120
	Total	**736** 4.3	**250**	—	**250**
4. All other British companies	Burmah	81	—	—	—
	ICI	491	122	75	250
	Thomson Scottish	254	240	—	240
	Tricentrol	97	—	60	102
	Scot/Lasmo	243	—	110	187
	RTZ	23	—	—	—
	Blackfriars	12	—	—	—
	Kleinwort	2	—	—	—
	Charterhouse	10	—	—	—
	Total	**1,213** 7.1	**362**	**245**	**779**
5. British state corporations	BNOC	1,241	825	—	825
	British Gas	133	—	—	—
	Total	**1,374** 8.0	**825**	—	**825**
6. Continental European companies	Deminex	411	119	75	247
	DNO (Norwegian)	27	25	—	25
	CFP	387	407	—	407
	Elf/ERAP	773			
	Total	**1,598** 9.3	**551**	**75**	**679**
	Grand total	**$17,164m** 100.0	**$3,129m** 79	**£500m** 21	**$3,980m = £2,340m** 100

Summary	Category	Capital expenditure $ million	Total known borrowings $ million	Percentage of known borrowings to capital expenditure
	The majors	9,830	1,042	10.6
	The large US independents	2,413	405	16.8
	Smaller US and Canadian companies	736	250	34.0
	All other British companies	1,213	779	64.2
	British state corporations	1,374	825	60.0
	Continental European companies	1,598	679	42.5
	Total	**$17,164m**	**$3,980m**	**23.2**

Sources: Lloyds Bank International; Wood Mackenzie.

C.5   The UK and international banks have been ready to regard the North Sea oil and gas fields as a potential source of sound lending business, in spite of the risks. Specialist staff have been engaged and innovative lending techniques have been developed in order to handle the complex technical, corporate and legal aspects of the financing arrangements. Some borrowers have not been able to qualify for bank finance in the first instance because of the small size of their balance sheets in relation to the scale of operations; but considerable ingenuity has been displayed in facing up to these problems. In some cases, guarantors have come forward, while in others the banks have been prepared to accept repayment solely from the oil proceeds of the fields, obtaining a royalty for their acceptance of risk; in addition, certain small companies have sold out to larger ones better placed to raise the necessary funds. Bank finance has thus always been available, even during a time of sharply rising costs, in order to develop any oilfield that has been declared commercial. Not all the oil companies have chosen to borrow, although finance was available to them, and the banks' willingness to lend has thus not been fully taken up in all cases. Even the uneertainty generated in 1974/75 about the North Sea tax structure and the details of UK state participation did not seriously impair the availability of development finance. In short, the banks have been well able to meet the demands made on them to play their part in financing the North Sea.

C.6   Banks account for nearly all the North Sea financial facilities, which are estimated to amount to at least £3.6 billion so far. This comprises £3,308 million to licensees and a further identifiable £301 million to non-licensees as shown in table 43. The figure of £3.6 billion is nearly half the total of £7.7 billion of capital expenditure to the end of 1978, and 36 per cent of the £10 billion of capital expenditure on the 18 fields now under development. Publicised facilities amounting to about £2.3 billion are shown in table 42. The clearing banks, as shown by the figures in table 43, accounted as at mid-August 1977 for a cumulative total of £1.2 billion in total facilities to North Sea licensees, and their share of total North Sea lending was 36 per cent. The Scottish banks accounted for a further 4 per cent, the American banks for 36 per cent, while the remaining 24 per cent was accounted for by all other types of bank in the United Kingdom. The clearing banks' lending to North Sea licensees accounted for 3 per cent of their total lending to UK residents.

North Sea lending and commitments   Table 43

17 August 1977*	Loans outstanding				Additional firm commitments †				Total facilities extended ‡			
£ million	Sterling	Foreign currency	Total	Per cent	Sterling	Foreign currency	Total	Per cent	Sterling	Foreign currency	Total	Per cent
To licensees												
London clearing bank groups	243	230	473	28.6	95	123	218	30.8	580	621	1,201	36.3
Scottish clearing banks	24	53	77	4.7	15	28	43	6.1	47	89	136	4.1
Accepting houses, other British banks and consortium banks	41	67	108	6.5	25	24	49	6.9	78	131	209	6.3
American banks	229	410	639	38.7	32	215	247	34.9	304	884	1,188	35.9
Other overseas banks	83	272	355	21.5	40	111	151	21.3	132	442	574	17.4
Total	**619**	**1,032**	**1,651**	**100.0**	**207**	**500**	**707**	**100.0**	**1,141**	**2,167**	**3,308**	**100.0**
**To non-licensees ** **												
London clearing bank groups	32	47	79		51	1	52		87	68	155	
Scottish clearing banks	100	26	125		19	2	21		Not available			
Total												
London clearing bank groups	**274**	**277**	**551**		**146**	**124**	**270**		**667**	**689**	**1,356**	
Scottish clearing banks	**123**	**79**	**202**		**34**	**30**	**64**		Not available			

*This table covers finance provided by banks in the United Kingdom for the UK sector only of the North Sea, including loans for gas fields. Loans and commitments are included:
  a. where lending is for an identifiable project; or
  b. where it is reasonable to assume that the purpose of the borrowing is to finance North Sea commitments.

†These are in addition to actual loans outstanding and are firm commitments, based on the existence of an agreed facility or of a loan not yet fully drawn down.

‡This is the gross total of all firm facilities agreed, whether drawn or not, from the commencement of North Sea oil financing, including those that have since been repaid.

**Lending and commitments are included only in cases where loan facilities of £250,000 or over exist. Leasing arrangements are included. Figures for other banks are not available.

Source: CLCB Statistical Unit.

C.7   The clearing banks have also extended £155 million in total facilities to non-licensees identifiably engaged in offshore construction and services, which raised their total North Sea facilities extended up to August 1977 to £1,356 million. The Scottish banks had, not unexpectedly, a somewhat higher figure of loans and commitments outstanding to non-licensees, namely £146 million compared with £131 million. Loans to non-licensees, such as rig and platform construction yards, have played an important part in the revival of economic activity in Scotland. The clearing banks also lend for refineries and chemical plants designed to use North Sea oil and feedstocks, which are not included in these figures. The clearing banks have thus played the major part that might have been expected of them.

C.8   North Sea lending has been partly in sterling and partly in dollars, mostly eurodollars but in some cases domestic US dollars. It is shown in table 43 that one-third has been in sterling and two-thirds in dollars, but for the clearing banks just under half has been in sterling; some borrowers have taken part of their loans in sterling, in view of their expenditure commitments in the United Kingdom. Until recently, UK exchange control regulations provided that not more than 30 per cent of any UK fixed investment by foreign companies outside the EEC might be financed in sterling, except for investment specifically located in development areas. However, some relaxation of the regulations has recently been made, allowing the development costs of oilfields to be financed in sterling. The clearing banks were able to accommodate all North Sea sterling loans within the 'corset' limits while these were in operation. They have been able to finance eurocurrency loans for the North Sea by taking deposits in the international money market, but the development of such lending in future will depend on other claims for eurocurrency finance, such as the new export scheme, given the prudential constraints that inevitably limit the size of the banks' total eurocurrency business.

C.9   The future demand for North Sea finance depends on a variety of factors. Perhaps the most important are the future demand for oil and its price, both in absolute terms and relative to other forms of energy. These will determine the pace of future exploration and development, as well as directly influencing the cash flow from fields already in production. Obviously the demand for finance will depend on how far exploration results in new discoveries, and also on what official policies are adopted on depletion, on the allocation of new licences and on government participation – in particular, the future role of the British National Oil Corporation. BNOC has a 51 per cent share in some fifth-round blocks, which requires it to fund 51 per cent of capital expenditure. The clearing banks have taken part in BNOC's first syndicated loan of $825 million. BNOC's future financial requirements will depend on its capital expenditure and on the extent to which it draws on the national oil account. The continuing availability of the interest relief grant scheme will also be an important factor. This has encouraged oil companies to place business with UK contractors, which the clearing banks have been happy to finance.

C.10 Consideration of the wider opportunities afforded to the UK economy by North Sea oil and gas has been excluded from this appendix. But it should be clear from the rest of the submission that the clearing banks stand ready to play their part in financing the 're-industrialisation' of Britain, whether this be in sectors related to the North Sea, such as refining and chemicals, or in other sectors not directly connected with oil and gas.

Appendix D
The property market

Introduction

D.1 Fixed property, in the form of dwellings, buildings of all kinds and civil engineering works, makes up more than two-thirds of the nation's stock of capital assets. Official estimates, based on capital expenditure over many years, adjusted for depletions and retirements as assets complete their useful lives, put the net capital stock of the United Kingdom at current replacement cost at some £393 billion at the end of 1976. Of this, vehicles, ships, aircraft, plant and machinery accounted for £122 billion (31 per cent); dwellings for £118 billion (30 per cent); and other buildings and works for £152 billion (39 per cent). Ownership of this capital stock is spread across all sectors of the economy. The personal sector and local authorities held 53 per cent and 40 per cent respectively of the stock of dwellings at the end of 1976; the ownership of other buildings and works is shown in table 44. Buildings have relatively long service lives and in a developed economy net additions to this part of the nation's capital are not normally large in relation to the existing stock. Given secure rights of private property, a well-conducted property market and a sound economic and monetary framework, there is likely to be reasonable stability in the prices of residential, commercial and industrial properties and in the capital valuations based on the future income to be derived from them. In an expanding economy, property values may be expected at least to be maintained in real terms. On such expectations, confirmed by experience over many years, long-term investments for rental income and loans against the security of property could generally be regarded as soundly based.

Ownership of property
Buildings and works, excluding dwellings

Table 44

1976	£ billion	Percentage
Personal sector	13.3	8.8
Financial companies and institutions	6.1	4.0
Industrial and commercial companies	50.1	33.0
Public corporations	31.5	20.7
Central government	18.9	12.4
Local authorities	32.1	21.1
Total	**152.0**	**100.0**

Source: National Income and Expenditure 1966–76.

D.2 In a developed economy with a developed financial system, this additional aspect of property ownership – the access to further sources of finance against the security of property – is of particular importance. A stock of buildings rising steadily in value represents a steadily expanding borrowing capacity for the whole community – a resource which efficient enterprises will seek to utilise as fully as possible for financing profitable operations. The extent to which they will do so is largely limited by prudential considerations, especially the need to maintain an appropriate relationship between borrowings and proprietors' resources. Given decades of uninterrupted growth and expansion of trade and industry, high gearing may be safe and advantageous, but in the United

Kingdom sharp changes in economic conditions, affecting both the cost of borrowing and the outlook for future income, have engendered a more cautious attitude on the part of borrowers and lenders alike. Events over the past five years have fully justified this caution, as the decline in business profitability and large increases in debt interest exacerbated the problems of businesses in economic recession. The collapse of the property market dealt a particularly heavy blow to confidence, sharply reducing borrowing capacity and narrowing, and in some extreme cases eliminating, security margins on the large volume of existing lending against property.

The property market since the war

D.3   The immediate need in 1946 was to catch up with the backlog of building and maintenance of the war years and to repair the damage resulting from enemy action. Building activity, initially held back by shortages of materials, subsequently expanded rapidly and by the 1950s the reconstruction and redevelopment of cleared sites was well under way. Rising economic prosperity in the 1960s created additional demand in all sectors of the property market which was met by large-scale redevelopment of residential property, shopping and office complexes and factory estates. Long-term finance from private and institutional investors was readily available to assist this process. Indeed, by the late 1960s insurance companies and pension funds were channelling about 20 per cent of the funds coming forward for investment directly into land, property and ground rents (see table 45). Property unit trusts were also emerging. From 1971 to 1973 a major property boom developed, stimulated by the cumulative effects of the relaxation of planning controls, the removal of restrictions on bank lending and the rapid increase in the money supply.

Institutional investment in property   Table 45

Net acquisitions of land, property and ground rents

£ million Figures in red are percentages		1968	1969	1970	1971	1972	1973	1974	1975	1976
Insurance companies		119	186	197	198	131	307	405	406	450
	Percentage of total net acquisitions of investments during the year	13	23	20	16	8	18	21	16	18
Superannuation funds		93	112	97	91	121	248	305	342	513
	Percentage of total net acquisitions of investments during the year	16	19	13	10	11	18	18	14	16
Property unit trusts	Net sales of units	50	39	34	45	66	31	−6	89	60
	Net transactions in property	40	43	25	23	39	57	15	34	71

Source: Financial Statistics.

D.4   A large part of the redevelopment was undertaken by property companies capable of mustering resources on the scale required to co-ordinate clearance and construction on major sites, to see a project through the complexities of planning and other controls and, over an extended time scale, to bring it to eventual fruition for sale or for letting. These companies rely to a very great extent on long-term loans to finance their activities, and were able to obtain these on acceptable terms against the security of their property holdings so long as the property market remained strong and there was confidence that values would be maintained. This was indeed the case until 1973. The strong belief that property was the best hedge against inflation encouraged demand in all sectors; prices rose consistently, underpinned to some extent by the acceleration in the costs of new construction from an annual rate of 7 per cent in 1970 to 11 per cent in 1971, to nearly 24 per cent in 1972, and to 26 per cent in 1973. The property companies, many of which had found opportunities for extending their operations internationally, shared in the property boom which accompanied the rapid and simultaneous growth in most of the industrialised countries in 1972/73, but suffered a severe set-back in the subsequent recession when high interest rates, over-reliance on short-term borrowings, government intervention and general lack of confidence produced a collapse of property markets world-wide.

D.5   It is perhaps worth emphasising that the property boom of 1971–73 and the subsequent collapse in 1974 was not confined to the United Kingdom. In the United States, the Real Estate Investment Trusts ran into difficulties when the financial and economic climate deteriorated sharply, with consequent problems for the banks which had financed them. In most European countries, tighter credit conditions, high interest rates and specific government intervention to check the boom eventually undermined confidence in their property markets. In Australia, the property and construction industries met similar problems. Even the lesser known markets such as Singapore and Hong Kong suffered serious setbacks and the withdrawal of foreign developers. The difficulties of British property companies with interests abroad were further aggravated by the weakness of sterling. Many of them had financed their overseas expansion largely with debt, often eurocurrency borrowings, relying on the equity they held in their UK properties. The fall in sterling therefore caused a weakening of their balance sheets over and above that caused by the fall in property prices.

The financial structure of property companies

D.6   In the latter half of 1973, companies in all sectors of the economy began to come under financial pressure and this intensified throughout 1974. But the reasons for the peculiar and additional problems of the property companies lie in their financial structure which differs considerably from that of companies engaged in manufacturing and distribution. Some degree of comparability is afforded by the *Business Monitor* series, published by the Department of Industry, which analyses the accounts of companies with net assets of £2 million or more or gross income of £200,000 or more in 1968, and which between them are thought to account for 60–65 per cent of the net assets of all industrial and commercial companies. The high gearing of property companies is illustrated in table 46 from which it can be seen that the ratio of total borrowings to shareholders' funds rose from 115 to 121 per cent between the accounting years 1970 and 1971. The fall to 89 per cent in 1972 was largely due to an increase in shareholders' funds through the addition of £1,205 million to capital and revenue reserves, reflecting revaluations of property holdings. In 1974 a £511 million reduction in reserves was the main factor behind the sharp rise in the gearing ratio to 142 per cent. These figures are, of course, averages for the property companies in the series; in many individual cases gearing was considerably higher. For companies in manufacturing and distribution, gearing, on this definition, rose from 47 per cent in 1970 to 53 per cent in 1971 and 1972. Substantially increased bank borrowings over the following two years took the ratio up to 62 per cent in 1974.

D.7   From 1972 onwards the property companies tended to rely to a greater extent on short-term borrowing to finance their expansion. Up to 1973 they were still raising considerable amounts by way of long-term loans, but at rapidly increasing cost. Published rates for local authority loans give a broad indication of the trend. At the end of 1971 local authority mortgage rates for large amounts and for terms of over five years were around 8 per cent and by the end of 1972 had hardened to 9½ per cent. Interest rates declined moderately in the first half of 1973 but then rose rapidly during the late summer and autumn. By the end of 1973, local authorities were paying 14½ per cent on five-year money and longer. The rate continued to rise, reaching 15½ per cent by the end of 1974. In 1972 and 1973 property companies were in fact facing the dilemma with which local authorities were already familiar. If the rise in interest rates was likely to be temporary then it would be preferable to borrow short and fund later as opportunity arose, rather than be committed to high rates of interest for five or more years ahead. In the event the rise both in short and long-term rates was sustained and so proved very expensive. For the property companies covered by the *Business Monitor* series, debt interest had absorbed about half of their gross income, before debt interest, in 1972. In 1973 the proportion had risen to about two-thirds and in 1974 to perhaps as much as 90 per cent—a classic illustration of the risks of high gearing, which by forcing the property companies to curtail their activities and to liquidate their property holdings to reduce borrowings would itself have soon brought the property boom to an end.

Property companies' financial structure
Comparison with manufacturing and distributive industries

Table 46

£ million Figures in red are percentages		1970		1971		1972		1973		1974	
Property companies	**Number of companies**	**100**		**95**		**90**		**85**		**85**	
	Shareholders' funds	1,459	47	1,795	45	3,130	53	3,407	48	2,920	41
	Long-term loans	1,440	46	1,618	41	1,901	32	2,295	32	2,425	34
	Bank overdrafts and loans	236	7	270	7	463	8	784	11	931	13
	Short-term loans			277	7	417	7	666	9	803	12
	Total	**3,135**	100	**3,960**	100	**5,911**	100	**7,152**	100	**7,079**	100
	Ratio of total borrowings to shareholders' funds	115		121		89		110		142	
Manufacturing and distribution	**Number of companies**	**1,919**		**1,825**		**1,754**		**1,665**		**1,649**	
	Shareholders' funds	19,119	68	20,465	65	23,022	65	25,824	64	28,297	62
	Long-term loans	5,326	19	5,887	19	6,615	19	7,377	18	7,592	17
	Bank overdrafts and loans	3,748	13	3,637	12	4,041	11	5,557	14	7,950	17
	Short-term loans			1,339	4	1,526	5	1,603	4	2,017	4
	Total	**28,193**	100	**31,328**	100	**35,204**	100	**40,361**	100	**45,856**	100
	Ratio of total borrowings to shareholders' funds	47		53		53		56		62	

Source: Department of Industry, Business Monitor series, M3 Company Finance.

Bank lending to property companies

D.8 Following the introduction of *Competition and Credit Control* in September 1971 the short-term money markets expanded dramatically, fuelled by the rapid increase in money supply in the 1972/73 dash for economic growth. Ample short-term finance was available from a wide range of competing banks and other institutions for which, as table 47 shows, demand from companies in manufacturing and distribution was distinctly sluggish in the earlier stages. The property industry was, however, a ready borrower and, as shown in table 61 on page 277, bank advances outstanding to the property sector rose from £343 million in November 1970 to £2,834 million in November 1974, with by far the larger part of the increase accounted for by non-clearing banks. It should be borne in mind that in the banking statistics the property sector includes housing estate developers (but not builders, who are included in the construction classification), housing associations and estate agents as well as companies

Property companies' sources of funds   Table 47

Comparison with manufacturing and distributive industries

£ million			1970	1971	1972	1973	1974
Property companies	Issues	Share capital (net)	59	91	87	65	18
		Long-term loans	131	187	274	353	150
	Increase in amount owing to banks		28	4	190	330	90
	Increase in short-term loans			63	134	245	161
	Increase in trade and other creditors		118	13	44	77	71
	Gross income from trading and other activities		168	191	254	280	231
	Other capital receipts		3	8	12	17	20
	Total sources of funds		**507**	**557**	**995**	**1,367**	**741**
Manufacturing and distribution	Issues	Share capital (net)	571	547	1,037	447	217
		Long-term loans	460	614	672	816	184
	Increase in amount owing to banks		601	−136	370	1,565	2,318
	Increase in short-term loans			80	111	102	442
	Increase in trade and other creditors		1,539	247	1,185	3,629	3,375
	Gross income from trading and other activities		4,799	5,397	6,778	8,373	8,677
	Other capital receipts		390	304	291	312	197
	Total sources of funds		**8,360**	**7,053**	**10,444**	**15,244**	**15,410**

Source: Department of Industry, Business Monitor series, M3 Company Finance.

specifically engaged in property ownership, development and management. It therefore covers a wide range of activities in residential, commercial and industrial property markets including an 'export' element from the overseas operations of property companies.

D.9 So far as the clearing banks are concerned, advances to property companies represent a relatively small proportion of their total lending to UK residents. For the parent banks, the proportion reached 8 per cent in 1972 and has subsequently declined to about 6 per cent, with a sizeable part comprising bridging loans pending funding from longer-term sources. The percentages for 1967 to 1974, which are shown in table 61 on page 277, are however somewhat higher than those which would be derived from figures published at the time, as the totals exclude advances under the special export schemes which, since 1975, have been reclassified as lending to overseas residents. Figures on a group basis, bringing in property lending by subsidiaries, first became available in 1973 and show that even at its peak the proportion for the clearing bank groups as a whole reached only 9 per cent. The clearing banks have always adhered closely to the official directives on bank lending. In the first of these issued under the new conditions of *Competition and Credit Control*, in August 1972, the Governor of the Bank of England referred to the growing demand from industry for finance and asked that, as necessary, credit should be less readily available to property companies and for financial transactions. The Governor added that he understood that the clearing banks were already taking steps in this direction. The ability of the clearing banks to effect an immediate reduction in their lending to property companies in response to this and subsequent directives on similar lines has, however, been limited by two major constraints: their obligation to honour commitments on credit lines already agreed and, later, a reluctance to withdraw facilities or to realise security which would result in forced sales of property on an already depressed market.

D.10 The rise which did take place in advances outstanding to the property sector clearly carried risks, but the clearing banks' exposure was not unduly high in relation to their resources and their ability to take a long-term view in supporting borrowers through difficult times. This, unfortunately, was not the case with a number of secondary banks which had indulged the financial appetite of property companies with loans and advances, financed by short-term deposits, beyond the limits of banking prudence. These weaknesses became apparent towards the end of 1973 when the failure of London and County Securities produced an acute loss of confidence in the secondary banks. Withdrawals of deposits obliged them to call in their loans from property companies. Those property companies relying unduly on short-term debt were faced with serious difficulties and some, whose short-term debt was found to constitute well over 60 per cent of total borrowings, were forced into liquidation. Others, with institutional support, were able to survive, but by early 1974 the damage had been done and the property market was in a state of collapse.

Other factors contributing to the collapse of the property market

D.11   Financial factors – high interest rates and short-term borrowing – were certainly the major reasons for the collapse of the property market and its wider repercussions, but there were other important contributory causes. The state of the property industry follows the general state of the economy, with some time lags. The excessive rate of monetary expansion introduced a speculative element to the 1972/73 boom, and the impact of the subsequent recession, deepened by the massive increase in oil prices, was therefore inevitably greater than in previous cycles. But confidence in the property market had been shaken by earlier blows. Rent controls had been applied with increasing severity with successive phases of prices and incomes policy from January 1973, with temporary freezes of residential rents but longer standstills on commercial rents which continued until May 1975. When taking action in November 1973 to restrict and control rents on commercial property, the government announced its intention to introduce measures to curb the profitability of property investment. In the following month, proposals were announced for a heavy development gains tax on the capital values of buildings covering first lettings. These proposals were modified by the Labour Government on taking office in February 1974 but were nevertheless implemented in more or less their original form. The White Paper on Land and the ensuing Community Land legislation were further causes of uncertainty and raised additional problems of property rights.

D.12   Realisation that government intervention might have been precipitate was, however, dawning. In December 1974, the late Mr Anthony Crosland, then Secretary of State for the Environment, recognised somewhat belatedly that "a healthy market in commercial property is necessary for the government's social and economic objectives" and that "much savings and pensions money, for example, depends on income from commercial property, which also constitutes an important credit base for industry". The road to recovery is nevertheless likely to be long and progress so far has been slow. The sharp rise in interest rates in the second half of 1976 demonstrated again the vulnerability of property companies to increases in borrowing costs, but there are now signs that the subsequent fall in interest rates and a brighter outlook for the economy generally have revived confidence in the market for first-class properties. At the present time, official directives on bank lending preclude support to speculative property development even if such applications were to re-emerge. For the rest, the clearing banks continue to support housebuilding and other projects where there are firm arrangements for repaying or funding bank borrowing or where the property financing is linked directly to the business of borrowers in the priority categories.

D.13   The past few years have seen significant declines in starts on new industrial and commercial building, especially for rental. Much of the space at present available is secondary, outdated and unattractive. New development is needed

Index

The reference numbers refer to chapter and paragraph numbers. The letters denote references in the appendices. As the entire submission is concerned with the clearing banks' activities there is no 'clearing bank' heading in the index. Where it has been considered necessary, however, the main headings have been qualified by a reference to the clearing banks. The preface, chapter summaries and appendices A and E are not covered in the index.

Tables

The undermentioned tables appear on the following fold-out pages:

Owing to rounding of figures, the sum of the separate items in tables will sometimes differ from the totals shown. The word 'billion' signifies 1,000 million in this submission. Unless otherwise stated, statistics give the sterling equivalent of currency items at middle market rates on reporting dates. The abbreviation 'LCB' is sometimes used for London clearing banks.